The Ancient Concept
of Progress
and other Essays

The Ancient Concept of Progress

and other Essays on Greek Literature and Belief

BY

E. R. DODDS

OXFORD
AT THE CLARENDON PRESS
1973

Oxford University Press, Ely House, London W.1

GLASGOW NEW YORK TORONTO MELBOURNE WELLINGTON
CAPE TOWN IBADAN NAIROBI DAR ES SALAAM LUSAKA ADDIS ABABA
DELHI BOMBAY CALCUTTA MADRAS KARACHI LAHORE DACCA
KUALA LUMPUR SINGAPORE HONG KONG TOKYO

© *Oxford University Press 1973*

*The paper 'The Ancient Concept of Progress'
is copyright (© 1972) by Charles Scribner's Sons*

*Printed in Great Britain
at the University Press, Oxford
by Vivian Ridler
Printer to the University*

PREFACE

ALL the pieces in this collection originated as lectures, and most of them bear clear marks of their origin. The lectures were delivered to audiences as various as the Cambridge Philological Society, the Society for Psychical Research, and the Sixth Form at Marlborough College, and in their written form they make correspondingly various demands on the reader. I have, however, excluded pieces which are of concern only or chiefly to professional scholars and have limited my choice to subjects of fairly wide general interest. In the majority of these papers I have kept Greek quotation and Greek terminology to the inescapable minimum, in the hope that the book may be of some value to that increasingly important if ill-defined person, the Greekless 'general reader'.

I hope also that widely as the papers differ in their immediate purpose and in their date of composition they will nevertheless be found to reflect a certain underlying consistency of standpoint. Since boyhood my curiosity has been excited by the variety in unity of human behaviour, the different yet related ways in which men have responded at different periods to comparable stresses. Hence my interest in ancient representations of strong personalities in extreme situations, like those of Prometheus or Oedipus, Clytemnestra or Medea; my interest in periods when new questions were breaking through the crust of inherited answers and provoking new patterns of response, as in the lifetime of Protagoras or in that of Plotinus; and finally, my interest in concepts which have shifted their ground and their meaning over the centuries, like the ambiguous notion of progress or the interpretation of those mysterious borderline phenomena we call 'supernormal'.

Papers which have been published previously, with the exception of No. X, are here reprinted without alteration save for correction of misprints and of a few obsolete references: *littera scripta manet*. Two unpublished older lectures, Nos. II and VI, I have also kept substantially in their original form, since each is tied in various ways to its date of delivery. Elsewhere I have allowed myself some freedom of revision and expansion.

Preface

For permission to reproduce articles that have appeared—or, in one case, will appear—elsewhere I am grateful to Messrs. Charles Scribner's Sons (I); the Cambridge Philological Society (III); the Clarendon Press and the Board of Management of *Greece & Rome* (IV); the Clarendon Press and the Classical Journals Board (V); the Society for the Promotion of Hellenic Studies (VII); the Society for the Promotion of Roman Studies (VIII); and the Society for Psychical Research (X).

My grateful thanks are also due to Mr. D. A. Russell, who read most of the material for this book, and to Professor A. W. H. Adkins, who kindly helped me with the proof-reading.

E. R. D.

Oxford
August 1972

CONTENTS

I.	The Ancient Concept of Progress	1
II.	The *Prometheus Vinctus* and the Progress of Scholarship	26
III.	Morals and Politics in the *Oresteia*	45
IV.	On Misunderstanding the *Oedipus Rex*	64
V.	Euripides the Irrationalist	78
VI.	The Sophistic Movement and the Failure of Greek Liberalism	92
VII.	Plato and the Irrational	106
VIII.	Tradition and Personal Achievement in the Philosophy of Plotinus	126
IX.	The Religion of the Ordinary Man in Classical Greece	140
X.	Supernormal Phenomena in Classical Antiquity	156
	Index of Passages Discussed	211
	General Index	212

I

The Ancient Concept of Progress[1]

THE title of this paper begs a question. 'The ancients had no conception of progress; they did not so much as reject the idea; they did not even entertain the idea.' So wrote Walter Bagehot in the year 1872, and his assertion has often been echoed since. Yet it was possible for Sir Henry Maine a couple of years later to declare that it was precisely the Greeks who 'created the principle of Progress'; and for the late Ludwig Edelstein to affirm in his posthumous book, *The Idea of Progress in Classical Antiquity* (1967), that 'the ancients formulated most of the thoughts and sentiments that later generations down to the nineteenth century were accustomed to associate with the blessed or cursed word—"progress"'.[2] How can we explain so flat a factual contradiction?

I think the answer lies partly in the Greek vocabulary and the Greek habit of thought, partly in the slipperiness of the concept itself. It must be conceded to Bagehot that the Greeks of the classical age had no real word for progress. Edelstein's candidate, the word *epidosis*, will hardly do: it is too general a term, meaning merely 'increase', whether of good or evil, and whether by human agency or otherwise. A closer equivalent is *prokopē*, 'pushing forward', which Cicero translates by *progressus* or *progressio*; but this term appears to be a Hellenistic coinage, though the verb

---

[1] A revised and extended version of the Frazer Lecture delivered in the University of Glasgow in 1969. A slightly different version will appear in the *Dictionary of the History of Ideas*, to whose publishers, Charles Scribner's Sons (New York), I am indebted for permission to include this paper in the present volume.

[2] *The Idea of Progress in Classical Antiquity*, xxxiii. Frequent occasions of disagreement must not obscure my considerable debt to this important though unfortunately unfinished book, especially in connection with the medical and scientific writers on whom Edelstein was an acknowledged authority. Other recent works which I have found particularly helpful include those of Gatz, Havelock and Spoerri, Guthrie's *In the Beginning* (chap. 5), and Mme de Romilly's paper on 'Thucydide et l'idée de progrès', *Annali di Pisa* (1966), 143-91, which covers more ground than its title suggests. I must also thank Geoffrey de Ste Croix for valuable advice on several points.

prokoptein is older. And this linguistic fact seems in turn to reflect a psychological attitude. The idea of progress involves a speculative view of the future as well as the past; and in the classical age of Greece, as van Groningen has pointed out,[1] while speculation about the past was abundant, explicit pronouncements about the future are surprisingly rare. Most people seem to have followed the advice of the poet Simonides: 'Being but man, never try to say what tomorrow brings.' The chief exceptions are to be found among the scientists, and their predictions are usually confined to the field in which they have expert knowledge. For the others we can as a rule do no more than infer their expectations about the future from their attitude to the past and the present—a legitimate procedure up to a point but seldom a secure one.

A further difficulty lies in the inherent ambiguity of the concept of progress. Progress implies a goal, or at any rate a direction; and a goal or direction implies a value judgement. By what scale of values, then, is progress to be measured? Is happiness to be the yardstick, or power over nature, or gross national product? Is moral advance the true criterion, or is it the advancement of learning? On this question the ancients were no more unanimous than men are today, and different criteria suggested conflicting conclusions. Then as now, the field in which past progress was most obvious was that of technology; but the view that technological advance has been accompanied by moral failure or moral regress was, as we shall see, at least as widely held in antiquity as it is at present. Some went further and posited a direct causal relation between the two: for them technological advance had actually induced moral decay, and was thus not a blessing but a curse—a line of thought which issued logically in an extreme form of primitivism.

The idea of progress, even in the restricted sense of technological progress, is in any case not one which comes early or easily to men. In primitive societies, custom-bound as they are and lacking historical records, progress does not readily develop a generalized meaning. Such societies may ascribe particular inventions or discoveries to individual culture-heroes or culture-gods, as popular Greek belief did from the Archaic Age onwards; but they do not think of them as forming a continuous ladder of

[1] B. A. van Groningen, *In the Grip of the Past* (1953).

ascent, and still less do they conceive such a ladder as extending into the present and the future. It is therefore not surprising that the idea of progress should be missing from the oldest Greek literature. And when it did emerge it found the field already occupied by two great anti-progressive myths which threatened to strangle it at birth, the myth of the Lost Paradise—called by the Greeks 'the life under Kronos', by the Romans the *Saturnia regna* or Golden Age—and the myth of Eternal Recurrence. The wide diffusion of these two myths, far beyond the limits of the Greco-Roman world, and their astonishing persistence throughout Antiquity and even down to our own day—one remembers how they fascinated Yeats—suggest that they must have deep unconscious roots in human experience: in the one case, perhaps, the individual experience of early infancy, when life was easy, nature supplied nourishment, and conflict did not exist; in the other, the eternally repeated drama of the recurrent seasons on which all agricultural life depends.

The first of these myths and probably the second also were already known to Hesiod about 700 B.C. His much-discussed tale of the Five Races[1] is a story of increasing though not uninterrupted degeneration, starting from the Lost Paradise 'under Kronos' and extending into the present and the future. Its backbone is the myth of the four metals—gold, silver, bronze, and iron—symbolizing four stages of material and moral decline, which he appears to have borrowed from an oriental source.[2] He has combined this with a historical tradition of the heroic world described in early Greek epic, which interrupts the pattern of continuous decline, and also (as Goldschmidt[3] has emphasized) with an aetiology of certain semi-divine beings who derive severally from the Golden, Silver, and Heroic Races. His story ends with the gloomy forecast of an increasingly corrupt and bitter future, very much in the style of an oriental apocalypse. But the poet's wish that he had either died before the present Iron Race or *been born later*[4] seems to betray the fact that the oriental myth was cyclic, ending with the completion of a Great

[1] *Works and Days* 106-201.
[2] R. Reitzenstein, *Studien zum antiken Synkretismus* (1926), 45; B. Gatz, *Weltalter, Goldene Zeit und sinnverwandte Vorstellungen* (1967), 7-27.
[3] V. Goldschmidt, *R.E.G.* 63 (1950), 33-9. I disregard here J. P. Vernant's six-stage interpretation, which seems to me to lack support in the text.
[4] *Works and Days* 174-5; cf. 180 f. where he foresees the end of the Iron Age.

Year and an abrupt return to the Lost Paradise. The cyclic interpretation of human history was not, however, what interested Hesiod; his concern was to emphasize the growing degeneracy of his own time. To a poet who lived the poverty-stricken life of a Boeotian peasant while his inner vision was filled with the glories of the heroic past no other view was really possible. And later poets who saw history in cyclic terms tended to follow Hesiod's example: they have much to say about the Lost Paradise, but almost nothing, until Virgil, about Paradise Regained. The cyclic theory is most often found in the service of pessimism.

How far Hesiod's contemporaries accepted his despairing prognosis we have no sure means of knowing. All we can say is that the first explicit statement to the contrary appears at the end of the Archaic Age in two well-known lines of the Ionian poet–philosopher Xenophanes:

> Not from the beginning did the gods reveal everything to mankind,
> But in course of time by research men discover improvements.[1]

This is a genuine affirmation of progress: the writer conceives it as a gradual process which extends into the present and presumptively into the future, and one which is dependent on man's own efforts, not on the arbitrary gift of any 'culture-god'. The first line looks rather like an echo of Hesiod's saying, 'The gods have hidden men's livelihood from them';[2] the second line looks like an answer to Hesiod. We do not know whether the couplet was a casual *obiter dictum* or formed part of a fuller historical statement. It may well have been prompted by Xenophanes' observation of recent cultural advances (we are told that he mentioned the recent invention of coinage by the Lydians and that he admired the astronomical discoveries of Thales). And it is perhaps also relevant to recall that he was a much-travelled man who took an interest in the red-haired gods of the Thracians and the snub-nosed gods of the Ethiopians. Such comparison of different cultures suggested to him, we know, the idea that religious beliefs are relative to the believer; it may also have sug-

---

[1] Xenophanes, frag. 18 Diels–Kranz. Xenophanes did not, however, anticipate *endless* progress. Having personally observed marine fossils on dry land, he inferred that the sea had once covered the earth and expected it one day to do so again, temporarily destroying all human life (A 33 Diels–Kranz).

[2] *Works and Days* 42.

gested the idea of man's slow and uneven upward movement from barbarism to civilization.

The pride in human achievement which we can feel in the few words of Xenophanes found more vivid expression a generation later in the great speech which Aeschylus put into the mouth of Prometheus.[1] It is true that Prometheus credits the achievement not to man but to himself: that was implicit in the dramatic situation. But the contrast between man as he once was and man as he now is has never been more eloquently expressed. Man is no exile from a Lost Paradise. On the contrary, he has come up from a state in which he was not yet capable of coherent thought but drifted aimlessly through life 'like a figure in a dream', unable to interpret the message of eyes and ears, his only shelter a cave. And consider him now! Not only has he set the animals to work for him, conquered the sea, discovered the secret mineral wealth of the earth, but he has learned to record his own achievements and has mastered difficult sciences—astronomy, arithmetic, medicine, divination.

This passage has surprised some critics, and has even been adduced as an argument against the authenticity of the play on the ground that it betrays sophistic influence.[2] That view rests on a misconception, as Reinhardt[3] and others have pointed out. Considered as a piece of anthropology, the speech is decidedly archaic and pretty evidently pre-sophistic. There is no attempt to mark the stages of evolution, no recognition of the decisive influence of the food-producing techniques (cattle-herding and agriculture), no reference to the origins of communal life. Technology takes a very minor place: even the potter's wheel, which Attic tradition associated especially with Prometheus, is left out as too unimportant or too banal. What the poet has chosen to stress is man's *intellectual* progress: the spur of economic necessity, which figures prominently in later Greek accounts, receives no emphasis from Aeschylus; instead, his hero undertakes to relate 'how I made men rational and capable of reflection, who till then were childish'. And the science on which he dwells at greatest length is that of divination, lovingly described

[1] P.V. 442–506.
[2] W. Schmid, *Untersuchungen zum Gefesselten Prometheus* (1929), 95 f.
[3] K. Reinhardt, *Aischylos als Regisseur und Theologe* (1949), 50 f. See also below p. 32.

in all its various branches. This is in keeping with Aeschylus' attitude elsewhere, but would be very surprising in a pupil of Protagoras.

But Aeschylus did at least recognize that man has risen, not fallen. Did he pick up the idea from Xenophanes? That is possible: in Xenophanes' old age the two poets may even have met in Sicily. But if so Aeschylus did not follow his 'source' at all closely: divination, which Xenophanes dismissed as a fraud,[1] is for Aeschylus the crown of man's scientific achievement. And need we postulate a source? The list of sciences was easy to make, and there is nothing in the description of man's original unhappy state which suggests special knowledge. If we ask how the poet came to substitute the idea of progress for the Hesiodic regress, part at least of the answer must surely lie in the triumphant *experience* of progress enjoyed by Aeschylus and his generation. The influence of this experience is equally apparent in the *Eumenides*, where Athena's gift of law is the counterpart and the completion of Prometheus' gift of reason. In that play Aeschylus appears not only to look back upon his country's past but to look forward with confidence to its present and its future.[2] For contrast, he had available to him the reports of barbarian peoples brought home by Greek travellers like Aristeas and Hecataeus, and several passages in his work show him making free use of them. Comparative anthropology was already in the air.[3]

One difficult question remains: did Aeschylus actually believe that the arts of civilization were taught to man by a divine being called Prometheus, or is his Prometheus just a symbol of human reason? The question may be thought illegitimate: so long as myth-making is a living mode of thought, to confront it with this sort of brutal 'either–or' is to force upon it a choice which destroys its being. But late Antiquity was in no doubt about the answer. For all Greek writers after Aeschylus Prometheus is purely a symbol of man's restless intelligence, to be admired or condemned according to the author's outlook. The earliest extant statement of this opinion seems to be a line from the comic poet Plato[4] which appears to equate Prometheus with 'the human

[1] Xenophanes A 52.   [2] See below, p. 62.   [3] See below, p. 98.
[4] Frag. 136 Kock. The text is uncertain, but the intention to equate *nous* with Prometheus can hardly be doubted.

intellect'. But it is suggestive that the line should have occurred in a play called *The Sophists*. It may well have been a sophist, perhaps Protagoras, who first made the symbolism explicit. It can, however, be argued that in Aeschylus it is already implicit. So far as we know, it was he who first made such an interpretation possible, by crediting Prometheus not merely with the gift of fire but with *all* the arts of civilization, including some which are assigned to other culture-heroes by other writers and even by Aeschylus himself in other plays.[1] By thus transfiguring the seriocomic trickster whom Hesiod had portrayed[2] he created one of the great symbolic figures of European literature. The symbolism, however, was not for him, as it was for Protagoras, something which could be stripped away without loss of significance. The belief that man's achievements are not purely his own but are the outcome and the expression of a divine purpose was to Aeschylus—at least in my view—a basic religious postulate.

After Aeschylus the literary tradition branches in two opposed directions. The religious interpretation of progress as a manifestation of divine providence appears in a speech that Euripides put into the mouth of Theseus, the type of Athenian conservative orthodoxy.[3] To refute the view of certain people who hold that there is more evil than good in human life Theseus lists the most obvious human assets and achievements, and asks if we should not be grateful to the god who so ordered man's life, raising it from incoherence and bestiality. He then proceeds to reprove those people who in their conceit of human intelligence 'imagine themselves wiser than the gods', i.e. think they know better what is good for them. This pretty certainly reflects some contemporary controversy, not the personal views of the poet. The opinions criticized may be those of the sophist Prodicus; the standpoint of the speaker is that of orthodox piety. He is no genuine progressive: he admits past progress only to enforce the old lesson that man should accept his station and be content. This line of thought developed into the argument from design which Xenophon attributed to Socrates, and issued ultimately

---

[1] A scholion on *P.V.* 457 tells us that Aeschylus elsewhere ascribed the invention of astronomy to Palamedes. See further A. Kleingünther, Πρῶτος εὑρετής (1933), 78 ff.
[2] *Theogony* 510–616; *Works and Days* 42–89.
[3] Eur. *Supplices* 195–218, probably written about 424–420.

in the Stoic and Christian conception of history as providentially guided.¹

For the first detailed statement of the opposing point of view we have to turn, surprisingly enough, to Sophocles. In a celebrated ode, *Antigone* 332–75, he set forth man's conquest of earth and sea, of beasts, birds, and fishes, of speech and thought and the arts of communal life, representing these things not as a providential endowment but as the result of man's own efforts. This has led some scholars to speak of Sophocles' 'humanistic philosophy' and to conclude that he is 'tinged with the rationalism of his age'.² But to draw that conclusion is to ignore the implications both of the lyric as a whole and of the play as a whole. The poet's praise of man's 'cleverness' (*deinotēs*, a morally ambiguous word) leads up to the warning that cleverness can bring destruction as easily as it can success; and the warning is reinforced in the next ode, where the picture of man's achievement is balanced by the companion picture of his utter helplessness when our human purposes come into conflict with the inscrutable purposes of God. Sophocles was no humanist, and the *Antigone* is no Protagorean tract for the times. We can, however, legitimately infer that by the date of the play (441 B.C.) the humanistic interpretation of progress was already current at Athens. And in later dramatists we can observe more direct echoes of such an interpretation. In a well-known fragment of the poet–politician Critias (d. 403 B.C.) a speaker explains, after the manner of an eighteenth-century *philosophe*, how 'some wise man' invented the gods as a prop to public morality.³ Later still, Chaeremon repeats in almost the same words the sentiment of Xenophanes; and Moschion, describing man's advance from cannibalism to civilization, treats Prometheus as the mythological equivalent of 'necessity' or 'experience', which were by then the accepted springs of progress.⁴

It has long been recognized that behind these numerous poetic utterances there must lie a substantial amount of serious anthro-

---

¹ On the history of the argument from design see W. Theiler, *Zur Geschichte der teleologischen Naturbetrachtung* (1925), 38 ff.; F. Solmsen, *Plato's Theology* (1942), 47 ff.; A.-J. Festugière, *Le Dieu cosmique* (1949), ch. iv.
² e.g. E. E. Sikes, *The Anthropology of the Greeks* (1914), 39; Solmsen, op. cit. 48; J. S. Morrison, *C.Q.* 35 (1941), 14.
³ Critias, frag. 1 Nauck (= frag. 25 Diels–Kranz).
⁴ Chaeremon, frag. 21 Nauck; Moschion, frag. 6 Nauck. On the latter fragment see below, p. 43.

pological speculation which had excited public interest. It is no surprise to learn from the *Hippias major*[1] that even in Sparta lectures on prehistory (*archaiologia*) were in great demand. And we know who the leading speculators were—Protagoras and Democritus, Anaxagoras and his Athenian pupil Archelaus. But of what they said on this subject we have only the scantiest attested fragments—for the most part too scanty in my opinion for any confident assignment of particular theories to individual thinkers. Since, however, scholarship, like Nature, abhors a vacuum, the views of Protagoras have been reconstructed on the basis of the myth which Plato put in his mouth,[2] and those of Democritus on the basis of what Diodorus some four centuries later attributed to 'the most generally recognized' of those natural scientists who hold that man and the cosmos had a beginning.[3] To discuss these reconstructions adequately would require a long separate essay. All I can do here is to indicate briefly some grounds for hesitation in accepting them.

The difficulty of using Plato's *Protagoras* myth as evidence lies in the impossibility of deciding with any certainty how much is Protagoras and how much Plato. Some scholars have treated the passage as an exact précis of Protagoras' views, or even as a verbatim excerpt from his alleged book *On Man's Original Condition*.[4] This is unjustified. Plato was no scissors-and-paste compiler but a great dramatic artist; the style (despite assertions to the contrary) is not notably different from that employed in other Platonic myths; and certain of the ideas and images appear much more Platonic than Protagorean.[5] The passage surely reflects not what Protagoras actually said but what Plato thought he might have said in a given situation. The utmost we can safely infer is that Protagoras did somewhere express opinions on the

---

[1] Plato, *Hipp. ma.* 285 d.   [2] Plato, *Protagoras* 320 c–328 d.
[3] Diodorus 1. 6. 3–1. 8. 9.
[4] Listed among Protagoras' works by Diogenes Laertius, 9. 55. But I cannot quite dismiss the gnawing suspicion which troubled Diels (on Protagoras B 8), that this title has been merely inferred from Plato's myth, just as the rather surprising title *On Wrestling* seems to have been inferred from a passage in Plato's *Sophist* (232 d).
[5] At 322 a the reference to man's kinship with God is so distinctively Platonic (cf. *Tim.* 90 a, *Laws* 899 d) that the more earnest 'Protagoreans' have felt obliged to excise it as an interpolation. For a survey of critical opinion on the whole question see the bibliography in E. A. Havelock, *The Liberal Temper in Greek Politics* (1964), 407–9.

origins of society; that in doing so he emphasized the poverty of man's physical endowment (which design-mongers like Xenophon admired so much) and insisted that early man owed his survival ultimately to his capacity for communal life; and that this in turn depended in his view on the development of the social virtues, *aidōs* and *dikē*—respect for the feelings and the rights of others. Since Protagoras also believed that 'virtue' can be taught, this may well have led him to take a rosy view of man's prospects; Plato makes him claim that the very worst citizen of modern Athens is already a better man than any savage.[1] In the same spirit Democritus seems to have held that man's natural endowment was malleable and could be 'reshaped' by education.[2] In the great days of the fifth century such optimism was natural; by the time Plato wrote, faith in the common heritage of *aidōs* and *dikē* had been shattered by the Peloponnesian War and its aftermath,[3] and the reproachful phantom of the 'Noble Savage' was waiting in the wings.

What Diodorus offers us is a short account of cosmogony, zoogony, and anthropology which he inserted rather loosely into the preface to his *Universal History*, written about 60 to 30 B.C. It is remarkable for its consistently rationalist approach and for its use of terms and concepts which seem to go back to fifth-century speculation. Reinhardt in 1912 argued ingeniously that its ultimate source was Democritus;[4] this view was long accepted, and the passage still appears among the fragments of Democritus in Kranz's edition. But doubts have since accumulated.[5] The cosmogony is non-atomist; the account of the origin of animal life has closer parallels in other Pre-Socratic texts than it has in Democritus; some features of the anthropology may be Democritean, but the author's reference to the crucial significance of the human hand, which has made man the only tool-using animal, seems to derive from Anaxagoras[6] (who happens to be

---

[1] 327 c–d. 'Protagoras' supports this by an anachronistic reference to the *Savages* of Pherecrates, produced in 421/420. But it seems more likely that Pherecrates' play was suggested by the speculations of Protagoras than that the historical Protagoras quoted it in support of these speculations.
[2] Frag. 33 Diels–Kranz. [3] Cf. below, p. 44.
[4] *Hermes* 47 (1912), 492–513, reprinted in *Vermächtnis der Antike* (1960), 114–32.
[5] The grounds for doubt, expressed earlier by Dahlmann, Cornford, and others, are most fully stated by W. Spoerri, *Späthellenistische Berichte über Welt, Kultur und Götter* (1959), 1–33.
[6] Aristotle, *de part. anim.* 4. 10, 687^{a}7.

also the only philosopher mentioned by name in the passage). In an earlier (unpublished) version of this paper I argued at some length that if we had to name a single source for the whole the likeliest was in fact Anaxagoras or his pupil Archelaus. But I should now be content to suggest that after all we should take Diodorus at his word and assume that he, or more likely some Hellenistic predecessor, being no philosopher, consulted a doxographic manual and out of what he found there put together a not very up-to-date summary of the opinions most often attributed to rationalist thinkers. If this is so, any hope of reconstructing in detail a 'Democritean' anthropology (as attempted most recently by Thomas Cole[1]) seems doomed to failure.

Less ambiguous evidence for the fifth-century faith in progress may be seen in the new importance attached to the concept of *technē*—that is to say, the systematic application of intelligence to any field of human activity. This was happening, and it was yielding results. Thucydides makes his Corinthian envoy warn the conservative Spartans that 'in politics, as in any *technē*, the latest inventions always have the advantage'.[2] Plato represents Socrates as agreeing with the sophist Hippias that there have been advances in all the *technai* such that 'the old practitioners cut a poor figure in comparison with to-day's'.[3] Were such advances expected to continue? The epic poet Choerilus of Samos could regret that he was born too late, in an age when 'everything has been assigned and the *technai* have reached their limits'.[4] But his was an obsolescent skill. The medical writers have an explicit faith in the future as well as pride in the past. Thus the author of the essay *On Ancient Medicine*, which is usually assigned to the latter part of the fifth century, asserts: 'Many splendid medical discoveries have been made over the years, and the rest will be discovered if a competent man, familiar with past findings, takes them as a basis for his inquiries.' And he goes on to make it clear that the progress of medicine is for him neither accidental nor god-given but is the fruit of cumulative observation.[5] In the same spirit another possibly fifth-century essay, that *On the Art of Medicine*, declares: 'To make new discoveries

[1] T. Cole, *Democritus and the Sources of Greek Anthropology* (1967).
[2] Thuc. 1. 71. 3.   [3] Plato, *Hipp. ma.* 281 d.
[4] Frag. 1 Kinkel.
[5] Hippocrates, *vet. med.* (1. 570 ff. Littré), chs. 2, 12, 14.

of a useful kind, or to perfect what is still only half worked out, is the ambition and the task of intelligence.'[1] A similar confidence in future possibilities is implied in the proposal of the town-planner Hippodamus that a special award of merit should be given to those 'who discovered something of advantage to the State'.[2] The passion for systematic research had been awakened: Democritus was not unique in feeling that he had rather solve a single problem than own the whole of Persia.[3]

But however buoyant the expectations of the anthropologists and the specialists, thoughtful minds in the fifth century were aware of the limitations imposed on progress by the human condition. Each of the two great historians expressed this awareness in his own way. Each of them, it is true, took pride in the past achievements of his people: for Herodotus the Greeks had long since outgrown the 'silly nonsense' associated with barbarism;[4] and Thucydides saw the past history of Greece as pursuing a gradual upward course. But Herodotus writes 'as one who knows the instability of human prosperity',[5] and this conviction haunts his imagination as it did that of his friend Sophocles. He explains it in the old religious manner: man is at the mercy of a Power which forbids him to rise above his station. Thucydides, on the other hand, finds the limitation in the psychological structure of man himself. Certain kinds of disaster, he tells us, 'occur and will always occur while human nature remains the same'; and he adventures the more general statement that 'in all human probability events of much the same kind (as those he is about to describe) will happen again in the future'.[6] It is a mistake to conclude from these passages, as one recent writer has done, that Thucydides 'finally adopted a cyclical view of history very much like Plato's'.[7] His expectation of recurrence is based not on cosmic cycles but on the permanence of the irrational and unteachable elements in human nature.[8] He was also deeply im-

---

[1] Hippocrates, *de arte* (6. 2 ff. Littré), ch. 1.
[2] Aristotle, *Politics*, 1268ᵃ6.   [3] Democritus, frag. 118.
[4] Hdt. 1. 60. 3. Cf. Thuc. 1. 6. 6: the early Greek way of life resembled that of present-day barbarians.
[5] Hdt. 1. 5. 4. Cf. my *Greeks and the Irrational* (1951), 29–31.
[6] Thuc. 3. 82. 2; 1. 22. 4.
[7] J. H. Finley, *Thucydides* (1942), 83. Cf. the criticisms of Momigliano, 'Time in ancient Historiography', *History and Theory*, Beiheft 6 (1966), 11 f. and Mme de Romilly, op. cit. [p. 1 n. 2 above], 177, 181 f.
[8] Cf. 3. 45. 4–7; 4. 108. 4.

pressed by the part which sheer chance has played and will play in history: as he puts it in one passage, 'it is possible for the fortunes of events to develop just as waywardly [*amathōs*] as the designs of men'.[1]

When we pass from the fifth century to the fourth we enter a perceptibly different atmosphere. There is no falling off in creative energy: the fourth century produced the greatest philosophers and the greatest orators of Antiquity; it invented new art forms, prose dialogue and domestic comedy; it witnessed great advances in mathematics and astronomy. Yet it is hard to deny (as Edelstein does) that something at least of the old confidence had been lost. The feeling of insecurity expressed itself in a variety of ways. Men looked over their shoulders to a supposedly more stable past, to what they called 'the ancestral constitution', or beyond that to a state of primal innocence no longer to be found save among remote peoples: Plato, as we shall see, celebrated the virtues of Stone Age man; Xenophon those of the early Persians; Ephorus discovered such virtues among the Scythians, while Ctesias attributed them to the Indians. Alternatively, the dream could be projected as a blueprint for the future, one of those 'rational Utopias' of which Plato's *Republic* is only the most famous example. Utopias of this kind are less a sign of confidence in the future than of dissatisfaction with the present; their authors seldom have much to say about the practical steps by which Utopia is to be achieved.

Others took a more radical line. Starting from the ideal of 'self-sufficiency' (*autarkeia*) which Socrates had commended, the Cynics preached rejection of all social conventions and a return to the simple life in its crudest form. They were the 'beatniks' or 'hippies' of Antiquity: they had opted out not only from the rat race but from all personal share in a civilization which they condemned.[2] Like their modern counterparts they were an unrepresentative minority, but like them they were symptomatic of a growing social malaise, something which was to become widespread in the Hellenistic Age. The Greek achievement still had its admirers, as we see in Isocrates; but in the century as

[1] 1. 140. 1. Cf. the long list of similar passages assembled by Kitto, *Poiesis* (1966), 339. For Thucydides the future is essentially unknowable.
[2] For 'opting out' in this period cf. also Aristippus, who according to Xenophon preferred to be 'everywhere an alien' rather than 'imprison himself in a community' (*Mem.* 2. 1. 13).

a whole primitivism was not 'on the wane' as Edelstein claims;[1] it was on the way to a revival.

The myth of the Eternal Return was also on its way to revival, assisted by Babylonian astrology. The doctrine of the Great Year had been imported or reimported from the East, apparently by the Pythagoreans, together with its sister doctrine of identically recurrent world periods separated by recurrent catastrophes. Both Plato and Aristotle know about the Great Year and attach some importance to it,[2] but they reject the idea of total world destruction and identical recurrence (which excludes all free will). In its place both of them postulate *partial* natural catastrophes which have destroyed and will destroy successive civilizations without destroying mankind. This curious theory appears first in the dialogues of Plato's old age (*Timaeus, Critias, Laws*); whether it was his own invention is uncertain.[3] The myths of Deucalion and Phaethon may have suggested it, but its value for Plato and Aristotle lay in enabling them to retain their metaphysical belief in the endless duration of the human race while recognizing that civilization, at any rate in Greece, was of comparatively recent origin.[4] The theory allowed for temporary and limited progress between catastrophes: the fifth-century picture of humanity's upward struggle need not be completely jettisoned. But it led Aristotle to the discouraging conclusion—discouraging at least to a modern mind—that 'in all likelihood every skill and every philosophy has been discovered many times over and again perished'.[5]

A more fundamental limitation on the idea of progress was imposed by the theory of Forms, both in the Platonic and in the Aristotelian version. For Plato all progress consists in approximation to a pre-existing model; the model has existed and will

---

[1] Op. cit. 69. Mme de Romilly is surely nearer the truth when she writes (op. cit. 183): 'Ce regret d'un passé glorieux va se propager, remplir tout le IVème siècle et, remontant le cours du temps, s'appliquer à un passé de plus en plus lointain et bientôt irréel.'

[2] Plato, *Tim.* 39 d; Aristotle, *Meteor.* 352^{a}28. Heraclitus was credited with some sort of belief in a Great Year, but its character and implications are disputed (see G. S. Kirk, *Heraclitus, the Cosmic Fragments*, 300–3, and M. L. West, *Early Greek Philosophy and the Orient* (1971), 155–8).

[3] See Cole, *Democritus*, 100 n. 5.

[4] Plato makes this clear at *Laws*, 677 c–d. The human race is as old as time (*Laws*, 721 c).

[5] Aristotle, *Metaph.* 1074^{b}10. Cf. *de caelo*, 270^{b}19, *Meteor.* 339^{b}27.

exist to all eternity in the unchanging world of transcendent Forms. There is thus, strictly speaking, no open future and no such thing as invention; what we call invention is but 'recollection' of a reality which is already there—nothing entirely new can ever come into being. The Platonist expresses his vision in a spatial metaphor, not a temporal one: he does not look forward like the early Christians from the Now to a promised Then, but upward from the Here to an ever-present There. For Aristotle, again, progress can never be more than the actualization of a Form which was already present potentially before the progress began. He traces, for example, the development of tragedy from rude beginnings to its contemporary state; but once it has 'attained its natural Form' development ceases, apparently for ever.[1] Similarly in nature his doctrine of immutable Forms excluded any possibility of biological progress: in the absence of any concept of evolution his *scala naturae* is a static sequence, not a ladder of ascent.

Despite the limitations inherent in Platonism, Edelstein has claimed Plato as a supporter of the idea of progress. This is hard to accept. It is true that he was no literal believer in the Lost Paradise, though he repeatedly toyed with the notion on a mythical level.[2] Up to a point he accepted the view of the fifth-century anthropologists that the emergence of civilization had been slow and difficult. But just as Engels projected his Utopian vision of the future on to the remote past in the form of an imaginary 'primitive communism', so Plato in the *Laws* projected on to the earliest human society certain features of his Ideal State: the same simplicity of living which he would impose on his ideal Guardians; the same absence of wealth and poverty which is his recipe for avoiding internal conflict; the same freedom from the corrupting influence of foreign trade. The experience of these early men was indeed incomplete, since they were ignorant alike of the vices and the virtues of city life,[3] but he claims that they were simpler, more courageous, more self-controlled, and in every way more righteous than the men of his own time.[4] With these words the aged Plato ushers in the Noble Savage.

[1] *Poetics*, 1449^{a}14. At most, he leaves open the possibility of minor improvements within the established Form (Edelstein, op. cit. 124).
[2] *Cratylus*, 398 a; *Politicus*, 271 c–272 d; *Laws*, 713 a–714 a; and the Atlantis myth in the *Critias*.
[3] *Laws*, 678 a–b.
[4] *Laws*, 679 e. Cf. *Philebus*, 16 c.

Subsequent history appears to him in this passage as a story of technical progress combined with moral regress—a pattern which we shall find constantly reasserted later. Elsewhere in the *Laws* he emphasizes, even more strongly than Thucydides, the role of chance in history, although to Plato this so-called chance may be, as Chamfort put it, 'a nickname for Providence'. 'Practically all human affairs', he tells us, 'are matters of chance.'[1] Everything mortal shifts and alters; one society grows better over the years while another deteriorates; there is no consistent direction of change.[2]

Aristotle's vision of history was less gloomy. His account of the growth of society from the individual household through the clan to the city state[3] follows the lines of fifth-century anthropology and is free from the equivocations of Plato's version. His interpretation of it is teleological: only in the city state does man become what nature intended him to be, a 'civic' animal, and only there can he live the good life. There is no suggestion of a Lost Paradise; on the contrary, early man was 'in all probability similar to ordinary or even foolish people to-day', and this is confirmed for him by the foolishness of such remnants of ancient custom as still survive. In this context Aristotle also mentions the great advances which have been achieved in sciences like medicine 'and in general in all professional skills and abilities'.[4] As we have seen, however, a limit is set to any advance by the attainment of 'the appropriate Form'. The city state was for Aristotle such a Form; he never envisaged any wider type of social organization, though a wider society was in fact in process of emergence in his own day. Progress on this showing is real enough, but it is the fulfilment of a predetermined and limited possibility, one which has been fulfilled many times before and will be fulfilled many times again.

It is noteworthy that Aristotle's pupils Theophrastus and Dicaearchus, while fully sharing his interest in cultural history, departed from his hard-headed attitude. Both of them idealized

---

[1] *Laws*, 709 a–c.
[2] *Laws*, 676 c. See further Lovejoy and Boas, *Primitivism and Related Ideas in Antiquity* (1935), chap. v; Havelock, *Liberal Temper*, 40–51.
[3] *Politics* I, chap. 2.
[4] *Politics*, 1268^{b}31–1269^{a}8. Cf. 1329^{b}25–31, where Aristotle expects each successive civilization to pursue a steady upward course from the provision of bare necessities to the graces of and avanced culture.

early man in a way which would surely have surprised their master. Theophrastus, writing on vegetarianism, traced the origin of corruption to the discovery of fire, which led to animal and human sacrifice and ultimately to war.[1] Dicaearchus, rationalizing Hesiod, asserted that 'the ancients' were the best endowed by nature and lived the best life, 'so that they were considered a Golden Race compared with the men of today'.[2] In this shift of value judgement they reveal themselves as true children of the Hellenistic Age.

The great social changes which followed the death of Alexander reinforced the new attitudes towards both the past and the future of which we have noted the early symptoms. The loosening of the traditional political and religious bonds which had attached the citizen to his small city state, and the development of vast monarchies bureaucratically administered, left the individual with an increased sense of isolation and helplessness and forced his thoughts inwards upon himself and his personal salvation. At the same time the new conditions of urban life, with the widening gap between the rich and the poor and the development of artificial wants stimulated by commercial greed, induced a nostalgia for a simpler and less 'civilized' existence which found literary expression in the Idylls of Theocritus, while its counterpart on the mythical level appears in Aratus' description of the Golden Age and in the Utopian accounts of distant or imaginary lands presented by writers like Onesicritus, Megasthenes, and Iambulus.

To sentiments of this kind the fashionable philosophies of the period gave intellectual and moral support. Cynic, Stoic, and Epicurean preachers alike tended to see their task as one of psychiatry: they were called to the healing of a sick culture. And since all else was subordinated to the aim of inducing freedom from anxiety (*ataraxia*) they had little interest in promoting scientific advance save in so far as it might contribute to this aim. Zeno is said to have considered 'the ordinary education' useless,[3] and Epicurus expressed a frank contempt for science as such.[4]

[1] Theophrastus, *de pietate*, cited by Porphyry, *de abstinentia*, 2. 5 ff.
[2] Dicaearchus, *Bios Hellados*, cited by Porphyry, *de abst.* 4. 2 (= frag. 49 Wehrli). Cf. Edelstein, op. cit. 134 f.
[3] Diogenes Laertius 7. 32. His successor Chrysippus took a less extreme view (ibid. 7. 129).
[4] Epicurus, *Epist.* 1. 79, 2. 85; frags. 163, 227 Usener.

The Stoics, moreover, were systematic determinists, and most of them accepted the theory of identically recurrent world periods, which excludes all genuine human initiative. It is therefore not surprising that the concept of progress played little part in the philosophical thinking of the early Hellenistic Age.

But there is one field in which the concept remained alive. The scientists of the time speak with another voice than the philosophers'. The greatest among them were not only proudly conscious of past and present progress; they expected it to continue. Thus Archimedes (about 287–212 B.C.) wrote that by using his method 'I apprehend that some either of my contemporaries or of my successors will be enabled to discover other theorems in addition, which have not as yet occurred to me'.[1] And the great astronomer Hipparchus (second century B.C.) compiled a list of all the fixed stars known to him in order that future astronomers might be able to compare his observations with their own and thus determine what changes, if any, had occurred in the population of the heavens.[2] Nor was this confidence entirely confined to scientific specialists. Polybius (about 200–118 B.C.) notes contemporary advances in technology and expects further improvements.[3] He also expects his own historical work to be of practical value to future generations, for example by providing posterity with the material for a final judgement on Roman rule.[4] And while holding (at least sometimes) a cyclic view of history he nevertheless describes the origins of civilization in terms which make no concession to primitivism. Starting like Plato from the theory of recurrent partial catastrophes, he offers an account of the genealogy of morals which is much more tough-minded than Plato's: man, he holds, is distinguished from the other animals only by his intelligence, which causes him to develop elementary ideas of right and wrong in the interests of self-preservation.[5]

The revived interest in human beginnings which shows itself in this passage of Polybius appears in the next century in the work of the Stoic Posidonius and the Epicurean Lucretius, both of whom have been acclaimed by some scholars as champions

---

[1] Archimedes, *Method*, p. 430 Heiberg.
[2] Pliny, *Nat. Hist.* 2. 95. See further Edelstein, op. cit. 140–55.
[3] Polybius 10. 43–7.   [4] 3. 4; 3. 31.
[5] 6. 5–7. See Cole, *Democritus* (1967), chap. vi, who goes so far as to call this passage 'probably the most satisfactory purely speculative reconstruction of the origin of society ever attempted'.

of the idea of progress. Posidonius is the greatest polymath of Antiquity, at once philosopher, historian, geographer, and natural scientist. He may also be called the first true *field* anthropologist. His interest in cultural origins seems to have arisen out of his personal studies among the semi-civilized Celts of Gaul and the barbarous tribes of Lusitania, in whose way of life he saw a clue to the original condition of mankind.[1] The rather odd picture of human development which resulted is known to us from Seneca's *Ninetieth Letter*, where his views are quoted and criticized. Posidonius knew too much about the ways of contemporary 'primitives' to treat man's earliest days as a Golden Age. But at some stage of the development—it is not clear just where—he postulated the emergence of wise philosophers (*sapientes*) who invented the useful arts and ruled the people for their good, not out of a lust for power but, like Plato's philosopher kings, out of a sense of duty; this was the true Golden Age when men were, in a phrase which echoes Plato, 'fresh from the hands of the gods'.[2] At a later date tyrannies arose, and thus the need for laws to hold them in check; but for Posidonius, as for Plato, the rule of law is only a second-best. His further account seems to have been mainly concerned (to Seneca's disgust) with the growth of the various practical skills, such as house-building, milling, weaving, etc. This interest in technology, nourished by his ethnographic observations, is a welcome change from the usual Greek contempt for manual occupations. But it hardly justifies us in crediting Posidonius with a belief in 'the idea of endless progress'.[3] No doubt, like the Alexandrine scientists, he expected a continuing increase in professional skills, but morally his own age seems to have represented for him a decline from the ideal standards of his *sapientes*. Whether these were originally suggested to him by the Platonic philosopher kings or by the 'learned men' to whom Democritus[4] had ascribed the origin of religion or by his own encounters with Gaulish druids, they show that for all his scientific empiricism he never completely liberated himself either from the myth of the Lost Paradise or from the moralizing tendencies of his school.

[1] Cf. Reinhardt, *Poseidonios* (1921), 397–9.
[2] 'a dis recentes', Seneca, *Epist.* 90. 44; cf. Plato, *Philebus* 16 c, and Sextus Empiricus, *adv. phys.* 1. 28.
[3] Edelstein, op. cit. 169. [4] Democritus, frag. 30 Diels–Kranz.

The same tension between the belief in technological progress and the belief in moral regress appears in an even more acute form in the fifth book of Lucretius, the fullest account of prehistory which has come down to us from Antiquity. As a good materialist Lucretius refuses to see the hand of Providence at any point in the story: the human race is the product of accident, and its achievements are its own, brought about in response to the spur of necessity by 'men who excelled in understanding and were strong in mind' (5. 1107). Progress in all the skills of civilization has been steady and gradual (*pedetemptim*, 5. 1453); some are still advancing (5. 332–7), but in general they are said to have attained their perfection (*summum . . . cacumen*, 5. 1457). All this is very much in the spirit of Democritus. But civilization has brought with it the seeds of corruption. Where necessity was once the mother of invention, invention has now become the mother of necessity: every fresh invention creates a new need (5. 1412–15), whereas the only true riches is 'to live frugally with a contented mind' (5. 1118 f.). Worse still, modern society offers new opportunities to senseless ambition (5. 1120 ff.), including what Lucretius had experienced in his own lifetime, the opportunity of large-scale war (5. 999 f., 1434 f.). Thus he plays off morals against technology, Epicurus against Democritus and against the Hellenistic scientists.

On one point the two conflicting currents in his thought appear to land him in flat self-contradiction. In one place we are told that the world is still in its first youth (5. 330 f.), with the implication that it still has great possibilities before it; yet elsewhere we learn that Nature is now worn out, like a woman past the age of childbearing, so that for all his modern tools the farmer can scarcely wring a livelihood from the soil which once yielded crops spontaneously and in abundance (2. 1150–74; 5. 826 f.). The idea that the generative powers of the earth have diminished was a traditional one,[1] but it is here given an alarmist turn which is seemingly new. Despite certain critics, Lucretius was no whole-hearted apostle of progress (it would have been a little surprising if he were, considering the times he lived in).[2]

[1] Cf. Diodorus 1. 7. 6, the earth can no longer generate large animals as it must once have done—a notion which may go back to Archelaus (60 A 4 Diels–Kranz).
[2] The best discussion of Lucretius' attitude to progress is still Robin's essay 'Sur la conception épicurienne du progrès', *Rev. de Métaphysique et de Morale*, 23 (1916), 697 ff., reprinted in his *La Pensée hellénique* (1942).

The age of civil war and corruption which destroyed the Roman Republic had a lasting effect on men's valuation of the past and present and on their expectation of the future; it reinforced existing anti-progressive tendencies and stimulated new ones. The immediate reaction was conveyed by Horace when he compressed into eleven lapidary words the advancing moral decline of four generations, of which the last and worst was still to come.[1] This is 'crisis poetry', comparable to the literature of the nineteen-thirties; Fraenkel has warned us not to read into it a general philosophy of history. But the mood of depression strengthened existing doubts about the values of Greek civilization. We see this in the popularity of the supposed *Letters of Anacharsis*, which Cicero did not disdain to quote; in Strabo's view (after Posidonius?) that the Greek way of life has corrupted even the neighbouring barbarians; in the opinion of Pompeius Trogus that Nature has done more for the Scythians than philosophy has for the Greeks; in the judgement of Dio Chrysostom that Prometheus was rightly punished for introducing man to the arts of civilization.[2]

Others, influenced by the prevailing belief in astrology, saw in the disturbing events of their time the symptoms of a *Weltwende*, a fresh turn of the Great Year. This could be interpreted in an optimistic sense: Virgil believed or half believed the Sibylline prophecy which announced the immediate return of the Golden Age.[3] To the Greco-Roman world this was, so far as we know, a novel idea: cyclic theories implied an eventual recurrence of the Golden Age, but no pre-Virgilian text suggests that it is imminent. And the vision soon faded to a formula. It became a standard form of flattery to describe the rule of the existing Emperor as a Golden Age (Seneca applied the term to Nero's reign). At the opposite extreme, Juvenal can find no metal base enough to symbolize man's present condition, and Lucian thinks that 'the Race of Lead' would be too flattering a description.[4] This is rhetorical hyperbole. But we must take more seriously the strange apocalyptic passage in Seneca's *Natural Questions*[5] where the displaced and disappointed ex-minister, drawing on

[1] *Odes* 3. 6. 46 ff.; cf. E. Fraenkel, *Horace* (1957), 286–8.
[2] Cicero, *Tusc.* 5. 90; Strabo 7. 3. 7; Justin, *Epitome*, 2. 2; Dio Chrysostom 6. 25.
[3] Virgil, *Ecl.* 4. 4 ff.; *Aen.* 6. 791 ff.
[4] Seneca, *Apocol.* 4. 1; Juvenal 13. 28–30; Lucian, *Saturnalia*, 20.
[5] Seneca, *N.Q.* 3. 27–30.

oriental sources, contemplates with something unpleasantly like glee the prospect of 'the single day which shall destroy the human race'. That such a day must come was traditional Stoic doctrine, and probably troubled believers no more seriously than the eventual cooling of the earth disturbed the optimism of nineteenth-century thinkers.[1] What is new, as in the case of Virgil, is Seneca's conviction that the day is not far off; what shocks us is his gloating description of it in terms which recall modern visions of atomic destruction: 'Cities that an age has built an hour obliterates.'

This passage is no doubt exceptional. But two other, more widely shared, anxieties tended to darken men's expectations of the future. One was the suspicion which we have already met in Lucretius that the earth itself is growing old and losing its vigour; it reappears in Seneca[2] and in many later writers. The other was the more specific feeling that the might of Rome—which good patriots from Virgil onwards declared to be eternal—had in fact like all things mortal its predetermined life-span and was already declining into impotent old age. This too figures in Seneca,[3] though his language is prudently obscure, and goes back beyond him to the age of civil war and even, in principle, to Polybius.[4] Both these premonitions of evil were later to be reinforced by Christian eschatological expectations, though both were in origin independent of Christianity.

Where sentiments of this sort prevail little interest in the idea of progress can logically be expected. Even the mystical faith in the eternity of Rome to which many clung for support in good times and bad, from Virgil down to the fifth-century poet Rutilius Namatianus,[5] did not carry with it any necessary belief in progress; it was essentially a faith in the perpetuation of a static present. Such testimony to progress as we find in the Roman Imperial Age comes, as in the Hellenistic period, chiefly from the scientists and technologists. Vitruvius in his book on architecture and Manilius in his poem on astronomy describe the gradual rise of their respective sciences from crude beginnings

[1] Guthrie, *In the Beginning* (1957), 78.
[2] Seneca, *Epist.* 90. 40, 44.
[3] As quoted by Lactantius, *Div. Inst.* 7. 15. 14 ff.
[4] Polybius 6. 9. 10–14. On the history of this idea see R. Häussler in *Hermes* 92 (1964), 313–41, and Gatz, *Weltalter* (1967), 108–13.
[5] Rutilius, *de reditu suo*, 1. 133 ff.

in terms which exclude any hint of a past Golden Age. Manilius shares Lucretius' pride in scientific achievement without his moral despondency. 'Man's capacity for learning', he tells us, 'has by effort vanquished every difficulty, and did not count its task finished until reason had scaled the heavens and grasped the deep nature of things and seen in its causes all that exists.'[1] As for the future, the elder Pliny—again in an astronomical context, *Nat. Hist.* 2. 62—remarks that no one should lose hope that the ages will continually make progress. But the most confident pronouncements come, to our surprise, from that same Seneca who predicted the early demise of the present world. Elsewhere in the *Natural Questions* he declares that science is still in its infancy: 'The day will come when time and longer study will bring to light truths at present hidden . . . when our descendants will be astonished at our ignorance of what to them is obvious.'[2] The same expectation of indefinite progress appears in other passages of *Nat. Q.*[3] and in the *Letters*, 64. 7, where we are assured that 'no one born a thousand ages hence will lack the opportunity to add to the store of knowledge'. But Seneca's enthusiasm is limited to pure science, whose aim is simply 'the knowledge of Nature'; applied science he thinks positively harmful; the liberal arts he judges in the old Stoic manner as worthless save in so far as they conduce to moral improvement.[4] And in his own day he sees only decadence: far from advancing, science and philosophy are actually on the retreat.[5] The question of his sources and of his consistency is too complex for discussion here.[6]

All the writers quoted in the preceding paragraph belong to the Early Empire. The two centuries which followed were the final period of consolidation and unification in all the sciences: thus medicine was unified and systematized by Galen, geography and astronomy by Ptolemy, Roman law by Papinian and Ulpian, and lastly philosophy by Plotinus. But in all these fields consolidation, necessary and valuable though it was, gradually turned to petrifaction. Men stood with their backs to the future; all wisdom was in the past, that is to say in books, and their

---

[1] Manilius 1. 95 ff.   [2] Seneca, *N.Q.* 7. 25.
[3] Ibid. 6. 5. 3; 7. 30. 5.
[4] Ibid. 6. 4. 2; *Epist.* 90. 7 ff.; *Epist.* 88.
[5] *N.Q.* 7. 32.
[6] Edelstein, op. cit. 169–77 and footnotes, supplies a partial bibliography of this vexed question.

only task was one of interpretation. Even Plotinus, the most original mind of the period, saw himself as a schoolman rather than a creative thinker.[1] Where men can build their systems only out of used pieces the notion of progress can have little meaning; the future is devalued in advance. And in the hands of the philosophers the devaluation was gradually extended to cover almost every aspect of human activity except the contemplative, of which mundane action is merely the outward shadow;[2] history is reduced to a transitory puppet-play,[3] so that future and past alike are drained of significance. It was, no doubt, the manifold material horrors of the third century that finally killed any rational expectation of progress. But its epitaph was already written by Marcus Aurelius. 'Our successors', said the Emperor, 'will see nothing new: in a sense, the man who has lived for forty years, if he has any intelligence at all, has seen all that has been and all that will be, since all is of one kind.'[4] οὐδὲν νεώτερον ὄψονται: that is the end of the story for a millennium and more.

As I warned the reader, this is a field where generalization is more than commonly hazardous. Nevertheless a few very simple conclusions may be thought to emerge from the evidence I have presented:

1. It is untrue that the idea of progress was wholly foreign to Antiquity; but our evidence suggests that only during a limited period in the fifth century was it widely accepted by the educated public at large.

2. After the fifth century the influence of all the major philosophical schools was in varying degrees hostile to the idea or restrictive of it.

3. At all periods the most explicit statements of the idea refer to scientific progress and come from working scientists or from writers on scientific subjects.

4. The tension between belief in scientific or technological progress and belief in moral regress is present in many ancient writers —most acutely in Plato, Posidonius, Lucretius, Seneca.

---

[1] See below, pp. 126 f.   [2] Plotinus 3. 8. 4.
[3] Marcus Aurelius 7. 3; Plotinus 3. 2. 15–18.
[4] Marcus Aurelius 11. 1. The sentiment itself was nothing new (cf. Lucr. 3. 945 *eadem sunt omnia semper*; Seneca, *tranq. animi*, 2. 15 *quousque eadem?*; *Epist.* 24. 26), but from the master of the Roman world it comes with singular force.

5. There is a broad correlation between the expectation of progress and the actual experience of progress. Where culture is advancing on a wide front, as in the fifth century, faith in progress is widely diffused; where progress is mainly evident in specialized sciences, as in the Hellenistic Age, faith in it is largely confined to scientific specialists; where progress comes to a virtual halt, as in the last centuries of the Roman Empire, the expectation of further progress vanishes.

II

The Prometheus Vinctus *and the Progress of Scholarship*

WHEN the Trustees of the Dill Memorial Fund did me the honour of inviting me to give the Dill Memorial Lecture for 1946,[1] I was moved to accept their invitation not only by my natural feeling of *pietas* towards the land which bred me but by a sense of what I owe to my fellow countryman, Sir Samuel Dill. I never, alas, knew him as a person, though I believe I once in boyhood heard him speak; but his book on *Roman Society from Nero to Marcus Aurelius*, received as a prize at school, opened a door for me into a fascinating world in which I have since spent a good deal of time, the world of later Greco-Roman culture where Greek rationalism fought its long losing battle against the revelations that came from the East, and under the shadow of the *pax Romana* the patterns of thought that were to rule men's minds for a millennium were slowly taking shape. I am grateful to Dill for this initiation and glad to have the opportunity today of expressing my gratitude.

More than forty years have passed since the publication of that book. They have been years of swift growth and even swifter destruction. The old Chinese curse, 'May you live in interesting times!' has descended on us with a vengeance. And at this moment as we emerge, still a little breathless, from our second World War it is inevitable that we should ask ourselves what future there is for those studies of Classical Antiquity to which Dill gave his life. Ought they indeed to have any future? Can we afford it? Beset as we are with the pressing problems of this new Age of Violence, feeling as many of us do that nothing less

[1] Since this lecture is firmly tied to its situation in time, has circulated in manuscript, and has been utilized by some later writers on the subject (Lloyd-Jones, Rose, Fitton-Brown), I have not attempted to bring it up to date but reproduce it here virtually as it stands in my original draft. I have, however, added a few notes in square brackets where it seemed desirable to supplement my argument or to call the reader's attention to important later publications.

than the future of civilization itself is at stake, can we afford to keep so much of our intellectual manpower employed in working the old mines—mines whose best ore, they tell us, has long since been minted and passed into common currency, mines which are certainly encumbered by mountainous slagheaps, the discarded leavings of past generations of workers? To these questions I shall attempt no direct answer: for Dill's studies are my studies, and I hold that no man can be a judge in his own cause. But there are two things which I should like to say, very briefly, for they are very simple.

The first is, that if we are concerned, as I think we should be, to repair the torn fabric of western European culture, to reaffirm the essential moral and intellectual values by which Western Man has lived for so many centuries, then we cannot afford to lose all contact with that ancient world within which those values were created; we cannot afford to let slip that tradition which is the common cultural inheritance of all the western lands and lies at the root of whatever cultural unity they still possess.

My second point is this. A cultural tradition cannot be transmitted passively. Unless new minds are always at work on it, so that it is continuously reinterpreted and revalued by and for the new generations, it becomes a dead thing, an encumbrance, a pedant's burden. If we aim merely at disseminating in predigested form, through translations and popular handbooks, so much of the results of the labours of former scholars as our children can swallow in their spare time, then I am sure the tradition will die on us. The condition of life is growth: a study which has ceased to progress ceases to attract enterprising minds, and therefore ceases to live.

Now I have sometimes heard it suggested that the study of Classical Antiquity has reached, or will soon reach, this stage: that all the work of major importance has long ago been done and the mine is approaching exhaustion, what remains being at best low-grade ore. Were I satisfied that this was true, I think I should give up teaching Greek and try to find a new profession. But the statement seems to me to be false, and I shall endeavour to illustrate its falsity. What is true, and what the outside critic does not always sufficiently realize, is that the questions which are central for the classical scholar today are for the most part materially different, and nearly always differently formulated, from those on which attention was focused a hundred or even fifty years ago. The public is apt to picture the classical scholar eternally chewing the cud of some stale problem which defeated the best efforts of Bentley and Porson, but such a picture bears very little relation to the facts. It is true that such perennial unsolved problems do exist and that we do from time to time return to them. But when we do so it is usually for one of two reasons: either because some fresh piece of evidence—a new papyrus or a new inscription or a new vase-painting—has put into our hands a critical weapon which Bentley and Porson lacked, or else because the new experience of a new generation of men has suggested a fresh angle of attack. In that way old problems are from time to time either solved or brought a stage nearer to solution. But in classical scholarship, as in all the historical sciences, the more usual and more important type of progress consists in the statement and solution of problems which are themselves entirely or partly new. That may happen through new discoveries which raise new questions. An obvious example is the complete restatement of the Homeric problem, partly in the light of Aegean archaeology, partly through the comparative study of oral poetry, which enables us to see not so much that Wolf and his successors gave the wrong answers as that they asked the wrong questions. But it can also happen without the stimulus of sensational discoveries, through a change in the focus of the scholar's eye. What we find in any document depends on what we are looking for, and what we look for depends on our own interests, which in turn are determined, at least in part, by the intellectual climate of our own age.

This kind of growth could be illustrated from many different fields, among them that in which Dill was a pioneer—the field of Greco-Roman social history. It would be easy to show how the broadening of modern historical interests to include social and economic, cultural and religious institutions, and the consequent shift of focus from the great figures on the public stage to the anonymous army of common men, has led to ever more systematic study of the scattered material to be found in inscriptions and papyri, with the result that today we know the mind and heart, the daily hopes and cares, of the ordinary citizen of the Roman Empire far better than our grandfathers could dream of doing. Or one could show how the modern analysis of logical concepts is at present giving new life to a part of ancient philosophy which in my youth appeared to be stone dead—the study of Aristotelian and Stoic formal logic. Or again, it would be possible to show how recent developments in social anthropology and social psychology open the way to a fuller understanding of Greek religion as an element in the complex pattern of Greek culture. In all these cases new insights have been achieved by putting fresh questions to old witnesses.

I propose in the remainder of this lecture to examine another and prima facie a much less favourable case—the interpretation of a Greek play. The masterpieces of the Attic dramatists have been studied intensively through many generations and have exercised the minds of the very greatest Greek scholars, men like Scaliger and Casaubon, Porson and Elmsley, Hermann and Wilamowitz. Is any further progress really possible here? Let me say at once that in so far as the questions we ask are the same as theirs we are most unlikely to do better than they, save where fortune has put into our hands new evidence or a new critical instrument. That has happened to some extent, especially with Euripides,[1] thanks to the publication of numerous papyrus fragments both of lost plays and of extant ones. The former have widened our knowledge of the poet's mind and style; the value of the latter has lain not so much in the new readings they offered, which have in general been disappointing, as in the light they threw on the history of the text and the nature and origin of the corruptions to which it has been exposed. We may reasonably hope for more such gifts of fortune in the future.

But for the play about which I have chosen to talk today we have at present no such adventitious aids: there are as yet no papyri of the *Prometheus Vinctus*. And unless really good papyri do turn up I doubt if we shall ever have a text of this play substantially better than the one which Wilamowitz edited just before the first World War. No fewer than five scholars of distinction have in fact edited the *Prometheus* since that date—Mazon, Smyth, Groeneboom, Thomson, Murray. But if my arithmetic is right the total number of new readings introduced into the text of the

---

[1] [Since this was written Menander has become for the first time a living figure and there have also been significant additions to our knowledge of Aeschylus and Sophocles.]

play by these five distinguished editors adds up to just six, or rather more than one new reading apiece.¹ And what is more significant than the number, not one of these five editors has accepted a single emendation proposed by any of the other four. Surely this suggests that the law of diminishing returns has begun to operate and that in restoring the text of the *Prometheus* we have got about as far as we are likely to get in the absence of fresh evidence. And while there are plays which offer more scope for conjectural emendation than the *Prometheus*, I think the conclusion is broadly true of Greek tragedy in general. This is also the lesson of the papyri. When a new papyrus of the *Bacchae* was published not long ago, it proved to support no fewer than thirteen corrections made by modern critics. That sounds like a pleasing testimony to our acumen. But before congratulating ourselves we should observe that most of these corrections were glaringly obvious and had been made before the end of the eighteenth century, and that the most recent critic of whose labours the papyrus takes any notice is Paley. On this sort of evidence my advice to those ambitious of immortalizing their names in an *apparatus criticus* would be that they should seek newer pastures: there is still plenty of work of this kind to be done on later texts, including for example such major authors as Strabo, Plutarch, and Plotinus.

This does not mean, however, that in the field of Greek tragedy scholars have no more to do than sit and wait for another papyrus to fall from Heaven. What it points to is a shift in the focus of attention from textual questions to the study of dramatic technique on the one hand, and on the other to the problem of relating the individual work of art to the social and cultural background out of which it grew. That shift has already taken place. It is exemplified on the one hand by books like Kranz's *Stasimon* and Professor Kitto's *Greek Tragedy*, on the other by Pohlenz's excellent book on tragedy (which ought to be translated) and in a more controversial way by Professor George Thomson's *Aeschylus and Athens*.

In the case of the *Prometheus Vinctus* a lively discussion has in our day been focused on three interconnected problems. These concern respectively its date and authenticity; the structure of

¹ [Murray's revised text (1955) incorporates in this play one additional new conjecture; Untersteiner's (1948), none.]

the trilogy (the *Prometheia*) of which it is presumed to have formed part; and the meaning of the work as a whole. I propose to offer some account of this controversy, because it illustrates so well the way in which contemporary issues are mirrored in the world of learning, and also the way in which the human weaknesses of scholars pervert their judgement and yet sometimes in the end contribute to the progress of scholarship.

Of the three questions I have mentioned it is historically convenient to start from the last—the question of the meaning of the work. Logically, we should not attempt to answer it until we have answered the other two; but in practice the views which scholars have held on this question have largely determined their opinion on the others. The discussion has its roots in the nineteenth century. Until then, readers of the *Prometheus Vinctus* had usually been content to interpret the play in the light of their immediate emotional response to it. And the nature of that response was never in doubt. To the imagination of the Christian Fathers the picture of the ancient Titan who suffers for his love of humanity had appeared as a prefigurement of the Christian Redeemer on the cross. To the imagination of the poets—of Goethe, Shelley, Byron—it had appeared as a symbol of the revolt of human intelligence against 'a world it never made', since, as a Greek poet put it, 'the Promethean part of man is his intellect'.[1] But nineteenth-century scholars would have none of that. Was not Prometheus the enemy of Zeus? And was not Zeus for Aeschylus the holiest of all names? Do not the Danaids in his *Supplices* pray to Zeus as 'King of Kings, most blessed of the blessed, among the perfect Power most perfect'?[2] Do not the old men in the *Agamemnon* cry out in a bewildered time that 'Only in the thought of Zeus can the heart be free from its vain burden of distress'?[3]

Hermann indeed declared stoutly that such contradictions did not matter: Aeschylus was a dramatist, not a theologian, and his attitude to Zeus just varied with the myths he handled. But the majority of nineteenth-century scholars thought otherwise, and concluded, with Schoemann,[4] that since Prometheus is a rebel against the supreme and holy God, our naïve sympathy with him cannot correspond to the poet's intention. Prometheus, said

[1] Plato comicus, frag. 136 Kock. [See above, pp. 6 f.]   [2] *Suppl.* 524 ff.
[3] *Ag.* 163 ff.   [4] *Gefesseltes Prometheus* (1844).

Schoemann, was quite mistaken in supposing that he had done a service to mankind by creating the arts of civilization; all he had invented was technology, a nasty thing which does people harm by making them rich and materialistic. Whether astronomy and medicine actually have this effect, whether this was really the view of 'technology' held by Aeschylus, whether it was even a possible view in the earlier part of the fifth century, Schoemann did not pause to inquire; but his argument was very gratifying to professors of Greek, resentful as they were against the growing claims of the upstart natural scientists, and they have often repeated it since.[1]

Correspondingly great efforts were made to whitewash the Zeus of the *Prometheus Vinctus*. Sikes and Willson express the accepted judgement of their time when they observe in their preface to the play: 'Prometheus had sinned, and was further sinning; Zeus was acting within his rights in punishing the sinner at the commencement of the play, and in adding to his punishment at the end ... The Judge had been stern, but not unjust.' Professor J. A. K. Thomson in a paper published in 1920 found it possible to go even further. 'The design of Zeus', he thought, 'may honestly be regarded as something higher and in the long run more beneficial to man himself than the hasty generosity of Prometheus.'[2] This seems to me a dark saying. The only design of Zeus for mankind about which the poet has told us was a design to liquidate the lot. 'Zeus', we are told, 'paid no regard to suffering humanity; he intended to wipe out the entire breed and replace it by another.'[3] To quote *this* design as an example of the higher beneficence one must be a pessimist indeed. But there is no trace of any other.

The first advance resulting from the modern discussion has been the fairly general abandonment of such attempts to distort

---

[1] Cf. the works of Schmid and Vandvik referred to below. George Thomson, from the opposite standpoint, praises Aeschylus for his 'bold materialism' (*Aeschylus and Athens* (1941), 327). But in fact the main stress in the great anthropological speech (441–506) is laid on *intellectual* achievements—astronomy, arithmetic, medicine, divination. The potter's wheel, which we might expect to find mentioned, is left out: apparently it was too βάναυσος, too 'technological', for Aeschylus. It would be easier (though for other reasons still wrong) to find 'bold materialism' in the Ode to Man in the *Antigone*. [See above, pp. 5 f.]

[2] 'The Religious Background of the *Prometheus Vinctus*', *Harv. Stud. in Class. Philol.* 31 (1920), 36.

[3] *P.V.* 231 ff.

the evidence, attempts which in origin seem to reflect the extremely conservative and monarchist tendencies of nineteenth-century universities, especially in Germany. They are not, however, wholly dead even now. As recently as 1943 a Norwegian scholar named Vandvik published a curious essay[1] in which he maintained that the account of the situation given by Prometheus is completely false and that the audience is meant to perceive its falsity. Since Zeus is just, it is impossible that he should have meant to destroy mankind; since he is all-powerful, it is impossible that Prometheus should have saved them; since he is omniscient, it is impossible that Prometheus should possess a secret which Zeus does not know. These are merely the delusions of the insane Titan, and both we and the Chorus are very silly to sympathize with him. The people with whom we ought to sympathize are Oceanus, who is a 'noble' character, and Cratos and Hermes, who represent 'the Olympian wisdom'. I mention this theory, not on account of its merits—for it seems to me to have none—but because it constitutes a logical *reductio ad absurdum* of the nineteenth-century interpretation.

For the objection to that interpretation is simply that it does not fit the facts as the poet has chosen to represent them. Far from attempting to whitewash Zeus, Aeschylus appears, as various critics have shown,[2] to have gone out of his way to exhibit him in the most unfavourable light. All that he has added to the Hesiodic tradition—Prometheus' new status as son of Themis, the goddess of Justice, and as inventor of all arts and sciences, his services to Zeus in the war against the Titans, and his frustration of the plan to destroy mankind, not to mention the Io scene—all this tends to exalt the character of Prometheus and to blacken that of his divine adversary. Had Aeschylus meant us to think of Zeus as 'stern but just', of Prometheus as (in the words of a German textbook) 'an impertinent reformer', he could and presumably would have written the play otherwise. He could, for example, have given Zeus more sympathetic advocates than the ugly brute Cratos, whose tongue, we are told, matches his appearance,[3] and the still nastier Hermes, who is,

[1] 'The Prometheus of Hesiod and Aeschylus', *Norske Videnskaps-Akademi*, Hist.-Filos. Klasse 1942 (Oslo, 1943).
[2] Cf. S. H. Butcher, *Harvard Lectures on Greek Subjects* (1904), 17 ff.; L. E. Matthaei, *Studies in Greek Tragedy* (1918), 10 ff.; O. J. Todd, *C.Q.* 19 (1925), 61 ff.; L. R. Farnell, *J.H.S.* 53 (1933), 40 ff. [3] *P.V.* 78.

and is surely meant to be, the worst sort of 'gentleman's gentleman'. If these are the employees, what, asks the audience, must the employer be? But except these two no one in the play perceives the divine justice which was so obvious to Victorian editors. Hephaestus does his work with a disgusted reluctance, and even the time-serving Oceanus calls Zeus 'a harsh and irresponsible ruler'.[1] As for Io, her sufferings could well have been attributed solely to Hera's malice, as in fact they are in the *Supplices*; but in the *P.V.* she names Zeus as their author and therefore longs for his dethronement.[2] There remains only the Chorus. The Chorus wobble, as Choruses do, torn between sympathy for Prometheus and alarm at his dangerous utterances: as Farnell put it, 'to sit on the fence and recommend prudence is the bourgeois function of Choruses'. But at the end they come off their fence and choose to sink into Tartarus with Prometheus rather than play the coward at the command of Hermes.[3] This is surely decisive evidence of the side on which our sympathies are meant to lie. And we cannot evade it by supposing, as certain scholars have done, that at the last moment they change their mind and run away: such a change would have to be indicated in the text. Vandvik, perceiving that the Chorus's decision is fatal to his whole view of the play, is driven to assume that the lines in which they announce it are an interpolation.

Short of such lame subterfuges there seems to be no escape from the conclusion that the *P.V.* as it stands is what the Russians would call an 'anti-God play'. For those who still hold that the devout Aeschylus cannot have written such a play there is only one road out of the dilemma—by proving that the *P.V.* is not his work. Once the nineteenth-century interpretation had collapsed, it was logical that this desperate attempt should be made; and it was made, as we should expect on social and political grounds, in Germany. The campaign was opened by Gercke, who in 1911 suggested that the play was composed in the early years of the Peloponnesian War by an admirer of Euripides. But a much weightier attack was launched in 1929 by a well-known scholar, Wilhelm Schmid of Tübingen, in his *Untersuchungen zum gefesselten Prometheus*. Schmid dates the play about 450–445, and claims it as 'our oldest evidence for the existence

---

[1] *P.V.* 324. [2] *P.V.* 757–60; contrast *Suppl.* 296.
[3] *P.V.* 1063–70.

of the sophistic movement and its radicalism about the middle of the fifth century at Athens'. Its purpose was to glorify the idea of progress and thus exalt Man in general, and technical education in particular, at the expense of God. It was intended as a counterblast to the *Prometheus Lyomenos*, which was a genuine work of Aeschylus. Owing to the bad taste of later generations the two plays got confused, and the *Vinctus* was preserved among the works of Aeschylus while the *Lyomenos* was lost. We do not know who composed the *Vinctus*, but he can hardly have been an Athenian gentleman, for it is evident that he sympathized with the industrial classes. Schmid would prefer to attribute the play to a metic, 'a business man with a colonial point of view', or to some alien like Ion of Chios.

Schmid supported these opinions with impressive batteries of learning. Yet he appears to have made very few converts, even in Germany. Nor is that surprising, for the difficulties of his theory are many and, I think, insuperable. I shall not spend time on listing them all. Perhaps it is enough to say that, apart from the unlikelihood of the sort of confusion Schmid postulates, the *Vinctus* was clearly meant to have a sequel (as its numerous loose ends and unfulfilled prophecies show) and trilogies were out of fashion in the 'forties; that the supposed links with the sophistic movement vanish on closer inspection;[1] and finally, that Oceanus and Danaus, Io's madness and Cassandra's, the geographical lecture in the *Vinctus* and the geographical digressions in the *Supplices* and the *Agamemnon*, are unmistakably creations of the same mind.

One may wonder why Schmid, an able and learned man, did not see all this for himself. The answer, I suppose, must be that the play appeared to him so dangerous, so subversive of all that a conservative German believed in, that it was essential to find reasons for excluding it from the Aeschylean canon. On that view his book affords what Housman called in another connection 'fresh and superfluous proof of the weakness of man's reason and the strength of his passions'. Yet scholarship sometimes draws

[1] The *word* σοφιστής is older than the movement it has come to denote for us. It occurs not only in the *P.V.* (62, 944) but in an undisputed fragment of Aeschylus (frag. 314 Nauck), where it describes an 'expert' musician; Herodotus applies it to Solon (1. 29) and Pythagoras (4. 95). [Cf. now Guthrie, *A History of Greek Philosophy*, iii. 27–34.] The typical concepts of sophistic anthropology, 'need' and 'utility', are significantly missing from the *P.V.*

unexpected profit from the human frailties of scholars. In the course of failing to prove that the *P.V.* was the work of an unknown atheist, Schmid did an important service to learning: he brought together a very substantial body of evidence tending to show that in metre, diction, style, and structure the *P.V.* stands apart from the rest of Aeschylus' work, and by doing this he set a new problem. Not indeed entirely new: Wackernagel[1] had already called attention to certain linguistic peculiarities, Ernest Harrison[2] to the presence of 'Sophoclean' rhythms in the trimeters, and as far back as 1869 the metrical singularity of some of the choral odes had led Westphal[3] to suggest that the play had been worked over by a later hand. But by his full statement of the evidence Schmid focused attention on the problem of accounting for it.

Some of his points are easily disposed of. That the *P.V.* should be 'the poorest in action of all Greek plays' need surprise no one: a person chained to a rock has little opportunity for action. Nor need we wonder that such words as φάραγξ, 'a gulley', πλάνη, 'wandering', χρίειν, 'to sting', occur repeatedly in the *P.V.* but nowhere else in Aeschylus: they would not have occurred here were it not that the scene is laid among mountains and that one character is a wanderer tormented by a gadfly. There remains, however, a good deal which cannot be so lightly dismissed. In particular, Schmid's investigations into the build of the iambic trimeters, since supplemented by the work of Denniston,[4] Yorke,[5] and others, prove that in a number of respects the *P.V.* shows a closer approximation to Sophoclean technique than any other play of Aeschylus, representing in several cases a more advanced development of tendencies which are observable in the *Oresteia*. Again, the *P.V.* has certain common words which Aeschylus elsewhere avoids but the other tragedians do not—notably λίαν, οἷός τε, καίτοι, and the interjection φέρε. Other features which seem to call for explanation are the brevity of the choral odes, compensated by Io's long monodies, and the prevalence of dactylo-epitrite metre; the very curious changes of metre in Prometheus' opening speech; and, perhaps most striking of all,

[1] 'Sprachgeschichtliches zu Aischylos, *Prometheus*', *Verhandlungen der Versammlung der Philologen* (1902), 65 f.
[2] *Proc. Camb. Philol. Soc.*, 1921.
[3] *Prolegomena zu Aeschylus' Tragödien* (1869).   [4] *C.Q.* 30 (1936), 73 ff., 192.
[5] Ibid. 116 ff., 153 f.

the Progress of Scholarship

the relative simplicity and clarity of the style as compared with any other play of Aeschylus.[1]

Since the publication of Schmid's book discussion has been largely centred on trying to account for these peculiarities. Some of them suggest the possible influence of Sophocles, whose first play was acted in 468, thirteen years before Aeschylus' death. That in a rapidly changing poetic climate a great poet can sharply modify his style late in life, partly under the influence of his juniors, has been shown in our own day by the example of W. B. Yeats; we may recall also how Propertius learned from Ovid. The dating of the *P.V.* soon after 470, which was accepted in the nineteenth century on not very conclusive grounds, has accordingly been called in question: George Thomson and others would put it at the very end of Aeschylus' life, between the *Oresteia* in 458 and his death in 456/5.[2] Among other advantages, such a date would enable us to assume that Aeschylus used three actors here, as he did in the *Oresteia*, and thus get rid of the grotesque and (as I think) unworkable hypothesis that Prometheus was represented by a wooden dummy.[3]

Further, tradition says that after the production of the *Oresteia* Aeschylus retired to Sicily; and if the play was written for production at Syracuse, this may account for some of its distinctive peculiarities. If he had in mind an audience unused to the high and elaborate style of Attic tragedy, Aeschylus may well have deemed it prudent to keep his diction simple and his choral odes short;[4] he may also have purposely introduced one or two local Sicilian words, as the scholiasts tell us he did.

These suggestions seem to me plausible as far as they go. Whether they go far enough is perhaps still open to dispute. Observing that so good a judge as Kranz[5] cannot believe all the choral odes to be the work of Aeschylus, Professor D. S. Robertson[6] put forward shortly before the war a hypothesis which I find tempting on several grounds. According to the *Suda*, a number of

---

[1] [I have quoted only a sample of the evidence. For the most complete statement and discussion of it see now C. J. Herington's indispensable book, *The Author of the 'Prometheus Bound'* (1970).]
[2] [In my judgement this dating has now been put on a firm foundation by Herington's work.]
[3] [This hypothesis still has its defenders, but see the objections of P. Arnott, *Greek Scenic Conventions* (1962), 96 ff., and Herington, 88 f.]
[4] Cf. F. Focke, *Hermes*, 65 (1930), 259 ff.
[5] *Stasimon*, 126 ff.
[6] *Proc. Camb. Philol. Soc.* 1938.

Aeschylus' plays were not performed in his lifetime but were staged posthumously by his son Euphorion (who also wrote plays of his own). Robertson suggested that the *P.V.* may have been among these posthumously staged plays, that it was unfinished, and that Euphorion supplied some of the odes as stopgaps.

I find this hypothesis seductive because it can be used to explain a number of difficulties besides those which its author had in mind. Ancient editors were notoriously conservative, even to the point of preserving obvious doublets; and I think we can reasonably assume that if Euphorion found a number of unfinished and unplaced passages among his father's drafts for the *P.V.*, he would probably do his best to work them in rather than let them be lost to posterity. Now there is one passage in the play which most scholars, since Badham pointed it out, have judged to be misplaced if not spurious, namely the lines about Atlas which so strangely interrupt the splendid ode on the universal mourning for Prometheus.[1] It cannot, I think, have been designed for this place; yet it is convincingly Aeschylean in style, there is nowhere else in the play where it could go, and it seems too long for a marginal adscript. On Robertson's hypothesis I should be disposed to guess that it was a fragment of an earlier draft, either for the *P.V.* itself or for some other uncompleted part of the tetralogy, which Euphorion inserted here because he did not want to waste it and the *metrical* context was more or less suitable. On the same principle one might also suspect that the odd patchwork of metres in the Titan's opening speech had its source in Euphorion's editorial activities.

Robertson's hypothesis would also relieve us of some embarrassing questions concerning the other plays of the tetralogy. We know that the *Vinctus* was followed by the *Lyomenos* (*The Unbinding of Prometheus*), and we have sufficient fragments of the latter to reconstruct a good part of its action in rough outline. But on the remaining plays of the set Antiquity is strangely silent. The satyr-play is nowhere mentioned; the only known satyr-play of Aeschylus dealing with Prometheus is the *Pyrkaeus*, and this, we know, was staged along with the *Persae* in 472. As for the remaining tragedy, it has been identified since Welcker with the play called *Prometheus Pyrphoros* in the Medicean list. But the *Pyrphoros* is a tantalizing ghost. Scholars have been unable to

[1] *P.V.* 425–30.

agree as to its subject or the position it occupied in the trilogy. The solitary line which is quoted as coming from it[1] tells us nothing, and appears in almost the same form in the *Choephoroe*. Nor does the opinion made fashionable by Westphal, which derives its name from the institution of a torchlight procession in honour of Prometheus, really help us very much: a procession does not make a play. Since we cannot decide what it was about, and since the Medicean table of *dramatis personae* for the trilogy appears to take account only of the *Vinctus* and the *Lyomenos*, I feel tempted to return to Hermann's view that the *Pyrphoros* of the list is merely an alternative title for the satyr-play *Pyrkaeus*[2]— which the list omits, though it certainly once existed. That would leave us with only two Prometheus tragedies, the *Vinctus* and the *Lyomenos*, which has generally been thought impossible, since we do not hear of Aeschylus or anybody else presenting 'dilogies'. If indeed the plays were intended *solely* for production at Syracuse, the objection is perhaps not decisive: we do not know the rules, if there were any, which governed Sicilian dramatic festivals.[3]

But Robertson's hypothesis suggests another possible explanation: the reason why we hear so little of the two remaining plays of the tetralogy may be simply that Aeschylus died before he had written them. He may have planned to prefix to the *Vinctus* a tragedy dealing with earlier events such as the theft of fire and Zeus' threat to destroy mankind, which are mentioned only briefly in the *Vinctus*; this would have made clear among other things the part played in these events by Ocean, to which there is an unexplained and puzzling allusion in our play.[4] As it was,

---

[1] Frag. 208 Nauck, cf. *Cho.* 582. [I agree with Fraenkel and Snell that *P. Oxy.* 2245 (frag. 278 in Lloyd-Jones's appendix to the Loeb Aeschylus) cannot be attributed to the *Pyrphoros*; such indications as we have point to a satyr-play, presumably the *Pyrkaeus*.]

[2] [An objection to identifying the *Pyrphoros* with the *Pyrkaeus* (which dealt with the theft of fire) has often been based on the tense of δεδέσθαι in schol. *P.V.* 94: ἐν γὰρ τῷ Πυρφόρῳ γ' μυριάδας φησὶ δεδέσθαι αὐτόν. But the tense of the scholiast's paraphrase need not be that used by Aeschylus (cf. the similarly loose use of φησὶ δεδέσθαι in the Hypothesis to our play, line 10). And in fact the figure of 30,000 years is incompatible, if literally meant, with the assumptions of the *Prometheia* (a space of 13 generations, *P.V.* 774). See Pohlenz, *Die griechische Tragödie* (1930), i. 70, and now A. D. Fitton-Brown, *J.H.S.* 79 (1959), 53.]

[3] Cf. Focke, loc. cit. [A similar view has since been put forward, partly at my suggestion, by the late Professor H. J. Rose in his *Commentary on the Surviving Plays of Aeschylus* (1957–8), i. 9 f.]

[4] *P.V.* 331.

Aeschylus died, the tetralogy remained a dilogy, and the so-called *Pyrphoros* is the ghost not of a lost play but of an unborn one.

All this, however, is sheer speculation, and likely, perhaps, always to remain speculation: I mention it only to show that even in so hackneyed a field of discussion there is still room for fresh ideas. We must now return to the question from which we started —the question what Aeschylus made of the Prometheus story as a whole and what significance he saw in it.

We know from the fragments of the *Lyomenos* and from the mythographical tradition that the conflict between Zeus and the Titan ended at last in a reconciliation. Heracles shot the torturing eagle; Prometheus yielded up his secret, perhaps on the advice of his mother Themis who is also Mother Earth; he was released from bondage and restored to a place of honour. What the terms of the reconciliation were we are, alas, not told. But I think it would now be fairly widely agreed that it cannot have been brought about simply by a one-sided surrender on the part of Prometheus. After the magnificent crescendo of defiance which we have witnessed in the *Vinctus* such an unmotived transition from pride to humility must have produced a painful and depressing effect of anticlimax. When the poet has used all his art to make his audience share the Titan's resentment against the divine tyrant, to thrill them with the spectacle of a moral and intellectual will unconquerable in its resistance to arbitrary might, if he then proceeded to exhibit the defeat and abject surrender of that will, what lesson could they draw save that the world is in the grip of an irresponsible and unscrupulous power against which all resistance is in vain? Besides being μιαρόν, morally shocking to Greek ideas, such a conclusion would indeed contradict all that Aeschylus has implied elsewhere about the relations between God and Man. And it would also make nonsense of certain passages in the *Vinctus*. Consider the prediction put into Prometheus' mouth at line 190:

> τὴν δ' ἀτέραμνον στορέσας ὀργὴν
> εἰς ἀρθμὸν ἐμοὶ καὶ φιλότητα
> σπεύδων σπεύδοντί ποθ' ἥξει,

'Subduing his stubborn temper, Zeus shall come at last to a pact of friendship with me, and the will shall be his and mine.' In a Greek play such a prophecy is virtually an undertaking given by the poet to the audience, an undertaking which he is expected to honour. And its fulfilment clearly requires more than a mere surrender on Prometheus' part. The pact is to be a voluntary treaty of peace, and one of its conditions is a change in the temper of Zeus. Such a change is again predicted at line 981. Prometheus has uttered a groan, ὤμοι, and Hermes has observed tauntingly that in the bright vocabulary of Zeus there is no such word as ὤμοι. 'Ah,' says Prometheus, 'but Time as he grows older teaches every lesson.' He plainly implies that Zeus will one day learn to say ὤμοι. That is again an undertaking which commits the poet.

We must suppose, therefore, as many scholars now do, that in the *Lyomenos* Aeschylus presented not only a changed Prometheus but a changed Zeus. And there is in fact some direct evidence of this: for in the interval between the two plays Zeus had decided to liberate Prometheus' fellow Titans, who formed the Chorus of the *Lyomenos*. That seems to mean that Zeus has already, before the *Lyomenos* opens, begun to 'subdue his stubborn temper'. In the *Vinctus* he is a raw, untried sovereign: with an emphasis which must be deliberate, and which surely has a bearing on the sequel, the insulting term νέος is applied to him no less than nine times in the course of the play. Among Greeks to call a ruler 'new' is an insult: it implies that his sovereignty lacks proper sanction. But it is also an excuse, for it implies inexperience. Wilamowitz[1] justifiably compared the man who excused the peculiar behaviour of Jehovah in the early books of the Old Testament; 'Ah, but the Lord God was young himself in those days.' The Zeus of the *Prometheia* visibly begins as the savage, unmoralized god of legend; we must believe that he ended as the god whom Aeschylus worshipped. The moral gulf to be bridged is wide, but so is the time-scale of the *Prometheia*: between the beginning of the action and its end thirteen human generations must intervene.[2] That slow but decisive change may in fact reflect the evolution of morals and religion in the mind of man; but to Aeschylus and his audience it necessarily appears as an objective evolution in Heaven.[3]

[1] *Aischylos: Interpretationen* (1914), 150. [That gods, like men, gain in experience with age is already assumed by Homer, *Iliad* 21. 440.] [2] *P.V.* 774.
[3] [It has sometimes been suggested that the change in Zeus should be read as a conscious symbol of the gradual change in men's religious ideas. But as G. Grossman has recently remarked (*Promethie und Orestie* (1970), 85), Aeschylus was

This notion of a 'progressive' Zeus seems strange to us, who are accustomed to associate progress not with God but with our beliefs about him. First suggested by Dissen as far back as 1824, it was rejected by the great Welcker, and among nineteenth-century scholars only a very few (most notably Lewis Campbell and Henri Weil) had the temerity to adopt it. In the present century it has won much wider acceptance;[1] but there is still an important minority who assert flatly that such a notion is 'un-Hellenic'.[2] Is not that because our idea of what is 'Hellenic' is still too much coloured by Plato and Aristotle? The doctrine of a changeless and eternal God took root in Greek thought only when Plato (following a hint in Parmenides) had expounded the conception of *aiōn* as a timeless mode of being, of which time is the 'moving image'. Later this doctrine was to be grafted on to Christianity through the influence of Platonizing thinkers like Saint Augustine. But the gods of earlier Greek belief are no more changeless than the early Jewish Jehovah. They are not timeless beings external to the cosmos; they are part of its furniture (cf. Hesiod, *Works and Days*, 108). And being within the cosmos they are within time and have each of them a personal history in time: Zeus, for example, had once been a child, and you could even visit his birthplace.

In the conception of such beings there was nothing to exclude the assumption of a moral development. And if belief in the old

not a modern 'Religionshistoriker': the change he depicts is an objective one and is situated in the mythical past before the Trojan War.]

[1] [To the long list of scholars who (with individual variations) have adopted this view, quoted by H. Lloyd-Jones, 'Zeus in Aeschylus', *J.H.S.* 76 (1956), n. 21, we may now add the names of N. Terzaghi, *Rendiconti Accad. Lincei* (1955); A. D. Fitton-Brown, *J.H.S.* 79 (1959), 52 ff.; G. Méautis, *L'Authenticité et la date du Prométhée Enchaîné* (1960); and G. Grossman, op. cit.]

[2] [So Farnell, *J.H.S.* 53 (1933), 47; Lloyd-Jones, op. cit.; Rose, *Commentary*, i. 11; L. Golden, *In Praise of Prometheus* (1962), 103 ff. But the most eloquent and influential proponent of this opinion has been Karl Reinhardt (*Aischylos als Regisseur und Theologe* (1949); 'Prometheus', *Eranos-Jahrbuch* 25 (1957)). Reinhardt's conception, however, of the Aeschylean Zeus as a mysterious two-faced *coincidentia oppositorum*, simultaneously tyrant and saviour, seems to me a good deal more anachronistic than the view here defended. And it gets little support from the text of Aeschylus, where, as *P.V.* 981 indicates, the element of time is all-important. In the *Vinctus* only the tyrant face is visible; in the *Lyomenos*, to judge from the fragments, only the saviour face appeared (cf. Grossman's criticism, op. cit. 102 ff.). Nor has Golden convinced me that the Zeus of the *P.V.* is just a symbol for 'the destructive forces of nature', totally distinct from the Zeus of the *Supplices*: what audience could read this riddle?]

the Progress of Scholarship

legends was to be reconciled with belief in divine justice, that assumption may well have appeared to certain thoughtful minds as not only possible but necessary. Stobaeus has preserved a long and interesting passage from a later tragedian, Moschion, in which someone speaks of a bygone time when 'Law took a humble seat and Violence [*Bia*] shared the throne of Zeus'.[1] Since the speaker mentions Prometheus a few lines lower down, it is not unlikely that Moschion had in mind Aeschylus' play, where Kratos and Bia are the agents of Zeus.

That to Aeschylus himself the idea of a possible change in the attitude of gods was not foreign, the *Eumenides* sufficiently testifies. There too we are shown a conflict between divine beings, which is brought to an end by an act of free generosity and by the conversion before the spectators' eyes of the spirits of vengeance into ministers of blessing. Nor is this all. In the course of that conflict one party to it points out that Zeus himself has sinned against the moral law which he now professes to uphold; he has imprisoned his own father. In reply the spokesman of Zeus neither denies the act nor seeks to justify it, but merely remarks that such deeds are not irrevocable: 'Fetters he can strike off.'[2] If this means anything it means that Zeus has not always been 'the most perfect of the perfect': he has done wrong in his time, but the wrong he did can be, and presumably has been, righted. Surely this is highly relevant to the Prometheus problem, especially when we remember that the Zeus of the *Vinctus* is still under his father's curse, as we learn from lines 910 ff. And relevant too, if I interpret them rightly, are the famous closing words of the trilogy, Ζεὺς ὁ πανόπτας / οὕτω Μοῖρά τε συγκατέβα, 'Thus Zeus the all-seeing and Fate's assignment have made their peace together.'[3]

The *Oresteia*, starting from an old tale of crime and punishment, celebrates the beginning of the reign of justice on earth. I think the *Prometheia*, starting from another such tale, celebrated

[1] Frag. 6. 15 Nauck. Cf. Thomson, *Aeschylus and Athens*, 339. [The word Διί in this passage may be a scribal conjecture, but it makes sense; the only suggested alternative, Canter's Δίκῃ, makes none—'Justice' has no place in a regime of cannibalism. But more direct evidence is now available in a new Aeschylean papyrus, *P. Oxy.* 2256, frag. 9a (= frag. 282 Lloyd-Jones), where Dike describes the *origin* of her partnership with Zeus—'Since that day Zeus has honoured me'—which implies that they have not always been partners.]
[2] *Eum.* 640–6.
[3] *Eum.* 1045–6. Cf. Cornford, *Plato's Cosmology* (1937), 361 ff.

its beginning in Heaven.[1] Aeschylus, like us, had lived through an Age of Violence among men, and tradition told him that there had once been a like Age of Violence among the gods. But his faith is that both on earth and in Heaven the rule of Violence is over. He can believe that Power in the person of Zeus is now at last reconciled with the Intelligence of which Prometheus is the mythical embodiment, and both of them with the supreme principle of Justice whose guardians are the Moirai and the Erinyes.[2] Such optimism was possible only for a generation like that of Aeschylus, a generation which had seen in the Persian Wars the victory, beyond all hope, of justice over brute force, and at Athens, in the years that followed, the swift blossoming of a civilization whose like had never been known before. It was a supreme moment in the history of Western Man. But it did not, it could not, last. Within the lifetime of the next generation the Peloponnesian War was to prove to all men that Power, Intelligence, and Justice were still at odds. With that realization the belief in human progress faded, and with it the mirror-image of a progressive Zeus. The *Vinctus* was still admired, as a symbol of Man's protest against the injustice of life. The *Lyomenos* was half forgotten, and eventually lost, because its lesson was no longer understood.

[1] Cf. F. Vian, *R.É.G.* 55 (1942), 216: 'Dans l'Olympe aussi, il faut que s'établissent les réformes de Clisthène.' [The parallel holds good so far, but I am wholly unconvinced by any of the recent attempts to discover political allegory in the *P.V.* (discussed by A. J. Podlecki, *The Political Background of Aeschylean Tragedy* (1966), ch. vi).]

[2] *P.V.* 511–16.

III

Morals and Politics in the Oresteia[1]

WHEN Aeschylus wrote, no distinction between morals and politics had yet been drawn.[2] But in our day the moral and the political element in the *Oresteia* have usually been examined separately. Thus, for example, Professor Dover, in his thoughtful paper on 'The Political Aspect of the *Eumenides*',[3] makes no attempt to connect this aspect with the moral issues raised in the earlier part of the trilogy. And Sir Richard Livingstone, in his paper on 'The Problem of the *Eumenides*', denied, if I understand him correctly, that any real link exists: 'The last 350 lines of the *Eumenides*', he says bluntly, 'are not an integral part of the trilogy. They are a loosely connected episode, stitched on its outside.'[4] If he is right, we may properly ask what motive was so strong, what need so urgent, as to induce the poet thus to botch the conclusion of his masterpiece. And if he is wrong, we should try to prove him wrong by making clear the nature of the link. To explore these alternatives is the chief purpose of the present paper.

I

The political implications of the *Oresteia* begin to force themselves on the reader's attention only in the scenes at Athens, a fact which is sometimes explained (if one can call it an explanation) by saying that Aeschylus wrote the first two parts of his trilogy for mankind, but the third part for the Athenians of 458 B.C.[5] Yet the language of contemporary politics is not wholly absent from the earlier parts.[6] Its most striking intrusion

---

[1] A paper read to the Cambridge Philological Society, 14 January 1960, and published in its *Proceedings*, No. 186 (1960), after revision in the light of subsequent discussion at an Oxford class on 'Politics in Greek Tragedy', to whose members I am indebted for much helpful criticism.
[2] Cf. Jaeger, *Paideia*, i. 323 (English edition, 1939).
[3] *J.H.S.* 77 (1957), 230 ff.   [4] *J.H.S.* 45 (1925), 123 f.
[5] So, e.g., W. Schmid, *Gr. Literaturgeschichte* (1929), I. ii, p. 253.
[6] This is well brought out by B. Daube, *Zu den Rechtsproblemen in Aischylos' Agamemnon* (1938); see especially pp. 45 ff., 135 f.

occurs at *Agamemnon* 883, where Clytemnestra describes her fear lest in the King's absence δημόθρους ἀναρχία βουλὴν καταρρίψειεν. Here the first two words surely mean (*pace* Fraenkel) 'the anarchy of popular clamour', and it is most natural to take βουλήν as meaning 'the Council'—a unique appearance of this political term in tragedy, but one which need not too greatly surprise us, since Aeschylus elsewhere admits semi-technical terms with a good deal of freedom.[1] It would be unwise to imagine here any conscious allusion to the contemporary conflict between δῆμος and Areopagus, and certainly wrong to draw any conclusion as to the poet's attitude towards it. But this passage and others in the *Agamemnon* do suggest that the author is already thinking in political as well as moral terms. References to the δῆμος are more frequent than we expect in a Mycenaean monarchy. What the citizens say about the Trojan war amounts to 'a curse decreed by the δῆμος' (456 f.); the loss of the fleet is 'a blow to the δῆμος' (640); Agamemnon fears what the δῆμος may say about him (938); and later the Chorus threaten both Clytemnestra (1409) and Aegisthus (1616) with 'the curses of the δῆμος'. Argos is not yet a democracy, as it will be in 458, but the opinions of the δῆμος are already important. We may notice also that the rule of Aegisthus is described in the language of politics: it is repeatedly called a τυραννίς (*Ag.* 1355, 1365; *Choephoroe* 973), from which Orestes 'liberates' Argos (*Choephoroe* 1046, cf. 809, 863). These things are no more than straws in the wind; yet I think they have some importance as suggesting that the political developments of the last play are not something 'stitched on the outside' of the trilogy, but were in the poet's mind from the first, and influenced his choice of words.

Argos is not yet a democracy. But Athens is, or so it would appear. The curious circumstance that in the *Eumenides*, alone among Greek tragedies, Athens lacks a king has hardly received the attention it deserves. True, 'the sons of Theseus' are casually mentioned at line 402; but even if this means Akamas and Demophon rather than the Athenians generally (a point which is open to doubt), they are plainly not sovereign. The only sovereign

---

[1] Cf. Fraenkel on *Ag.* 534–7, Lloyd-Jones on *Sept.* 1006 (*C.Q.* N.S. 9 (1959), 94), and H. G. Robertson's long list of technical phrases in the *Supplices*, *C.R.* 50 (1936), 104 n. 3. The alternative rendering, 'deliberation', suits ill with the vividly pictorial word καταρρίψειεν, 'fling to the ground'. If Aeschylus had meant 'reject deliberation', I suspect he would have used ἀποῤῥίψειεν, as at *Eum.* 215.

is Athena, χώρας ἄνασσα (288). She it is who, exercising the same royal function as Pelasgus in the *Supplices*, weighs the grounds for accepting or rejecting the suppliant's claim; she it is who in the trial scene takes the place of the ἄρχων βασιλεύς. In mythical time, as her first words show (397–402), we are still within a few years of the Trojan war, but in historical time we have leapt forward to a new age and a new social order. This telescoping of the centuries is characteristic of the *Eumenides*, and as I believe essential to its purpose. The Athenian audience must have begun to be aware of it when at line 289 Orestes provides a mythological αἴτιον for the recent alliance with Argos; and when in the next breath he speculates on the possible presence of Athena in Libya, 'helping her friends' (295), I imagine they asked themselves 'What friends?' and quickly guessed the answer: 'Of course, our other ally, those Libyans whose king we are just now helping to break the yoke of Persia.' (That the actual campaigns of 459 and 458 were fought not in Libya but in the Delta is true, so far as our limited knowledge goes, but surely unimportant. The ancients had no war correspondents and no maps of the front. Probably neither the poet nor the majority of his audience would be in a position to know just where the battles were taking place; what they would know is that many of their kinsfolk were overseas, fighting for the Libyans. The phrase χώρας ἐν τόποις Λιβυστικῆς (292) is in fact studiously vague,[1] while the reference to Lake Triton is added only for the sake of the necessary mythological link.)

Whether there were any contemporary goings-on in Chalcidice, where also Athena might have been (295 f.), or in the Troad, where she actually was (398), I do not know; the supposition can be neither proved nor ruled out.[2] But when we come to the foundation of the Areopagus, no audience in 458 could fail to be reminded of contemporary goings-on. Nearly everyone agrees (the chief exception is Groeneboom) that there is

[1] Despite Dover, op. cit. 237, it should be remembered that 'Libya' was a general name for the African continent, and that its frontiers were uncertain (Pind. *Pyth.* 9. 9 and schol., Hdt. 2. 16).
[2] Cf. *Ath. Trib. Lists*, iii. 321 n. 88: 'Very possibly lines 295–6 will refer to some sort of trouble in Pallene, and this would surely mean Poteidaia. It is not impossible that Poteidaia remained recalcitrant till Kimon made his Five Years' Truce in 451.' As for the Troad, Sigeum seems to have been threatened by Persian encroachments in 451/0 (*I.G.*² i. 32, and B. D. Meritt in *Hesperia*, 5 (1936), 360 f.), and it is *possible* that the trouble began earlier.

a political point here; but after a century of controversy there is still no agreement on what the point is. I believe myself that this is exactly what the poet would have wished: he was writing a political play, yes; but a propagandist play, no. It is very difficult to suppose with K. O. Müller and Blass that he was fighting a conservative rearguard action. That view is virtually excluded by his three emphatic references to the Argive alliance; on this subject I have nothing to add to Dover's careful discussion. But in the light of Athena's foundation-speech I find it almost equally difficult to see Aeschylus as a consistent and committed supporter of radical reform. Stale though the controversy is, we must consider again the two vital sentences, 690–5 and 704–6.

The first of these says that on Ares' hill awe and terror will restrain the people from wrong-doing, whether open or secret, so long as the citizens themselves do not (do something bad to) the laws. The corrupt participle cannot be restored with certainty, but the next two lines make it plain that its sense was pejorative. To what action did it refer? To Ephialtes' action in cutting down the powers of the Areopagus? That used to be the common view, and if it is right, the poet here emerges, to our confusion, as an out-and-out reactionary. To avoid this, Dover suggests equating the ἐπιρροαί of line 694 with the ἐπίθετα of *Ath. Pol.* 25. 2: the bad action will then be, as Verrall thought, the supposed action of the Areopagus in assuming unconstitutional powers; Aeschylus will be echoing the propaganda of the radicals. But will this really do? 'The citizens themselves' cannot mean merely the members of the Areopagus (who are ἀστῶν . . . τὰ βέλτατα, 487); we expect it to mean the whole body of citizens sitting in the Assembly. But there is no evidence that the Areopagus either acquired or was thought to have acquired its ἐπίθετα by legislation in the Assembly; most historians believe that the powers in question were in fact preSolonian. And in the absence of such evidence I fear that this interpretation will not stand. I still incline personally to a third view, that the action the poet has in mind is something as yet in the future, though already a topic of discussion at the time the play was produced, namely the admission of the Zeugitae to the archonship, and thereby to membership of the Areopagus —a measure which was carried through in the year 458/7. I have argued for this view in print,[1] and I will not repeat my arguments here. If I am right, Aeschylus is neither justifying the recent reforms nor grumbling about them; he is offering something more practical and less overtly partisan, a quiet word of warning for the future.

The other crucial passage is lines 704–6. These are the final words in which Athena declares the Areopagus established and defines its purpose; they are as it were the trust-deed or charter of the new institution. And it is not easy to read them in a restrictive sense, as limiting its functions to those of a murder court. The only way to make this plausible is to accept the scholiast's view that εὑδόντων means 'the dead'. Wilamowitz at one time did so, but repented later, with good reason.[2] I know no real parallel in Attic Greek for such a use; and if there were one, the metaphor would be quite inappropriate here. With those dead who sleep quiet in their graves a murder court has no concern; its only clients among the ghosts are precisely the unquiet dead, the βιαιοθάνατοι, and to call these 'the sleepers' would be strangely misleading, even if we could reconcile that sense with the wider function implied in φρούρημα γῆς. It is possible that εὑδόντων is intended literally, if Lucian's repeated statement[3] that the Areopagus sat by night is anything more than a mistaken inference from the present passage. But it seems more likely that we are to think of the citizens as inactive 'sleeping partners' who entrust their security to the vigilance of the Areopagus: this metaphorical use of εὕδειν and καθεύδειν is common enough; we find it at *Ag.* 1357 and *Cho.* 881. On either of these views the functions of the Areopagus would seem to be conceived in wider terms than those of a murder court, which does indeed protect the security

[1] *C.Q.* N.S. 3 (1953), 19 f. Jacoby has objected (*Frag. gr. Hist.* III b Suppl. ii, p. 528) that Aeschylus could not imply, even indirectly, that the Zeugitae were, even relatively to the λαμπροί, 'mud'. I am not sure on what this judgement is based. If it means that Aeschylus could not *entertain* an undemocratic sentiment, it begs the question under discussion. If it means that in 458 he could not risk *expressing* an unpopular opinion, I should reply that in the *Persae* he had taken at least as grave a risk: in 472, when Themistocles, if not already ostracized, had certainly fallen from popular favour, it was surely an act of moral courage to recall so frankly his services to Greece.

[2] Wilamowitz's other suggestion (*Arist. u. Athen.* (1893), ii. 334), that in founding the Areopagus Athena was 'really' thinking of the Heliaea, must be still more firmly rejected; it has no support in the text (cf. H. Bengl, *Staatstheoretische Probleme in der attischen Tragödie*, 54), and in 458 such a confusion was surely impossible.

[3] Lucian, *Herm.* 64, *dom.* 18. Did the Areopagus provide the model for Plato's Nocturnal Council (which meets in fact at dawn, *Laws,* 961 b)?

of the individual, but scarcely that of the country as a whole. The poet's language is vague (I think intentionally so); but the powers of the historical Areopagus are described in equally vague phrases. The *Ath. Pol.* calls it φύλαξ τῶν νόμων (4. 4) and ἐπίσκοπος τῆς πολιτείας (8. 4); and similarly Plutarch terms it ἐπίσκοπον πάντων καὶ φύλακα τῶν νόμων (*Sol.* 19). Aeschylus' phrase, ἐγρηγορὸς φρούρημα γῆς, is most naturally taken as referring to the same powers. And if that is right, the play is no more propaganda for Pericles than it is propaganda for Cimon. It looks to me as if the famous saying about the superiority of τὸ μέσον—which Aeschylus put so oddly into the mouth of the Erinyes (530)—might in fact be taken, not as a political catchword of Right or Left, or even as 'recommending a reflective attitude to politics',[1] but as an honest and correct description of the author's own position. It has often been noticed that in the passage of which it forms part the goddesses appear to speak less for themselves than as the poet's persona; they echo the choruses of the *Agamemnon*, exhort mankind in the second person singular, and anticipate the wisdom of Athena.[2]

I add a word about the theory of Miss Smertenko, tentatively revived by Dover,[3] that the curse of the Pelopidae should be seen as a mythological prototype of the curse of Cylon, and Apollo's purification of Orestes as a prototype of his purification of the Alcmaeonids. My difficulty about this is not so much the absence of direct evidence that the Alcmaeonids were ever purified as the feeling that if Aeschylus had meant to be so understood he would have made the purification of Orestes at Delphi much more important than it is in our play. As it is, its importance seems to be deliberately *minimized*. When Orestes arrives at Athens after long wanderings by sea and land (*Eum.* 75–7, 240), he has experienced not one purification but 'many' (277), a phrase which allows for the local traditions of his purification at Trozen, Megalopolis, and various other places.[4] Now he is no longer

[1] Dover, op. cit. 233.
[2] Compare 520–1 with *Ag.* 180–1, 532–7 with *Ag.* 758–62, 538–42 with *Ag.* 381–4, 552–65 with *Ag.* 1005–13; also 517–19 and 526–8 with *Eum.* 696–8. Cf. Kranz, *Stasimon* (1933), 172 f., and on the 'paraenetic' second person singular Dover, op. cit. 232.
[3] Clara M. Smertenko, 'The Political Sympathies of Aeschylus', *J.H.S.* 52 (1932), 233 ff.; Dover, op. cit. 236. Cf. also A. Plassart, *R.E.A.* 42 (1940), 298 f.
[4] Cf. L. Radermacher, *Das Jenseits im Mythos der Hellenen* (1903), 138 f.; A. Lesky in P.–W. s.v. 'Orestes', cols. 988 ff.; P. Amandry, *Mél. Grégoire* (1949), 37.

προστρόπαιος (237), but this is not due to the unaided efforts of the καθαρταί. Time has also done his part (286): Orestes has 'rubbed off' his pollution on the cities and roads of the world (238–9), so that now 'the blood is getting sleepy and fading from his hand' (280). (It is futile to delete line 286, for its content is already implicit in lines 238–9 and 280.) Orestes is in fact noticeably vague about the efficacy of pig's blood. The Erinyes are not. For them it has no efficacy. In their view Orestes is still a polluted creature, food for vampires (302), unfit for any contact with gods or men (653–6). And finally, even when they are reconciled and settled at Athens, the doctrine of inherited guilt is *not* abolished; it is reaffirmed at lines 934–5. If Aeschylus was really thinking about the curse of Cylon, the encouragement he offers the Alcmaeonids is singularly limited.

I turn now to the closing scene between Athena and the Erinyes, where for brevity's sake I shall confine my discussion to two passages, both of which have troubled conscientious editors. The first is lines 858–66, where the goddess begs the Erinyes not to start a civil war in Attica. Dindorf excised the entire passage; Weil transposed it to follow line 912. The transposition is impossible; for at 912 the Erinyes are already reconciled, and concerned only with blessings. For the excision a better prima-facie case can be made than for much of the surgery to which the text of Aeschylus has been subjected. It can be argued on the ground of sense, since the Erinyes have never in fact threatened to start a civil war; on that of logical sequence, since τοιαῦτα in 867[1] clearly refers back to the promises made in lines 854–7; and on that of symmetry (such as we expect in an 'epirrhematic' passage), since the omission of these lines will make Athena's four persuasive speeches roughly equal in length—they will contain respectively 14, 13, 13, and 11 lines. On the other hand, who but Aeschylus would introduce those typically Aeschylean mixed metaphors, that wild notion about the cock's heart, and those Aeschylean turns of phrase, οὐ μόλις (cf. *Ag.* 1082) and οὐ λέγω (cf. *Cho.* 989)? My own guess is that the lines were interpolated by the poet himself, who at some moment when the threat of civil war had grown acute inserted them into an already completed draft, at the cost of dislocating the context and

---

[1] Dindorf made the mistake of deleting 867–9 as well as 858–66, thus depriving himself of his best argument.

damaging the symmetry. Their author certainly has his own day in mind, as appears from the allusion to foreign war, οὐ μόλις παρών.[1] And that Aeschylus did at this time fear civil war is plain enough from lines 976–87, lines which would naturally be taken by his first audience as a reminder of the fairly recent murder of Ephialtes and an appeal to the radicals not to pursue a vindictive policy. Such fears were not groundless, as we know from Thucydides' words (1. 107. 4) about the treachery planned by certain pro-Spartan oligarchs—a kind of treachery which the old poet had experienced once before in his life, in the year 508. This time the danger was averted, but there may well have been moments of real anxiety.

Should we go further than this, and say with Livingstone that since Athena's advice to the Erinyes is in effect the poet's advice to the Athenian oligarchs, we have here a sort of 'allegory'? I have sometimes been tempted to do so, especially in view of lines 851–2, where Athena's words, 'If you go to a foreign country, you will long for Attica', seem to fit oligarchs contemplating voluntary exile better than they do the Erinyes. But, as Dover points out,[2] the Erinyes cannot be thus suddenly reduced to allegorical figures when the audience has come to accept them as real beings and active participants in the drama. What we *can* perhaps say is that their case is paradigmatic: their eventual choice is an *exemplum*, showing that even the bitterest feud can and should end in reconciliation. As Zuntz has expressed it, 'In the mirror of the myth, tragedy puts before the city of Pallas the image of what she ought to be and to do'.[3]

The remaining passage to which I would call attention is lines 996–1002, where the Erinyes invoke a blessing upon Athens *in nomine patris et filiae*. It begins with a reference to αἰσιμίαι πλούτου. The word αἰσιμία is otherwise unknown, but presumably means 'just apportionment' rather than simply 'fated apportionment' (which would have little point in the context). The phrase

---

[1] We possess a casualty-list of the tribe Erechtheis for one of the years 460–458, giving the names of those 'killed in action in Cyprus, Egypt, Phoenicia, Halieis, Aegina and Megara in the same twelvemonth' (*I.G.*² i. 929, Tod 26). And it is no mere coincidence that the feelings of parents and wives who saw their men 'changed for a handful of dust' are unforgettably painted in the second ode of the *Agamemnon*.

[2] Dover, op. cit. 236 f.

[3] G. Zuntz, *The Political Plays of Euripides* (1955), 11.

Morals and Politics in the Oresteia 53

recalls a number of passages about wealth in the choruses of the *Agamemnon*, particularly lines 773–80 where Justice is said to honour the ἐναίσιμος, whereas she has no respect for 'the power of wealth mis-stamped with praise'.[1] Solmsen has observed, quite correctly, that 'in the statements of Aeschylus' choruses the κέρδος motive looms larger than in his plots'; money questions have no real place in the tragedy of the House of Atreus. He is inclined to attribute this irrelevant emphasis to the influence of Hesiod and Solon, in whose scheme of justice wealth does, for good reasons, play an important role.[2] That may indeed be the true explanation, or part of it; but the present passage suggests that the poet had in mind not only the economic conflicts of Solon's day but others more recent, which he prays may now be ended. For in this last scene, as Weil already saw, 'fabulae pars fiunt ipsi spectatores'.[3]

More important than this, however, are the implications of line 1000, σωφρονοῦντες ἐν χρόνῳ. Blass and Groeneboom tell us that ἐν χρόνῳ is 'meaningless' here, and print instead Weil's conjecture ἔμφρονος. In this they are certainly mistaken. I cannot find that ἔμφρων is used anywhere in Greek literature as an epithet for a god, nor should we expect it to be. It commends the human being who is 'in his right mind', sane or rational; but it would be a poor compliment to the goddess of wisdom to call her ἔμφρων. ἐν χρόνῳ, on the other hand, though less common than the simple dative, is a perfectly good Aeschylean phrase: it is used at line 498 of this play and at *Cho.* 1040 with the meaning 'in course of (future) time'. Here the reference must be to the present—the actual present, not the mythological one—and the implication must be that the Athenians have acquired 'over the years' a σωφροσύνη which they have not always possessed. I shall try to show that this idea of the slow and painful acquisition of wisdom provides the necessary connection between the moral questions of the first two plays and the political answers of the *Eumenides*. To eliminate ἐν χρόνῳ is, in my view, to destroy an essential clue to the meaning of the trilogy.

---

[1] Cf. also *Ag.* 381 ff., 471, 1008 ff.
[2] F. Solmsen, *Hesiod and Aeschylus* (1949), 220 n. 160. Cf. also D. Kaufmann-Bühler, *Begriff u. Funktion der Dike in den Tragödien des Aischylos* (1951), 64.
[3] H. Weil, *De tragoediarum graecarum cum rebus publicis coniunctione* (1844), 11.

II

The moral issues raised by the *Agamemnon* are notoriously complex. For simplicity's sake, I shall limit myself to the two principles which the Chorus of Elders enunciate with such solemnity—παθεῖν τὸν ἔρξαντα and πάθει μάθος. Both are associated with the name of the supreme god. It is said of the first that while the rule of Zeus endures it too will endure as a law (1563–4); and of the second, that it was laid down by Zeus, who thereby set mankind on the road to wisdom (176–8). Neither principle, of course, was invented by Aeschylus.[1] But he appears to have designed them as clues which the audience is expected to follow, for we are repeatedly reminded of them in the course of the trilogy. That the doer shall suffer is applied by the Herald to the case of Troy (532–3) and by Clytemnestra to the case of Agamemnon (1527); in the *Choephoroe* it is restated at the beginning of the great κομμός, where the Chorus call it a τριγέρων μῦθος (313–14); later they apply it to the case of Orestes (1009). The connection of suffering with wisdom is reaffirmed at *Ag.* 250 and implied at *Eum.* 520. All this has long been recognized. But, strangely enough, it is only in recent years that scholars have seriously asked themselves in what sense these principles operate in the drama of the House of Atreus as the poet has presented it.[2] To this question I now address myself.

First, then, 'the doer shall suffer'. Before the trilogy opens this maxim has already been verified in the cases of Thyestes and Paris; the audience will see it verified for Agamemnon, for Clytemnestra and Aegisthus, even for Cassandra;[3] and for Orestes also, provided we do not arbitrarily limit the meaning of πάθος. But are we to think of it as universally valid? What, for example,

---

[1] The antecedents of πάθει μάθος have been scrupulously examined by H. Dörrie, 'Leid und Erfahrung', *Abh. Mainz* (1956), Nr. 5. The rule παθεῖν τὸν ἔρξαντα is formulated in a line ascribed to Hesiod (frag. 174), εἴ κε πάθοι τά τ' ἔρεξε, δίκη κ' ἰθεῖα γένοιτο.

[2] Cf. Daube, op. cit. 148–50; Kaufmann-Bühler, op. cit. 59–107; A. Lesky, *Die tragische Dichtung der Hellenen* (1956), 93–8; H. D. F. Kitto, *Form and Meaning in Drama* (1956), chaps. i–iii; H. Lloyd-Jones, 'Zeus in Aeschylus', *J.H.S.* 76 (1956), 61–5; D. L. Page, Introduction to *Agamemnon*, xx–xxix; F. Solmsen, *Gnomon*, 31 (1959), 472 f.

[3] Cassandra sees her destruction as Apollo's act of vengeance for her offence against him (*Ag.* 1269–76). Yet in the next moment she predicts that she shall be avenged on Apollo's unconscious agents (1279–80).

of Atreus? We hear much of his crime, but nothing of his πάθος. And what of those many Greeks and Trojans who suffered for what they did not do, ἀλλοτρίας διαὶ γυναικός? And a further, more disturbing question: does the maxim apply without distinction of circumstance? Is the crime of Agamemnon, who was the unconscious agent of Zeus, or that of Orestes, who was the conscious agent of Apollo, to be equated with the crime of Clytemnestra?

If we are to bring this confused picture into any sort of focus, we must recognize that the moral and logical presuppositions behind it are not those which we take for granted today. I will list a few of them.

(1) Guilt is inherited, and because the son's life is a prolongation of his father's (*Cho.* 503-4), the guilty man may suffer in his son's person, as Atreus suffers in the person of Agamemnon (*Ag.* 1577-82). We must not say that Aeschylus somehow 'transcended' this assumption, for it is implicit in passages like *Ag.* 1338-42, and at the end of the *Eumenides* it is explicitly affirmed by Athens herself (932-7).

(2) Guilt is infectious, not only in the formal sense of contagious impurity but in the sense that the punishment of a guilty individual may require the destruction of an entire community: πολλάκι καὶ ξύμπασα πόλις κακοῦ ἀνδρὸς ἐπαυρεῖ. The fate of Troy is a case in point. When this happens, however, a fresh guilt is created: τῶν πολυκτόνων γὰρ οὐκ ἄσκοποι θεοί (*Ag.* 461). The offence of an individual can thus give rise to a situation in which crime is *inevitable*. Of that situation Orestes' dilemma is the classic example. If he refuses his office as avenger of blood, the Erinyes of his father will get him (*Cho.* 283 ff.); if he accepts it, the Erinyes of his mother. Either way, he is doomed and damned.

(3) This sinister capacity of guilt for producing fresh guilt is 'projected' as an evil spirit, or a company of evil spirits, for whom the terms δαίμων, ἀλάστωρ, and ἐρινύς are used more or less interchangeably. It is idle to ask whether Aeschylus believed in the objective existence of such beings: this is the sort of question which no dramatist can be made to answer, for it is the function of every dramatist to think in images. But their reality and causative activity is a presupposition of the story as Aeschylus unfolds it. They are not everywhere at work (*Ag.* 761-2); we are to think of them as generated by a specific deed of blood (*Cho.*

327–8, correctly explained by Wilamowitz, cf. 402), or by the curses of its victim (*Eum.* 417, cf. *Sept.* 70, *O.C.* 1375–6). But once generated they are henceforth active in the human heart, 'constraining' it to fresh crime with the voice of Temptation, Πειθώ (who is herself a daemon).[1] Such temptation is described as ἄφερτος,[2] 'more than our nature will bear' (*Ag.* 386); and yet it does not relieve us of responsibility. That is surely made plain once and for all in the passage where the Queen claims that not she was the killer but the ἀλάστωρ, using her body as its instrument, and the Chorus reject her claim: the fiend may have been a συλλήπτωρ, but the guilt is hers (*Ag.* 1497–1508). It is the same judgement which Darius pronounces concerning the δαίμων who tempted Xerxes (*Pers.* 353–4, 724–5): ἀλλ' ὅταν σπεύδῃ τις αὐτός, χὠ θεὸς συνάπτεται (*Pers.* 742)—without some flaw in our nature the δαίμων could not gain entrance. As Arthur Adkins puts it, 'though some may be predisposed towards evil by supernatural agency, none are so predestined'.[3]

(4) But finally, behind all this intricate interplay of human and daemonic purposes there is still something else, the purpose of Zeus, παναιτίου πανεργέτα· τί γὰρ βροτοῖς ἄνευ Διὸς τελεῖται; (*Ag.* 1485–8). How seriously are we to take that? Very seriously, I think: that whatever happens is the will of God has been said, and seriously meant, many times since; it is a recurrent datum of the religious consciousness. But the people who say it have never meant it as a denial of human causation or of human responsibility.[4] Nor did Aeschylus. We have to recognize here the same willingness to accept 'over-determination' which we already recognize in Homer.[5] Where Plato said αἰτία ἑλομένου· θεὸς ἀναίτιος, Aeschylus is prepared to say αἰτία ἑλομένου· θεὸς

[1] Cf. the well-known scyphos by Macron which shows her tempting Helen.
[2] This word is found no less than nine times in the *Oresteia*, and nowhere else in the whole of Greek literature. It would seem that Aeschylus coined it (Fraenkel on *Ag.* 386) as a unique descriptive term for the unique situation created by the curse.   [3] Arthur W. H. Adkins, *Merit and Responsibility* (1960), 124.
[4] Most of them would, I think, say with Paul Tillich that 'God's directing creativity always acts through the freedom of Man'.
[5] On 'over-determination' in general see *The Greeks and the Irrational*, 30 f., 51 f. Its modalities in Homer have been worked out by Prof. Lesky in the paper which he read to the Third International Congress of Classical Studies at London. That something of the kind must also be admitted for the *Oresteia* is now recognized by the more perceptive critics: cf. Daube, op. cit. 172–8; Lesky, 'Der Kommos der Choephoren', *Sitzb. Wien*, Phil.-Hist. Kl. 221 (1943), Abh. 3, 122–3; Kitto, *Form and Meaning*, 71–2.

παναίτιος. We may call this a pre-logical or a post-logical way of thinking; but if we do not accept it for the *Oresteia* we risk being gravely misled.

For example, logic may assure us that Agamemnon at Aulis can neither have made a choice nor have incurred any intelligible guilt; for it was the will of Zeus that Troy should fall (*Ag.* 60–8), and what Zeus wills must come to pass and must be right.[1] If we follow the promptings of logic, we shall conclude that δράσαντι παθεῖν stands for something as dramatically senseless[2] as it is morally revolting—the suffering wantonly inflicted by an all-powerful deity upon a human marionette. But may it not be better to follow the text instead? There we see the King go through all the motions of a man in the act of choice. Like Pelasgus in the *Supplices* (472 ff.), or like any other man caught in a dilemma, he weighs the alternatives, and dislikes them both: βαρεῖα μὲν..., he says, βαρεῖα δὲ... τί τῶνδ᾽ ἄνευ κακῶν; (206–11). The considerations which influence him are purely human, and surely he *believes* himself to be making a choice between them; for he does not know that he is the agent of Zeus. And the Chorus too believes it; for it describes his act in terms which have no meaning save in relation to an act of choice. He hesitated, they say ('a veering wind blew through his heart', 219), and changed his mind (μετέγνω, 221); but a man who has no choice can do neither of these things. But what then of 'the harness of necessity' (218, ἀνάγκας ἔδυ λέπαδνον)? I reply, with Bruno Snell,[3] that the man who wears such harness has indeed lost his freedom, but the man who *puts it on* might have refused to do so. The next sentence shows what is meant: by making the wrong choice Agamemnon placed himself in the power of the alastor, here called παρακοπὰ πρωτοπήμων (223). Henceforth he will listen, not to his own good sense, but to the voice of the tempter: he has *given away* his freedom.

---

[1] Cf. Page, Introd. to *Ag.*, xxiii ff.

[2] The *O.T.* should not be cited as an example to the contrary. The dramatic value of that play depends not on the acts which Oedipus once committed as the puppet of destiny, but on the choices which we see him make as a free agent. [See below, pp. 70 f.]

[3] *Aischylos u. das Handeln im Drama* (Philol. Supp. 20, 1, 1928), 143. A different way of meeting Page's objections is offered by Kitto, *Gnomon*, 30 (1958), 168, who thinks that Agamemnon at Aulis is 'helpless but not innocent' because his fatal choice has already been made, at the moment when he decided to attack Troy. But if so, why the parade of weighing alternatives?

I have dwelt on this passage because in my view the existence of a moment of choice is something which the poet wished not merely to admit but to emphasize. As Fraenkel says,[1] that is why he suppressed the reasons commonly given for the anger of Artemis: had the sacrifice of Iphigeneia been a punishment for boasting, as in the *Cypria*, or for killing a sacred deer, as in Sophocles' *Electra*, or had it been, as in other versions, the fulfilment of a rash vow, then Agamemnon would really have had no choice. But Aeschylus wanted him to have a choice, and though he could not show it on the stage, he has described it for us rather fully and carefully. Certain other moments of choice we are made to witness. The first is in what we must no longer call the carpet-scene. There we see Agamemnon first refuse and then agree to provoke the φθόνος of gods and men by 'treading on purple'. Why does he agree? Out of a trivial vanity, or from sheer weakness of will? Neither, I think. He agrees because ever since Aulis τὸ παντότολμον φρονεῖν μετέγνω (221). He has given away his power of judgement; now he must follow where the tempter leads, on the path of ὕβρις whose end is the palace door—the gateway to death.[2] Like all that happens at Argos, his choice is the outcome of that older choice. And then comes a parallel[3] scene in which we see Cassandra first refuse and then agree to enter that same gateway. But what the King chose blindly, at his wife's prompting or at the alastor's, Cassandra chooses with full knowledge, yet by a free act of will—ἰοῦσα πράξω· τλήσομαι τὸ κατθανεῖν (1289). Helpless slave though she is, in that act she asserts her status as a human being. But the most dramatic moment of choice is that in the *Choephoroe*, when Orestes hesitates to kill his mother, and Pylades speaks for the first and last time, uttering the will of Apollo (899–903). It was, of course, to kill his mother that Orestes came to Argos; yet it is a real moment of choice, the resolution of an internal conflict of which, if we are at all sensitive, we have been conscious throughout the earlier part of the play. (Schadewaldt succeeded for a time in persuading most scholars that no such conflict exists, but I think his view has been convincingly refuted by Lesky.)[4]

---

[1] *Agamemnon*, ii. 98 f.   [2] 1291 Ἅιδου πύλας.
[3] The parallelism is brilliantly brought out by Reinhardt, *Aischylos als Regisseur u. Theologe*, 90–105.
[4] W. Schadewaldt, 'Der Kommos in Aischylos' Choephoren', *Hermes*, 67 (1932), 312 ff.; Lesky, *Sitzb. Wien*, 221.

Is there a moment of choice in the *Eumenides*? Not for Orestes: his time for choosing is over; he is now, as Wilamowitz said,[1] *corpus delicti* and nothing more. As for the jury, they fail to choose; and in the light of Aeschylus' presuppositions that is inevitable. Orestes' act can neither be simply condemned as a crime nor simply justified as a duty, for it is both; the logic of the vendetta, brought to the test of this limiting case, breaks down in flat contradiction. It is Athena who decides Orestes' case, but on an arbitrary personal ground which seems to deprive the decision of moral significance. The crucial choice in this play is surely that made by the Erinyes when they first refuse and then accept Athena's offer. This is the final liberating moment; not, like the others, a choice between evils, but a choice of Good, and one made by deathless beings, not by transient mortality. Moreover, as we have seen, it is so presented as to suggest its paradigmatic value for the poet's own day. The moral issues of the myth are living issues which have still to be faced in the Athens of 458.

What of Aeschylus' other law, πάθει μάθος? The older commentators were strangely incurious about its working out in the *Oresteia*, and often strangely vague about the meaning of μάθος. It was left to Mr. Lloyd-Jones and Professor Page to observe that if μάθος involves moral improvement it does not work out at all. As Lloyd-Jones says, Agamemnon, Clytemnestra, Aegisthus, 'are not purified or ennobled; they are simply killed';[2] and Orestes (one may add) is not perceptibly nobler after his sufferings than he was before. We must conclude that μάθος does not signify what is vulgarly meant by 'moral improvement'. But it seems equally clear that to Aeschylus the saying does not mean merely what is doubtless meant originally, 'A burnt child dreads the fire': that sense would be equally irrelevant to the tale of the House of Atreus. The poet's language suggests that μάθος has an intellectual content: he paraphrases it by φρονεῖν or σωφρονεῖν (*Ag.* 176, 181; *Eum.* 521).[3] Let us consider then what it is that the characters of the drama can be said to learn.

Of Agamemnon we can say only that up to (and during) his brief appearance on the stage he learns *nothing*; and ὤμοι,

---

[1] In the Einleitung to his translation of the *Eumenides*, 42.
[2] H. Lloyd-Jones, op. cit. 62; cf. Denniston and Page on *Ag.* 184 ff.
[3] As Headlam rightly said in his note on *Eum.* 520, 'σωφρονεῖν is synonymous with γνῶναι σεαυτόν, *to know your place* in relation to the gods and to your fellow-men'.

πέπληγμαι conveys no final flash of insight. But the poet has told us why Agamemnon learns nothing: he is a man already blinded by the alastor, incapable of φρόνησις since the fatal hour at Aulis when τὸ παντότολμον φρονεῖν μετέγνω. Hence the painful impression of mingled arrogance and stupidity which he makes on most readers.[1] He is a παράδειγμα, not of πάθει μάθος, but of that δολόμητις ἀπάτα θεοῦ which slowly strangles all sense in the man who incurs it.

It is otherwise with Clytemnestra: her education—her πάθος which is also her μάθος—is played out before us, if we have eyes to perceive it. It is not an education in morals. At no point does she exhibit the slightest repentance for her deed or pity for her victims. It is an education in insight—insight into the rules of the nightmare world that she inhabits. In her first speeches after the killing she claims sole responsibility for her act, and glories in it as an act of simple justice. Then slowly she comes to see it, first as a sacrifice to the evil spirits whom she still refuses to fear (1432–4), then as a deed done at the prompting of the daemon (1475–80), finally as the daemon's own act, of which she was but the instrument (1496–1504). That this last *is* insight and not 'cold irony' seems to me certain, not only from the parallel with *Cho.* 910, where she makes a comparable[2] claim in no ironic mood, but also from the parallel with Cassandra's insight; for Cassandra too perceives her own action as the action of a supernatural being possessing her and working through her (1269), and Cassandra should know the rules of the nightmare world if any mortal does. In the end, what breaks Clytemnestra down is the Chorus's word, παθεῖν τὸν ἔρξαντα (1564). At that point she offers blood-money to the being in whose power she has placed herself; but in vain, for now she too has 'put on the harness of necessity' and must walk to the end the road she chose. In the *Choephoroe* we see her as a broken woman, haunted by evil dreams, vainly seeking to appease the dead man's ghost, and

---

[1] Fraenkel's picture of Agamemnon as 'a great gentleman, possessed of moderation and self-control' is very hard to reconcile with the indications of the text. Cf. Denniston and Page on *Ag.* 810 f. and 931 ff.

[2] It is uncertain whether παραιτία at *Cho.* 910 means 'contributory cause' (like μεταίτιος and συναίτιος), or 'parallel cause', or simply 'cause' (as in later usage). The use of the word at frag. 44. 7 seems to favour the second or the third view, which would make Clytemnestra maintain the position she took up at *Ag.* 1497 ff.

perceiving everywhere the action of the daemon.¹ She has gained her insight, unwillingly; but it is an insight only into the daemonic level of causation, and it serves only to torture her.²

Orestes' case³ is again different. We see him stand where his mother once stood, in the palace doorway; once again a man and a woman lie dead at the Avenger's feet; but where Clytemnestra carried a bloody sword Orestes carries a θαλλός and a wreath (*Cho.* 1035). The parallelism is intentional and significant; so is the difference. Outwardly, his situation resembles hers; inwardly, there is a deep gulf between them. It is not merely that Orestes is humble where she was arrogant, or that his motives are 'purer' than hers; like her, he has simple human motives, which he does not conceal (299–304). The deeper difference is that the divine purpose, of which both Agamemnon and Clytemnestra were unconscious and guilty agents, is for Orestes something consciously known and humbly, though not easily, accepted. He is aware that his act is a crime, even before he has committed it (930, τὸ μὴ χρεών, cf. 1016–17 and 1029); but receiving it as a duty, he stands as a type of all those who take upon themselves 'the necessary guilt of human action'. Orestes has not merely suffered his situation, he has understood and in a sense mastered it; it is his μάθος which makes him worthy of salvation.

Thus far we seem to have a fairly logical progression, from Agamemnon, the blind instrument of justice, who never learns, through Clytemnestra, the half-blind instrument, who learns too late and incompletely, to Orestes, the conscious instrument, whose insight comes before the deed and achieves contact with the divine will. Is there a fourth term in the progression? My thoughts return to the great central ode of the *Eumenides*, with its renewed insistence that it is good for men σωφρονεῖν ὑπὸ στένει, 'to learn wisdom under pressure', and to those Athenians at the end of the play, σωφρονοῦντες ἐν χρόνῳ. May not this be the fourth and final term—πάθει μάθος no longer illustrated in the

---

¹ *Cho.* 691–9 is certainly spoken by Clytemnestra; and comparison with *Ag.* 1497 ff. and 1660 suggests that it is seriously meant. Cf. Lesky, *Hermes* 66 (1931), 207.
² Cf. *Cho.* 68–9: Ate keeps the guilty one alive 'until he is filled to the brim with sickness'.
³ Cf. Kaufmann-Bühler's discussion, op. cit. 99–102; and K. v. Fritz in *Studium Generale*, 8 (1955), 197–9.

life-history of individuals, but writ large in the destiny of a whole people and ushering in a new age of understanding? Such a hope can only be an act of faith; and the poet has set it in a devotional context. It is a hope for the people of the Virgin, 'whose seat is near to Zeus';[1] and should we not here remember what we were told at the outset, that he who has faith in Zeus shall attain to perfect understanding (*Ag.* 175 τεύξεται φρενῶν τὸ πᾶν)?[2] I will risk the guess that it was this hope for Athens—the hope of achieving a truer insight into the laws that govern our condition—this, rather than the particular squabble about the powers of the Areopagus, that shaped the composition of the *Oresteia*.

To say, as Jacoby said,[3] that 'Aeschylus wrote his trilogy because of the Areopagus' is to distort the pattern by divorcing the 'political' application from the underlying religious and moral ideas that give it lasting significance.[4] But may we not say that he wrote it in the way he did 'because of Athens'? When he sat down to compose it, his country had just passed through the greatest internal revolution since Cleisthenes, and had just embarked on the greatest foreign adventure she had ever undertaken. It was a moment of high hope, but also of grave danger—both from enemies abroad and from extremists at home. All turned on what Athena prays for (*Eum.* 1012), the ἀγαθὴ διάνοια of the people. Given that, Athens might achieve a position such as no Greek state had ever held since Agamemnon's day; without it, the whole adventure might collapse in στάσις and defeat. Is it surprising if behind the lineaments of prehistoric Argos the pressing problems of another and a dearer city thrust themselves

---

[1] *Eum.* 998 ἴκταρ ἥμενοι Διός—not in any genealogical or topographical sense, but because 'whom the wings of Pallas shelter, her Father cherishes' (1001–2). Bothe's ἡμένας would express the thought more perspicuously, at the cost of turning poetry into prose.

[2] Solmsen has lately put the same question in a more general form, asking 'Have not these weighty utterances of the Chorus [in the *Agamemnon*] their significance also for the entire trilogy, and especially for the last piece?' (*Gnomon*, 31 (1959), 472 f.). The answer is surely 'Yes'.

[3] *Frag. gr. Hist.* III b 1, p. 25.

[4] The present paper is concerned with those aspects of the *Oresteia* which tie it down to a particular locus in time and place. But it should be unnecessary to add that underneath its time-bound purpose and its archaic presuppositions the *Oresteia* is also an enduring symbol of certain moral tests and torments which will always be part of the human condition. Great works of art can be understood on more than one level of significance.

upon the imagination of the old poet, faintly and fitfully at first, then with growing insistence, until finally his vision of the past was completely interfused with his hopes and fears for the present, and in the closing scene of the trilogy the two images became one?

IV

On Misunderstanding the Oedipus Rex[1]

ON the last occasion when I had the misfortune to examine in Honour Moderations at Oxford I set a question on the *Oedipus Rex*, which was among the books prescribed for general reading. My question was 'In what sense, if in any, does the *Oedipus Rex* attempt to justify the ways of God to man?' It was an optional question; there were plenty of alternatives. But the candidates evidently considered it a gift: nearly all of them attempted it. When I came to sort out the answers I found that they fell into three groups.

The first and biggest group held that the play justifies the gods by showing—or, as many of them said, 'proving'—that we get what we deserve. The arguments of this group turned upon the character of Oedipus. Some considered that Oedipus was a bad man: look how he treated Creon—naturally the gods punished him. Others said 'No, not altogether bad, even in some ways rather noble; but he had one of those fatal ἁμαρτίαι that all tragic heroes have, as we know from Aristotle. And since he had a ἁμαρτία he could of course expect no mercy: the gods had read the *Poetics*.' Well over half the candidates held views of this general type.

A second substantial group held that the *Oedipus Rex* is 'a tragedy of destiny'. What the play 'proves', they said, is that man has no free will but is a puppet in the hands of the gods who pull the strings that make him dance. Whether Sophocles thought the gods justified in treating their puppet as they did was not always clear from their answers. Most of those who took this view evidently disliked the play; some of them were honest enough to say so.

The third group was much smaller, but included some of the more thoughtful candidates. In their opinion Sophocles was

---

[1] A paper read at a 'refresher course' for teachers, London Institute of Education, 24 July 1964, and published in *Greece & Rome*, 13 (1966).

'a pure artist' and was therefore not interested in justifying the gods. He took the story of Oedipus as he found it, and used it to make an exciting play. The gods are simply part of the machinery of the plot.

Ninety per cent of the answers fell into one or other of these three groups. The remaining ten per cent had either failed to make up their minds or failed to express themselves intelligibly.

It was a shock to me to discover that all these young persons, supposedly trained in the study of classical literature, could read this great and moving play and so completely miss the point. For all the views I have just summarized are in fact demonstrably false (though some of them, and some ways of stating them, are more crudely and vulgarly false than others). It is true that each of them has been defended by some scholars in the past, but I had hoped that all of them were by now dead and buried. Wilamowitz thought he had killed the lot in an article published in *Hermes* (34 [1899], 55 ff.) more than half a century ago; and they have repeatedly been killed since. Yet their unquiet ghosts still haunt the examination-rooms of universities—and also, I would add, the pages of popular handbooks on the history of European drama. Surely that means that we have somehow failed in our duty as teachers?

It was this sense of failure which prompted me to attempt once more to clear up some of these ancient confusions. If the reader feels—as he very well may—that in this paper I am flogging a dead horse, I can only reply that on the evidence I have quoted the animal is unaccountably still alive.

I

I shall take Aristotle as my starting-point, since he is claimed as the primary witness for the first of the views I have described. From the thirteenth chapter of the *Poetics* we learn that the best sort of tragic hero is a man highly esteemed and prosperous who falls into misfortune because of some serious ($\mu\epsilon\gamma\acute{\alpha}\lambda\eta$) ἁμαρτία: examples, Oedipus and Thyestes. In Aristotle's view, then, Oedipus' misfortune was directly occasioned by some serious ἁμαρτία; and since Aristotle was known to be infallible, Victorian critics proceeded at once to look for this ἁμαρτία. And so, it appears, do the majority of present-day undergraduates.

What do they find? It depends on what they expect to find. As we all know, the word ἁμαρτία is ambiguous: in ordinary usage it is sometimes applied to false moral judgements, sometimes to purely intellectual error—the average Greek did not make our sharp distinction between the two. Since *Poetics* 13 is in general concerned with the moral character of the tragic hero, many scholars have thought in the past (and many undergraduates still think) that the ἁμαρτία of Oedipus must in Aristotle's view be a moral fault. They have accordingly gone over the play with a microscope looking for moral faults in Oedipus, and have duly found them—for neither here nor anywhere else did Sophocles portray that insipid and unlikely character, the man of perfect virtue. Oedipus, they point out, is proud and over-confident; he harbours unjustified suspicions against Teiresias and Creon; in one place (lines 964 ff.) he goes so far as to express some uncertainty about the truth of oracles. One may doubt whether this adds up to what Aristotle would consider μεγάλη ἁμαρτία. But even if it did, it would have no direct relevance to the question at issue. Years before the action of the play begins, Oedipus was already an incestuous parricide; if that was a punishment for his unkind treatment of Creon, then the punishment preceded the crime—which is surely an odd kind of justice.

'Ah,' says the traditionalist critic, 'but Oedipus' behaviour on the stage reveals the man he always was: he was punished for his basically unsound character.' In that case, however, someone on the stage ought to tell us so: Oedipus should repent, as Creon repents in the *Antigone*; or else another speaker should draw the moral. To ask about a character in fiction 'Was he a good man?' is to ask a strictly meaningless question: since Oedipus never lived we can answer neither 'Yes' nor 'No'. The legitimate question is 'Did Sophocles intend us to think of Oedipus as a good man?' This *can* be answered—not by applying some ethical yardstick of our own, but by looking at what the characters in the play say about him. And by that test the answer is 'Yes'. In the eyes of the Priest in the opening scene he is the greatest and noblest of men, the saviour of Thebes who with divine aid rescued the city from the Sphinx. The Chorus has the same view of him: he has proved his wisdom, he is the darling of the city, and never will they believe ill of him (504 ff.). And when the catastrophe comes, no one turns round and remarks 'Well, but it was your own fault: it must have been; Aristotle says so.'

In my opinion, and in that of nearly all Aristotelian scholars since Bywater, Aristotle does *not* say so; it is only the perversity of moralizing critics that has misrepresented him as saying so. It is almost certain that Aristotle was using ἁμαρτία here as he uses ἁμάρτημα in the *Nicomachean Ethics* (1135^b12) and in the *Rhetoric* (1374^b6), to mean an offence committed in ignorance of some material fact and therefore free from πονηρία or κακία.[1] These parallels seem decisive; and they are confirmed by Aristotle's second example—Thyestes, the man who ate the flesh of his own children in the belief that it was butcher's meat, and who subsequently begat a child on his own daughter, not knowing who she was. His story has clearly much in common with that of Oedipus, and Plato as well as Aristotle couples the two names as examples of the gravest ἁμαρτία (*Laws* 838 c). Thyestes and Oedipus are both of them men who violated the most sacred of nature's laws and thus incurred the most horrible of all pollutions; but they both did so without πονηρία, for they knew not what they did—in Aristotle's quasi-legal terminology, it was a ἁμάρτημα, not an ἀδίκημα. That is why they were in his view especially suitable subjects for tragedy. Had they acted knowingly, they would have been inhuman monsters, and we could not have felt for them that pity which tragedy ought to produce. As it is, we feel both pity, for the fragile estate of man, and terror, for a world whose laws we do not understand. The ἁμαρτία of Oedipus did not lie in losing his temper with Teiresias; it lay quite simply in parricide and incest—a μεγάλη ἁμαρτία indeed, the greatest a man can commit.

The theory that the tragic hero must have a grave moral flaw, and its mistaken ascription to Aristotle, has had a long and disastrous history. It was gratifying to Victorian critics, since it appeared to fit certain plays of Shakespeare. But it goes back much further, to the seventeenth-century French critic Dacier, who influenced the practice of the French classical dramatists, especially Corneille, and was himself influenced by the still older nonsense about 'poetic justice'—the notion that the poet has

---

[1] For the full evidence see O. Hey's exhaustive examination of the usage of these words, *Philol.* 83 (1927), 1–17, 137–63. Cf. also K. von Fritz, *Antike und Moderne Tragödie* (1962), 1 ff.

a moral duty to represent the world as a place where the good are always rewarded and the bad are always punished. I need not say that this puerile idea is completely foreign to Aristotle and to the practice of the Greek dramatists; I only mention it because on the evidence of those Honour Mods. papers it would appear that it still lingers on in some youthful minds like a cobweb in an unswept room.

To return to the *Oedipus Rex*, the moralist has still one last card to play. Could not Oedipus, he asks, have escaped his doom if he had been more careful? Knowing that he was in danger of committing parricide and incest, would not a really prudent man have avoided quarrelling, even in self-defence, with men older than himself, and also love-relations with women older than himself? Would he not, in Waldock's ironic phrase, have compiled a handlist of all the things he must not do? In real life I suppose he might. But we are not entitled to blame Oedipus either for carelessness in failing to compile a handlist or for lack of self-control in failing to obey its injunctions. For no such possibilities are mentioned in the play, or even hinted at; and it is an essential critical principle that *what is not mentioned in the play does not exist*. These considerations would be in place if we were examining the conduct of a real person. But we are not: we are examining the intentions of a dramatist, and we are not entitled to ask questions that the dramatist did not intend us to ask. There is only one branch of literature where we *are* entitled to ask such questions about τὰ ἐκτὸς τοῦ δράματος, namely the modern detective story. And despite certain similarities the *Oedipus Rex* is not a detective story but a dramatized folktale. If we insist on reading it as if it were a law report we must expect to miss the point.[1]

[1] The danger is exemplified by Mr. P. H. Vellacott's article, 'The Guilt of Oedipus', which appeared in *Greece & Rome*, 11 (1964), 137-48 shortly after my talk was delivered. By treating Oedipus as a historical personage and examining his career from the 'common-sense' standpoint of a prosecuting counsel Mr. Vellacott has no difficulty in showing that Oedipus must have guessed the true story of his birth long before the point at which the play opens—and guiltily done nothing about it. Sophocles, according to Mr. Vellacott, realized this, but unfortunately could not present the situation in these terms because 'such a conception was impossible to express in the conventional forms of tragedy'; so for most of the time he reluctantly fell back on 'the popular concept of an innocent Oedipus lured by Fate into a disastrous trap'. We are left to conclude either that the play is a botched compromise or else that the common sense of the law-courts is not after all the best yardstick by which to measure myth.

In any case, Sophocles has provided a conclusive answer to those who suggest that Oedipus could, and therefore should, have avoided his fate. The oracle was *unconditional* (line 790) : it did not say 'If you do so-and-so you will kill your father'; it simply said 'You will kill your father, you will sleep with your mother.' And what an oracle predicts is bound to happen. Oedipus does what he can to evade his destiny: he resolves never to see his supposed parents again. But it is quite certain from the first that his best efforts will be unavailing. Equally unconditional was the original oracle given to Laius (711 ff.) : Apollo said that he *must* (χρῆναι) die at the hands of Jocasta's child; there is no saving clause. Here there is a significant difference between Sophocles and Aeschylus. Of Aeschylus' trilogy on the House of Laius only the last play, the *Septem*, survives. Little is known of the others, but we do know, from *Septem* 742 ff., that according to Aeschylus the oracle given to Laius *was* conditional: 'Do not beget a child; for *if* you do, that child will kill you.' In Aeschylus the disaster *could* have been avoided, but Laius sinfully disobeyed and his sin brought ruin to his descendants. In Aeschylus the story was, like the *Oresteia*, a tale of crime and punishment; but Sophocles chose otherwise—that is why he altered the form of the oracle. There is no suggestion in the *Oedipus Rex* that Laius sinned or that Oedipus was the victim of a hereditary curse, and the critic must not assume what the poet has abstained from suggesting. Nor should we leap to the conclusion that Sophocles left out the hereditary curse because he thought the doctrine immoral; apparently he did not think so, since he used it both in the *Antigone* (583 ff.) and in the *Oedipus at Colonus* (964 ff.). What his motive may have been for ignoring it in the *Oedipus Rex* we shall see in a moment.

I hope I have now disposed of the moralizing interpretation, which has been rightly abandoned by the great majority of contemporary scholars. To mention only recent works in English, the books of Whitman, Waldock, Letters, Ehrenberg, Knox, and Kirkwood, however much they differ on other points, all agree about the essential moral innocence of Oedipus.

II

But what is the alternative? If Oedipus is the innocent victim of a doom which he cannot avoid, does this not reduce him to a mere puppet? Is not the whole play a 'tragedy of destiny' which denies human freedom? This is the second of the heresies which I set out to refute. Many readers have fallen into it, Sigmund Freud among them;[1] and you can find it confidently asserted in various popular handbooks, some of which even extend the assertion to Greek tragedy in general—thus providing themselves with a convenient label for distinguishing Greek from 'Christian' tragedy. But the whole notion is in fact anachronistic. The modern reader slips into it easily because *we* think of two clear-cut alternative views—either we believe in free will or else we are determinists. But fifth-century Greeks did not think in these terms any more than Homer did: the debate about determinism is a creation of Hellenistic thought. Homeric heroes have their predetermined 'portion of life' ($\mu o \hat{\iota} \rho \alpha$); they must die on their 'appointed day' ($\alpha \ddot{\iota} \sigma \iota \mu o \nu \ \tilde{\eta} \mu \alpha \rho$); but it never occurs to the poet or his audience that this prevents them from being free agents. Nor did Sophocles intend that it should occur to readers of the *Oedipus Rex*. Neither in Homer nor in Sophocles does divine foreknowledge of certain events imply that all human actions are predetermined. If explicit confirmation of this is required, we have only to turn to lines 1230 f., where the Messenger emphatically distinguishes Oedipus' self-blinding as 'voluntary' and 'self-chosen' from the 'involuntary' parricide and incest. Certain of Oedipus' past actions were fate-bound; but everything that he does on the stage from first to last he does as a free agent.

Even in calling the parricide and the incest 'fate-bound' I have perhaps implied more than the average Athenian of Sophocles' day would have recognized. As A. W. Gomme put it, 'the gods know the future, but they do not order it: they know who will win the next Scotland and England football match, but that does not alter the fact that the victory will depend on the skill, the determination, the fitness of the players, and a little on luck.'[2] That may not satisfy the analytical philosopher, but it seems to have satisfied the ordinary man at all periods. Bernard Knox aptly quotes the prophecy of Jesus to St. Peter, 'Before the cock crow, thou shalt deny me thrice.' The Evangelists clearly did not intend to imply that Peter's subsequent action was 'fate-bound'

[1] Sigmund Freud, *The Interpretation of Dreams* (London, Modern Library, 1938), 108.
[2] A. W. Gomme, *More Essays in Greek History and Literature* (1962), 211.

in the sense that he could not have chosen otherwise; Peter fulfilled the prediction, but he did so by an act of free choice.[1]

In any case I cannot understand Sir Maurice Bowra's[2] idea that the gods *force* on Oedipus the knowledge of what he has done. They do nothing of the kind; on the contrary, what fascinates us is the spectacle of a man freely choosing, from the highest motives, a series of actions which lead to his own ruin. Oedipus might have left the plague to take its course; but pity for the sufferings of his people compelled him to consult Delphi. When Apollo's word came back, he might still have left the murder of Laius uninvestigated; but piety and justice required him to act. He need not have forced the truth from the reluctant Theban herdsman; but because he cannot rest content with a lie, he must tear away the last veil from the illusion in which he has lived so long. Teiresias, Jocasta, the herdsman, each in turn tries to stop him, but in vain: he must read the last riddle, the riddle of his own life. The immediate cause of Oedipus' ruin is not 'Fate' or 'the gods'—no oracle said that he must discover the truth—and still less does it lie in his own weakness; what causes his ruin is his own strength and courage, his loyalty to Thebes, and his loyalty to the truth. In all this we are to see him as a free agent: hence the suppression of the hereditary curse. And his self-mutilation and self-banishment are equally free acts of choice.

Why does Oedipus blind himself? He tells us the reason (1369 ff.): he has done it in order to cut himself off from all contact with humanity; if he could choke the channels of his other senses he would do so. Suicide would not serve his purpose: in the next world he would have to meet his dead parents. Oedipus mutilates himself because he can face neither the living nor the dead. But why, if he is morally innocent? Once again, we must look at the play through Greek eyes. The doctrine that nothing matters except the agent's intention is a peculiarity of Christian and especially of post-Kantian thought. It is true that the Athenian law courts took account of intention: they distinguished as ours do between murder and accidental homicide or homicide committed in the course of self-defence. If Oedipus had been tried before an Athenian court he would have been acquitted—of murdering his father. But no human court could

[1] B. M. W. Knox, *Oedipus at Thebes* (1957), 39.
[2] C. M. Bowra, *Sophoclean Tragedy* (1944), ch. v.

acquit him of pollution; for pollution inhered in the act itself, irrespective of motive. Of that burden Thebes could not acquit Oedipus, and least of all could its bearer acquit himself.

The nearest parallel to the situation of Oedipus is in the tale which Herodotus tells about Adrastus, son of Gordies. Adrastus was the involuntary slayer of his own brother, and then of Atys, the son of his benefactor Croesus; the latter act, like the killing of Laius, fulfilled an oracle. Croesus forgave Adrastus because the killing was unintended (ἀέκων), and because the oracle showed that it was the will of 'some god'. But Adrastus did not forgive himself: he committed suicide, 'conscious', says Herodotus, 'that of all men known to him he bore the heaviest burden of disaster'.[1] It is for the same reason that Oedipus blinds himself. Morally innocent though he is and knows himself to be, the objective horror of his actions remains with him and he feels that he has no longer any place in human society. Is that simply archaic superstition? I think it is something more. Suppose a motorist runs down a man and kills him, I think he *ought* to feel that he has done a terrible thing, even if the accident is no fault of his: he has destroyed a human life, which nothing can restore. In the objective order it is acts that count, not intentions. A man who has violated that order may well feel a sense of guilt, however blameless his driving.

But my analogy is very imperfect, and even the case of Adrastus is not fully comparable. Oedipus is no ordinary homicide: he has committed the two crimes which above all others fill us with instinctive horror. Sophocles had not read Freud, but he knew how people *feel* about these things—better than some of his critics appear to do. And in the strongly patriarchal society of ancient Greece the revulsion would be even more intense than it is in our own. We have only to read Plato's prescription for the treatment to be given to parricides (*Laws* 872 c ff.). For this deed, he says, there can be no purification: the parricide shall be killed, his body shall be laid naked at a cross-roads outside the city, each officer of the State shall cast a stone upon it and curse it, and then the bloody remnant shall be flung outside the city's territory and left unburied. In all this he is probably following actual Greek practice. And if that is

[1] Herodotus 1. 45. Cf. H. Funke, *Die sogenannte tragische Schuld* (Diss. Köln, 1963), 105 ff.

how Greek justice treated parricides, is it surprising that Oedipus treats himself as he does, when the great king, 'the first of men', the man whose intuitive genius had saved Thebes, is suddenly revealed to himself as a thing so unclean that 'neither the earth can receive it, nor the holy rain nor the sunshine endure its presence' (1426)?

III

At this point I am brought back to the original question I asked the undergraduates: does Sophocles in this play attempt to justify the ways of God to man? If 'to justify' means 'to explain in terms of *human* justice', the answer is surely 'No'. If human justice is the standard, then, as Waldock bluntly expressed it, 'Nothing can excuse the gods, and Sophocles knew it perfectly well.' Waldock does not, however, suggest that the poet intended any attack on the gods. He goes on to say that it is futile to look for any 'message' or 'meaning' in this play: 'there is no meaning', he tells us, 'in the *Oedipus Rex*; there is merely the terror of coincidence.'[1] Kirkwood seems to take a rather similar line: 'Sophocles', he says, 'has no theological pronouncements to make and no points of criticism to score.'[2] These opinions come rather close to, if they do not actually involve, the view adopted by my third and last group of undergraduates—the view that the gods are merely agents in a traditional story which Sophocles, a 'pure artist', exploits for dramatic purposes without raising the religious issue or drawing any moral whatever.

This account seems to me insufficient; but I have more sympathy with it than I have with either of the other heresies. It reflects a healthy reaction against the old moralizing school of critics; and the text of the play appears at first sight to support it. It is a striking fact that after the catastrophe no one on the stage says a word either in justification of the gods or in criticism of them. Oedipus says 'These things were Apollo'—and that is all. If the poet has charged him with a 'message' about divine justice or injustice, he fails to deliver it. And I fully agree that there is no reason at all why we should require a dramatist—even a Greek dramatist—to be for ever running about delivering banal 'messages'. It is true that when a Greek dramatic poet had

---

[1] A. J. A. Waldock, *Sophocles the Dramatist* (1951), 158, 168.
[2] G. M. Kirkwood, *A Study of Sophoclean Drama* (1958), 271.

something he passionately wanted to say to his fellow citizens he felt entitled to say it. Aeschylus in the *Oresteia*, Aristophanes in the *Frogs*, had something to say to their people and used the opportunity of saying it on the stage. But these are exceptional cases—both these works were produced at a time of grave crisis in public affairs—and even here the 'message' appears to me to be incidental to the true function of the artist, which I should be disposed to define, with Dr. Johnson, as 'the enlargement of our sensibility'. It is unwise to generalize from special cases. (And, incidentally, I wish undergraduates would stop writing essays which begin with the words 'This play *proves* that . . .' Surely no work of art can ever 'prove' anything: what value could there be in a 'proof' whose premisses are manufactured by the artist?)

Nevertheless, I cannot accept the view that the *Oedipus Rex* conveys *no* intelligible meaning and that Sophocles' plays tell us nothing of his opinions concerning the gods. Certainly it is always dangerous to use dramatic works as evidence of their author's opinions, and especially of their religious convictions: we can legitimately discuss religion *in* Shakespeare, but do we know anything at all about the religion *of* Shakespeare? Still, I think I should venture to assert two things about Sophocles' opinions:

First, he did not believe (or did not always believe) that the gods are in any human sense 'just';

Secondly, he did always believe that the gods exist and that man should revere them.

The first of these propositions is supported not only by the implicit evidence of the *Oedipus Rex* but by the explicit evidence of another play which is generally thought to be close in date to it. The closing lines of the *Trachiniae* contain a denunciation in violent terms of divine injustice. No one answers it. I can only suppose that the poet had no answer to give.

For the second of my two propositions we have quite strong *external* evidence—which is important, since it is independent of our subjective impressions. We know that Sophocles held various priesthoods; that when the cult of Asclepius was introduced to Athens he acted as the god's host and wrote a hymn in his honour; and that he was himself worshipped as a 'hero' after his death, which seems to imply that he accepted the religion of the State and was accepted by it. But the external evidence does not stand alone: it is strongly supported by at least one passage in the

Oedipus Rex. The celebrated choral ode about the decline of prophecy and the threat to religion (lines 863–910) was of course suggested by the scene with Creon which precedes it; but it contains generalizations which have little apparent relevance either to Oedipus or to Creon. Is the piety of this ode purely conventional, as Whitman maintained in a vigorous but sometimes perverse book?[1] One phrase in particular seems to forbid this interpretation. If men are to lose all respect for the gods, in that case, the Chorus asks, τί δεῖ με χορεύειν; (895). If by this they mean merely 'Why should I, a Theban elder, dance?' the question is irrelevant and even slightly ludicrous; the meaning is surely 'Why should I, an Athenian citizen, continue to serve in a chorus?' In speaking of themselves as a chorus they step out of the play into the contemporary world, as Aristophanes' choruses do in the *parabasis*. And in effect the question they are asking seems to be this: 'If Athens loses faith in religion, if the views of the Enlightenment prevail, what significance is there in tragic drama, which exists as part of the service of the gods?' To that question the rapid decay of tragedy in the fourth century may be said to have provided an answer.

In saying this, I am not suggesting with Ehrenberg that the position of Oedipus reflects that of Pericles,[2] or with Knox that he is intended to be a symbol of Athens:[3] allegory of that sort seems to me wholly alien to Greek tragedy. I am only claiming that at one point in this play Sophocles took occasion to say to his fellow citizens something which he felt to be important. And it *was* important, particularly in the period of the Archidamian War, to which the *Oedipus Rex* probably belongs. Delphi was known to be pro-Spartan: that is why Euripides was given a free hand to criticize Apollo. But if Delphi could not be trusted, the whole fabric of traditional belief was threatened with collapse. In our society religious faith is no longer tied up with belief in prophecy; but for the ancient world, both pagan and Christian, it was. And in the years of the Archidamian War belief in prophecy was at a low ebb; Thucydides is our witness to that.

I take it, then, as reasonably certain that while Sophocles did not pretend that the gods are in any human sense just he

---

[1] C. H. Whitman, *Sophocles* (1951), 133–5.
[2] V. Ehrenberg, *Sophocles and Pericles* (1954), 141 ff.
[3] B. M. W. Knox, op. cit., ch. ii.

nevertheless held that they are entitled to our worship. Are these two opinions incompatible? Here once more we cannot hope to understand Greek literature if we persist in looking at it through Christian spectacles. To the Christian it is a necessary part of piety to believe that God is just. And so it was to Plato and to the Stoics. But the older world saw no such necessity. If you doubt this, take down the *Iliad* and read Achilles' opinion of what divine justice amounts to (24. 525–33); or take down the Bible and read the Book of Job. Disbelief in divine justice as measured by human yardsticks can perfectly well be associated with deep religious feeling. 'Men', said Heraclitus, 'find some things unjust, other things just; but in the eyes of God all things are beautiful and good and just.'[1] I think that Sophocles would have agreed. For him, as for Heraclitus, there is an objective world-order which man must respect, but which he cannot hope fully to understand.

IV

Some readers of the *Oedipus Rex* have told me that they find its atmosphere stifling and oppressive: they miss the tragic exaltation that one gets from the *Antigone* or the *Prometheus Vinctus*. And I fear that what I have said here has done nothing to remove that feeling. Yet it is not a feeling which I share myself. Certainly the *Oedipus Rex* is a play about the blindness of man and the desperate insecurity of the human condition: in a sense every man must grope in the dark as Oedipus gropes, not knowing who he is or what he has to suffer; we all live in a world of appearance which hides from us who-knows-what dreadful reality. But surely the *Oedipus Rex* is also a play about human greatness. Oedipus is great, not in virtue of a great worldly position—for his worldly position is an illusion which will vanish like a dream—but in virtue of his inner strength: strength to pursue the truth at whatever personal cost, and strength to accept and endure it when found. 'This horror is mine,' he cries, 'and none but I is strong enough to bear it' (1414). Oedipus is great because he accepts the responsibility for *all* his acts, including those which are objectively most horrible, though subjectively innocent.

To me personally Oedipus is a kind of symbol of the human intelligence which cannot rest until it has solved all the riddles—

[1] Heraclitus, frag. 102 Diels–Kranz.

even the last riddle, to which the answer is that human happiness is built on an illusion. I do not know how far Sophocles intended that. But certainly in the last lines of the play (which I firmly believe to be genuine) he does generalize the case, does appear to suggest that in some sense Oedipus is every man and every man is potentially Oedipus. Freud felt this (he was not insensitive to poetry), but as we all know he understood it in a specific psychological sense. 'Oedipus' fate', he says, 'moves us only because it might have been our own, because the oracle laid upon us before birth the very curse which rested upon him. It may be that we were all destined to direct our first sexual impulses towards our mothers, and our first impulses of hatred and violence towards our fathers; our dreams convince us that we were.'[1] Perhaps they do; but Freud did not ascribe his interpretation of the myth to Sophocles, and it is not the interpretation I have in mind. Is there not in the poet's view a much wider sense in which every man is Oedipus? If every man could tear away the last veils of illusion, if he could see human life as time and the gods see it, would he not see that against that tremendous background all the generations of men are as if they had not been, ἴσα καὶ τὸ μηδὲν ζώσας (1187)? That was how Odysseus saw it when he had conversed with Athena, the embodiment of divine wisdom. 'In Ajax's condition', he says, 'I recognize my own: I perceive that all men living are but appearance or unsubstantial shadow.'

ὁρῶ γὰρ ἡμᾶς οὐδὲν ὄντας ἄλλο πλὴν
εἴδωλ', ὅσοιπερ ζῶμεν, ἢ κούφην σκιάν.[2]

So far as I can judge, on this matter Sophocles' deepest feelings did not change. The same view of the human condition which is made explicit in his earliest extant play is implicit not only in the *Oedipus Rex* but in the *Oedipus Coloneus*, in the great speech where Oedipus draws the bitter conclusion from his life's experience and in the famous ode on old age.[3] Whether this vision of man's estate is true or false I do not know, but it ought to be comprehensible to a generation which relishes the plays of Samuel Beckett. I do not wish to describe it as a 'message'. But I find in it an enlargement of sensibility. And that is all I ask of any dramatist.

[1] Sigmund Freud, op. cit. 109.   [2] *Ajax* 124–6.
[3] *O.C.* 607–15, 1211–49.

V

Euripides the Irrationalist[1]

I WISH to make it clear at the outset that the present paper, despite its title, is not primarily intended as a direct answer to the late Dr. Verrall: indeed, up to a point, the suggestions I am going to offer are quite compatible with his thesis, though they do not involve it. Verrall used the term 'rationalist' in the Victorian sense: I propose to use it in the seventeenth-century sense. When the Victorians talked about 'rationalists', they generally meant anti-clericals; what Verrall wished to emphasize, and I am not concerned to deny, was the anti-clericalism of Euripides. For the purpose of this paper I must ask you to dismiss that use of the word 'rationalist'. I shall give the word its older and wider meaning, as a description of that type of philosophy which in various transformations has on the whole (except for one long and very curious break) dominated European thought since Socrates. This philosophy makes three affirmations:

First, that reason (what the Greeks called rational discourse, λόγος) is the sole and sufficient instrument of truth—as against the views which assign that function to sense-perception, or to faith, or to something called 'intuition,' or deny that any sufficient instrument exists at all.

From this it follows, secondly, that reality must be such that it can be understood by reason; and this implies that the structure of reality must be itself in some sense rational.

Lastly, in such a universe values as well as facts will be rational: the highest Good will be either rational thought or something closely akin to it. Hence the tendency of rationalism is to say that moral, like intellectual, error can arise only from a failure to use the reason we possess; and that when it does arise it must, like intellectual error, be curable by an intellectual process.

These are what I shall call the three affirmations of rationalism: reason as the instrument of truth; as the essential character of

[1] A paper read before the Classical Association, 12 April 1929, and published in the *Classical Review*, 43 (1929).

reality; as the means to personal redemption. The philosophy thus summed up in its most generalized traits was the decisive contribution of the Greeks to human thought. The history of early Greek philosophy is the history of the progressive emergence of rationalism out of the old hylozoism; but I think it would be generally agreed that the earliest representation of the Cosmos and of Man's place in it which is rationalist not merely by implication but consciously and consistently is to be found in the teaching of Socrates. And the question which I shall attempt to answer in the present paper is this: How does Euripides stand in relation to that intellectual revolution which after centuries of effort was at length being consummated in his own day and in his own city—whose leader, moreover, was one of his personal friends?

In such an inquiry two objections meet us at the outset. It may be asked, in the first place, why a dramatist should relate himself at all to intellectual revolutions. Sophocles, so far as we can see, never did. And the business of a dramatic poet is, in Aristotle's words, to represent 'men in action', not theories in discussion. The answer to this is simply that while Sophocles is a dramatist, Euripides happens to be, like Bernard Shaw and Pirandello, a philosophical dramatist.[1] It is credibly affirmed by various ancient authorities that Euripides began life as a student of philosophy; and that he numbered among his friends Anaxagoras and Socrates, Protagoras and Prodicus. It was in Euripides' house, according to one story, that Protagoras gave the first public recital of his famous treatise *Concerning the Gods*,[2] which made as much stir in Periclean Athens as Darwin's *Origin of Species* once did in England. And if the value of such statements be doubted, we still have the evidence of Euripides' own work, which clearly shows acquaintance with the ideas not only of Anaxagoras and Protagoras but of less known philosophers like Diogenes of Apollonia and of older thinkers like Heraclitus. That being so, we have a prima-facie ground for seeking in his plays some trace of his reaction to the teaching of Socrates.

But the fact remains that Euripides wrote plays, not treatises: how then are we to tell when his characters are uttering their

[1] 'Euripides, auditor Anaxagorae, quem philosophum Athenienses scenicum appellaverunt' (Vitruv. 8, *praef.* § i).
[2] [See below, pp. 96 f.].

author's thoughts and when their own? This is a real difficulty; but to the careful student not, I think, an insuperable one. To begin with, in Euripides, as in Shaw, we can generally distinguish the characters who are only characters, a Theseus or a Broadbent, an Admetus or a Burge-Lubin, from those who are also, like their author, thinkers; John Tanner or Father Keegan, Medea or Phaedra or Hecuba or Electra (for it is a peculiarity of Euripides that his thinkers are nearly always women). If we find further, as on the whole we do find, that, despite profound differences of individual temperament and dramatic circumstance, the thoughts of these various thinking characters spring from the same fundamental attitude towards life, which is not determined for them by their history or situation, then we are justified in assuming that this attitude was the author's. Where the speaker's philosophical opinions are determined in advance by his profession or his previous history (as with the professional seer Teiresias or the temple-bred boy Ion) they must of course be correspondingly discounted. Where, on the other hand, his opinions are conspicuously inappropriate to his personality or his dramatic situation—where the διάνοια breaks loose from the μῦθος—there we have especial reason to suspect the intervention of the author. When, for instance, Hecuba, on hearing the moving recital of her daughter's martyrdom, responds with a disquisition on the relative importance of heredity and environment as elements in the formation of character, after which with a much-needed apology she recalls herself to the matter in hand[1]—when this happens we may be sure that the disquisition is the work of Euripides the philosopher, who must then make his excuses as best he can to Euripides the dramatist.

The opinions hardest to assess are those of the Chorus. It is certain that in many cases the Chorus are content to draw the conventional moral from the events of the play, although it is equally certain that this was not the moral that Euripides meant us to draw. There are Choruses in Euripides who affirm their belief in the oracle of Delphi, in the inherited curse, in the importance of ritual, in such myths as the divine birth of Heracles—all of them things which we have good reason to think that Euripides did not believe in. On the other hand, there are many places where Euripides does seem to speak through his Chorus,

[1] *Hec.* 592 ff.

even at the sacrifice of dramatic appropriateness, as when he makes the villagers of prehistoric Pherae describe themselves as deeply read in poetry and philosophy and convinced necessitarians.[1]

Bearing these cautions in mind, let us see whether we can discover in the extant plays and fragments any evidence of Euripides' attitude towards our three affirmations of rationalism. And since it is obviously the theory of conduct which concerns a dramatist most deeply, let us begin with the ethical affirmation: that virtue, being a kind of knowledge, is teachable, and that wrongdoing is the result of ignorance.

Why did Medea murder her children? Was it because she was a barbarian, who knew no better? We have her own answer in lines 1078 ff. 'I recognize', she says, 'what evil I am about to do, but my $θυμός$ [my passion] is stronger than my counsels: $θυμός$ is the cause of Man's worst crimes.' Her reason can judge her action, which she frankly describes as a 'foul murder',[2] but it cannot influence it: the springs of action are in the $θυμός$, beyond the reach of reason. Helplessly she beseeches her $θυμός$ to have mercy: 'No! for God's sake, my $θυμός$, do not this thing: touch them not, O desperate one—spare my children!'[3] It is the traditional appeal of the victim to the tyrant: only here victim and tyrant are bound together in one personality—which is, nevertheless, in some dreadful way not one but two. Jason, like the conventional Greek he is, would fain put the blame on an ἀλάστωρ;[4] but Medea *is her own* ἀλάστωρ.

Consider next the *Hippolytus*. At the beginning of the play Hippolytus goes out of his way to inform us, *à propos de bottes*, that true σωφροσύνη comes from φύσις, not from teaching.[5] And later, when Theseus asks bitterly why, among all the countless discoveries of Man, no one has yet discovered a way of teaching moral sense (φρονεῖν) to those who have no νοῦς, Hippolytus rejoins: 'Clever indeed is the sophist you describe, who is able to force a moral sense upon those who lack it.'[6] This sounds very much like a hit at Prodicus and his kind, who claimed to teach men ἀρετή. But where, then, does this ineradicable evil come from? Theseus, a hopelessly superficial person, merely puts it down to lack of νοῦς; but Phaedra, who has often lain awake

[1] *Alc.* 962. [2] *Med.* 1383. [3] Ibid. 1056–7.
[4] Ibid. 1333. [5] *Hipp.* 79 f. [6] Ibid. 921–2.

all night thinking about this question,¹ knows as well as Medea that it has nothing to do with our intellect:

τὰ χρήστ' ἐπιστάμεσθα καὶ γιγνώσκομεν,
οὐκ ἐκπονοῦμεν δέ.

Something gets in the way—either ἀργία, so that the good principles are inoperative, or else ἡδονή, setting up a rival principle of conduct.² We are reminded of Aristotle's analysis of the ἀκρατής and the ἀκόλαστος a century later. As the Nurse puts it, you can be σώφρων, and yet desire evil:³ just as Medea was σοφή, and yet did evil. The Chorus may ascribe it all to the ancestral curse;⁴ but Euripides knows better. The moral impotence of the reason is emphasized repeatedly in the fragments.⁵

I have already referred to the passage where Hecuba asks whether moral differences are due to heredity or environment:

ἆρ' οἱ τεκόντες διαφέρουσιν ἢ τροφαί;⁶

Her answer is the common-sense one that both have their importance. But we see from other passages that the influence of environment is strictly limited. μέγιστον ἡ φύσις: no amount of training will make good men out of children with a bad heredity.⁷ Adrastus in the *Supplices*⁸ makes the poet's idea of moral education more precise: courage *can* be taught; but only by ἄσκησις, by practice, in the same way as babies learn to speak and understand. One is tempted to think that Euripides has in mind here discussions like those in Plato's *Laches*: at any rate, both here and in frag. 1027 he seems to emphasize the principle of ἄσκησις, which the Socratic intellectualism tended to undervalue, and which lies at the base of most modern educational reforms.

For Euripides the evil in human nature is thus indestructible and rooted in heredity (which with him, as with Ibsen, takes the place of the Aeschylean ancestral curse); the intellect is powerless to control it, though early education may have some effect in favourable cases. Euripides' characters do not merely enunciate these principles; they also illustrate them in action. The *Medea*, the *Hippolytus*, the *Hecuba*, the *Heracles*: what gives to all these plays their profoundly tragic character is the victory

---

¹ *Hipp.* 375.   ² Ibid. 380 ff.   ³ Ibid. 358.   ⁴ Ibid. 756 ff.
⁵ Cf., for example, frags. 572, 840, 841 (the numeration followed is that of Nauck's second edition).
⁶ *Hec.* 899.   ⁷ Frags. 333, 810, 1068.   ⁸ 911 ff.

Euripides the Irrationalist

of irrational impulse over reason in a noble but unstable human being. *Video meliora proboque, deteriora sequor*: it is here that Euripides finds the essence of man's moral tragedy. Hence the scientific care which, as an ancient critic remarks, he devoted to the study of ἔρωτάς τε καὶ μανίας—the dark irrational side of man's nature. The accuracy with which he observed the symptoms of neurosis and insanity appears from such scenes as Phaedra's first conversation with the Nurse,[1] or the awakening of Agave out of her Dionysiac trance personality,[2] or again in the figure of Heracles, whose insanity is clearly marked as belonging to the manic–depressive type. But I can only mention these things in passing, as exemplifying the fascinated precision with which Euripides explored those dark tracts of the spirit that lie outside the narrow illuminated field of rational thought.

We have seen that in Euripides the intellect does not help us to right conduct. Does it help to the attainment of truth? There are many passages which suggest that it does not. In the first place, the bad characters in Euripides argue as ingeniously and plausibly as the good: hence Aristophanes can accuse him of making the worse appear the better cause. 'A clever speaker can argue both for and against any proposition whatever', says somebody in the *Antiope*,[3] echoing a famous remark of Protagoras. Such a speaker wields a terrible power; the power of Persuasion, that goddess whose altar, as we are told in another fragment, is set in the human heart.[4] Why do we not abandon all other studies, asks Hecuba, and hire teachers of Persuasion[5]—teachers like Gorgias, in fact? But persuasion is not proof: in the end, πράγματα are stronger than λόγοι;[6] λόγοι cheat us just as hopes do;[7] the σοφοὶ καὶ μεριμνηταὶ λόγων come to a bad end.[8] What then is left us but the 'enlightened scepticism' (σώφρων ἀπιστία) recommended by the messenger in the *Helena*?[9] I remark here that the rationalist Plato denounces the sophists quite as vigorously as Euripides

---

[1] *Hipp.* 198–251. Cf. *C.R.* 39 (1925), 102.
[2] *Bacch.* 1264–84. Noteworthy here are (1) the amnesia which comes on in line 1272 (as with patients awakening from a hypnotic trance), and the gentle skill with which Cadmus reinstates the lost memory by the help of association; (2) Agave's attempt to retreat into her dream rather than face the truth of which she is already subconsciously aware (1278; cf. 1107–9, where Pentheus is simultaneously thought of as an animal and as a human spy, and the similar clash of dream and reality in Pentheus' own mind, l. 922).
[3] Frag. 189. [4] Frag. 170. [5] *Hec.* 814 ff. [6] Frag. 206.
[7] Frag. 650. [8] *Med.* 1225; cf. *Hec.* 1192. [9] 1617.

does. But there is this difference: Plato, because he is a rationalist, believes that he has a technique for discriminating the genuine philosophers from the hollow sophists: Euripides' characters, on the other hand, constantly complain that no such technique exists:

> οὐδεὶς ὅρος ἐκ θεῶν
> χρηστοῖς οὐδὲ κακοῖς σαφής.[1]

There is a story in Diogenes Laertius that Socrates, who always attended the first production of a new play by Euripides, had come to see his *Electra*. He sat it out until the actors reached the place where Orestes, discussing this very question of the criterion of goodness, declares that it is better to give it up:

> κράτιστον εἰκῇ ταῦτ' ἐᾶν ἀφειμένα.[2]

At that point Socrates rose and left the theatre in disgust. The anecdote is very likely an invention; but it points to the truth that the whole Socratic–Platonic political philosophy depends on the possibility of sorting out with certainty the good from the bad, the guardians from the common people; and this possibility is just what Euripides denies. Time, he admits, will show,[3] but no other test is any use.

Is intelligence to be desired as a means to happiness? From the case of Medea, it would seem not. Medea is the typical clever woman: 'All the Greeks recognized that you were σοφή', says her husband.[4] But her cleverness has brought about her ruin: εἰμὶ δ' οὐκ ἄγαν σοφή, she cries—'I am not so very clever after all.'[5] Her advice to parents is, not to bring up their children to be περισσῶς σοφοί: they will get nothing by it but unpopularity.[6] The same thought, that 'the too much wisdom of the wise brings its own penalty', recurs in the *Electra*; but there it receives a deeper interpretation: the wise suffer more than other men because they feel more profoundly the pity of life.[7] In the light of these two passages we can understand the curious prayer of the Chorus in the *Hippolytus*,[8] who wish for an insight into life which shall be true, indeed, but *not too precise*:

> δόξα δὲ μήτ' ἀτρεκὴς μήτ' αὖ παράσημος ἐνείη.

To see too deeply into the nature of the world is very dangerous.

---

[1] H.F. 669; cf. Med. 516, Hipp. 925.   [2] 379.   [3] Hipp. 428, etc.
[4] 539.   [5] 305.   [6] 294 ff.; cf. frag. 635.   [7] 294 ff.   [8] 1115.

Against this we may set a famous passage in praise of the student's life, frag. 910. ὄλβιος ὅστις ..., it begins: 'Blessed is he who ...' This is the traditional formula for introducing a beatitude; but what it introduces here is a little surprising:

> ὄλβιος ὅστις τῆς ἱστορίας
> ἔσχε μάθησιν.

'Blessed is he who has learned the methods of research.' The chief ground of his blessedness, however, seems to be that he is thereby kept out of mischief, 'without impulse to hurt his fellows, or to any unrighteous dealing, but contemplating the ageless order of undying Nature, how it arose and whence: such men have no temptation to ugly deeds.' The same spirit breathes in Amphion's prayer: 'Give me the gift of song and subtle utterance: let me not meddle at all in the distempers of the State.'[1] The contemplative life, as distinguished from the noisy propaganda of the sophists, is a sheltered and beautiful one; but for all that it is the refuge of despair, like that sheltering wall behind which Plato's Good Man crouches from the storm, leaving the wicked to their wickedness. Here for once Plato and Euripides speak with the same voice—a voice which forebodes the apparition of the Stoic philosopher and the Christian monk.

But it is by no means the same 'ageless order' which Plato and Euripides contemplate. The Platonic contemplative is at home in the universe, because he sees the universe as penetrated through and through by a divine reason, and therefore penetrable to human reason also. But for Euripides Man is the slave, not the favourite child, of the gods;[2] and the name of the 'ageless order' is Necessity. κρεῖσσον οὐδὲν Ἀνάγκας ηὗρον, cry the Chorus in the *Alcestis*.[3] All else is guesswork. Is 'Zeus' some physical principle, like the ether?[4] or is he a mythological projection of what is highest in ourselves? or just another name for Necessity?[5]

---

[1] Frag. 202.   [2] *Or.* 418.
[3] 965; cf. *Hel.* 513 f., and the repeated insistence that Man is subject to the same cycle of physical necessity as Nature, frags. 330, 415, 757.
[4] Frag. 877; cf. 839, 919, 941.
[5] *Tr.* 885:

> ὅστις ποτ' εἶ σύ, δυστόπαστος εἰδέναι,
> Ζεύς, εἴτ' ἀνάγκη φύσεος εἴτε νοῦς βροτῶν.

The interpretation I have ventured to give to the ambiguous νοῦς βροτῶν is supported by l. 988, where the same speaker tells Helen that her own corrupt mind

Euripides lets his puppets speculate, but Euripides does not know. His own position seems to be fairly summed up in one of the fragments:[1] 'Men are not masters of these high arguments. He that pretends to have knowledge concerning the gods has in truth no higher science than to persuade men by assertion.' And with that the whole of the traditional Greek mythology crumbles to the ground. That, in fact, Apollo and the Furies and the rest of the denizens of Olympus and Tartarus are for Euripides no more than dramatic fictions has been abundantly proved by Verrall and others: there is no need for me to labour the point.

What is more important is to emphasize that, in spite of all this, Euripides remains in the wider sense of the word a deeply religious poet. The state religion meant little or nothing to him; and concepts like Αἰθήρ and Ἀνάγκη seem to offer small handhold for faith. Yet it is clear that there are forces in the world—inhuman and non-rational forces—which he recognizes as divine. Consider the *Hippolytus* again, and take first the Nurse's lines (189 ff.):

All the life of Man is pain, and there is no rest from trouble. But that Other—whatever it be—that is more precious than life, darkness enshrouding covers it in cloud. A nameless thing that shines across the world: and 'tis plain that for this we are sick with longing, because we have no knowledge of another life, because we have no revelation (ἀπόδειξις) of the things under earth, but still drift vainly upon a tide of legend.

This is not the religion of the state, or the religion of the Orphic societies, or the religion of Socrates: all these believed that they had in some sense an ἀπόδειξις of the things under earth. But the essential mark of the religious temperament is here—the affirmation of a something 'Other' which is 'more precious than

---

(νοῦς) *turned into* Aphrodite: Aphrodite is only a hypostatized lust, and Zeus himself may be a like figment. The famous line

ὁ νοῦς γὰρ ἡμῶν ἐστιν ἐν ἑκάστῳ θεός (frag. 1018)

is similarly ambiguous. Nemesius (*Nat. Hom.* 348) took it to mean τὸν νοῦν τὸν ἐν ἑκάστῳ προνοεῖν ἑκάστου, θεῶν δὲ μηδένα. Is this 'paltering in a double sense' deliberate and prudential? Cf. also the much discussed lines *Hec.* 799–801, where Hecuba seems to say that the gods are the servants (or symbols?) of the Law of Justice which governs human society, and that religion derives its strength from morality. Whether the 'Law' is meant to be cosmic *as well as* human, I cannot feel sure.

[1] 795; cf. also 391, 480.

life.' We shall meet it again in the *Bacchae*. Consider next the figure of Kypris in the *Hippolytus*. Mythologize the force which made the tragedy of Phaedra—turn Kypris into a person—and you get not a goddess but a petty fiend, whose motives are the meanest personal jealousies. Mythologize the interplay of this force with the opposite force of chastity, and you get a ludicrous picture of the Balance of Power in the chancelleries of Olympus, such as is sketched for us in lines 1329 ff. But from behind this transparent satire on the Olympians there emerges a deeper conception of Kypris and Artemis as eternal cosmic powers: the very point of the satire is to show that they must be interpreted as principles, not as persons—εἰ θεοί τι δρῶσιν αἰσχρόν, οὐκ εἰσὶν θεοί. That is just what the Nurse says:[1] 'Kypris, it appears, is no goddess, but something bigger.' Further on she is more explicit: 'Kypris haunts the air; in the waves of the sea she hath her dwelling; of her are all things born. She is the sower, she the giver of desire; and children of desire are all we upon earth.'[2] The Kypris of the *Hippolytus* is none other than the Venus Genetrix of Lucretius, the Life Force of Schopenhauer, the *élan vital* of Bergson: a force unthinking, unpitying, but divine. Opposed to her, as the negative to the positive pole of the magnet, stands Artemis, the principle of aloofness, of refusal, ultimately of death. Between these two poles swings the dark and changeful life of Man, the plaything which they exalt for a moment by their companionship, and drop so easily when it is broken:

μακρὰν δὲ λείπεις ῥᾳδίως ὁμιλίαν,

says Hippolytus bitterly.[3]

If with this thought in our minds—the thought of the divinity of natural forces—we approach the *Bacchae*, I think we shall find that great but puzzling play somewhat less difficult to understand. If I am right in my general view of Euripides, the *Bacchae* is neither the pious testimony of a deathbed conversion (as the Victorians supposed) nor the last sneer of the dying atheist (as Verrall supposed). To my mind it is neither a recantation nor a development of Euripides' earlier views on the Olympians and their cult: because, as Professor Murray has emphasized, it has very little to do with the Olympians; it is a study of an orgiastic nature-religion. Euripides is dealing here with something

[1] 360. [2] 447. [3] 1441.

based neither on reason nor on Homeric tradition, but on an immediate personal experience—an experience in which 'the heart is congregationalised',[1] so that the worshipper is made one with his fellow worshippers, one also with the wildness of brute nature,[2] and one with Dionysus, the spirit of that wildness.[3] Euripides confronts us here with an irruption into normal life of the mystery behind life, the 'something other that is more precious than life'. Beside that Other, sing the Chorus, the wisdom of the sophist is folly (τὸ σοφὸν οὐ σοφία);[4] beside it the wisdom of the true philosopher is but a groping in darkness:

τὸ σοφὸν οὐ φθονῶ·
χαίρω θηρεύουσα· τὰ δ' ἕτερα μεγάλα
φανερά.[5]

'The Other Things are great and shining.' But this is precisely the Nurse's doctrine, only more confidently enunciated! And the scorn poured on false σοφία is entirely in keeping with what we have met elsewhere in Euripides.

Perhaps the nearest modern parallel[6] to the *Bacchae* (if one may compare great things with smaller) is Shaw's *Major Barbara*. But the difference of treatment in the two plays is as striking as the similarity of subject. Shaw approaches salvationism as a psychologist; Euripides studies Bacchism both as psychologist and as poet. That is why he can deal faithfully alike with the surpassing beauty and the inhuman cruelty of irrationalist religion, where Shaw sees only its humour and its pathos. That the deep religious feeling shown in the choruses is not the result of any eleventh-hour conversion appears from a fragmentary chorus of an earlier play, *The Men of Crete*, in which the mysteries of the Kouretes, closely akin to those of Dionysus, are treated in the same reverent spirit.[7] That these songs are instinct with a personal emotion seems to me unmistakable. But in none of his greater plays does Euripides violate the law of experience by

[1] 75, θιασεύεται ψυχάν: the rendering is Verrall's.
[2] 726, πᾶν δὲ συνεβάκχευ' ὄρος καὶ θῆρες.
[3] 115, Βρόμιος ὅστις ἄγῃ θιάσους (I accept Murray's reading and interpretation of the line). [I now doubt both: see my commentary ad loc.]
[4] 395.   [5] 1005.
[6] Or, rather, not a parallel but an echo; for it was Professor Murray's translation of the *Bacchae* which set Shaw exploring the truncated manifestations of orgiastic religion in our own day.
[7] Frag. 472.

putting all the moral weights into one scale of the balance. Reverence does not blind him to the inhumanity of the great Nature-Powers. 'Gods *ought* to be wiser than men', says the old serving-man in the *Hippolytus* to the cosmic principle Kypris.[1] 'Gods *ought* not to be like men in their anger', says the broken old man Cadmus to the cosmic principle Dionysus.[2] But the human 'ought' has no meaning for cosmic principles. There is indeed an immanent 'Justice' in the universe—Euripides throughout his life asserted that—but it is no paternal government by the father of gods and men.[3] It is the justice of Kypris, the justice of Dionysus, an unpitying, unreasoning justice that pauses for no nice assessment of deserts, but sweeps away the innocent with the guilty, Phaedra with Hippolytus, Cadmus with Pentheus. This is the religion of Euripides—pessimistic and irrationalist, as his ethics and cosmology are pessimistic and irrationalist.

What are we to think of such a *Weltanschauung*? What is its historical significance? That it is diametrically opposed to the Socratic thesis is plain enough. Socrates affirmed the supremacy of reason in the governance of the universe and in the life of man; in both these spheres Euripides denied it:

πολὺς ταραγμὸς ἔν τε τοῖς θείοις ἔνι
κἀν τοῖς βροτείοις.[4]

The question how far Euripides developed his own view in *conscious* opposition to that of his friend is a difficult one to answer (nor is it a question of the first importance). I should say myself that some of the passages about the relation between knowledge and conduct do at any rate look like a conscious reaction against the opinion of Socrates, or of other persons who thought like Socrates; but that the rest of the Euripidean outlook on things probably shaped itself independently, and its positive inspiration, in so far as it is not original, derives from the work of the last physicists (like Diogenes of Apollonia) and the first sophists (like Protagoras). Some of the characteristic features of this outlook appear already in the *Alcestis*, produced in 438; and it is very

---

[1] *Hipp.* 120.   [2] *Bacch.* 1348.
[3] Cf. especially the remarkable fragment 506 (which should perhaps be brought into connection with *Hec.* 799–801).
[4] *I.T.* 572.

doubtful if Socrates had emerged as an independent thinker at so early a date.

Probably, if the works of Protagoras and others of that kidney were extant, we should find the philosophical opinions of Euripides less surprising. As it is, Euripides remains for us the chief representative of fifth-century irrationalism; and herein, quite apart from his greatness as a dramatist, lies his importance for the history of Greek thought. The disease of which Greek culture eventually died is known by many names. To some it appears as a virulent form of scepticism; to others, as a virulent form of mysticism. Professor Murray has called it the Failure of Nerve. My own name for it is systematic irrationalism. Its emergence has been variously accounted for: some put it down to the influx of oriental ideas following Alexander's eastern conquests; others, to the decay of the city state; others, to malaria or the will of God. To my mind, the case of Euripides proves that an acute attack of it was already threatening the Greek world in the fifth century, when the city state was still flourishing and intercourse with the East was still relatively restricted. He shows all he characteristic symptoms: the peculiar blend of a destructive scepticism with a no less destructive mysticism; the assertion that emotion, not reason, determines human conduct; despair of the state, resulting in quietism; despair of rational theology resulting in a craving for a religion of the orgiastic type. For the time being the attack was averted—in part by the development of the Socratic–Platonic philosophy; in part, no doubt, by other agencies which escape us, since they did not express themselves in a literary form. But the germ survived, became endemic, and spread over the whole Greco-Roman world as soon as social conditions were favourable to its development. Greek rationalism died slowly (even Plotinus is in many respects a rationalist); but it was already more than half dead when Christianity and the other Oriental religions administered the *coup de grâce*. Considerable elements of it were taken over into Christianity; but the next emergence of a complete or nearly complete rationalism is in the work of Descartes and Spinoza. Since then it has in many guises dominated our thought. But I need hardly remind you that at the present time its supremacy is threatened from a great variety of quarters: by pragmatists and behaviourists, by theosophists and by spiritualists, by followers of Freud and Jung.

Euripides the Irrationalist

That is perhaps one reason why Euripides, who seemed so poor a creature to Schlegel and to Jowett, whom Swinburne could describe as a scenic sophist and a mutilated monkey, is for our generation one of the most sympathetic figures in the whole of ancient literature.

VI

The Sophistic Movement and the Failure of Greek Liberalism[1]

WHAT we call the verdict of history is never the final verdict. It is best represented not by a full stop but by a zigzag line, a graph of the successive impressions made by a stationary object on a series of moving observers. Each generation empanels a new jury to retry the old cases, sometimes in the light of fresh material evidence, more often on the ground that the last jury was misdirected. This is the normal process of historical judgement, a judgement which is for ever in the making because the present is for ever in the making and we cannot see the past except by the light of the present. But occasionally the normal process is held up for a time: a man of genius utters his personal verdict, and because he is a man of genius posterity accepts it as final. So it was that Plato fixed for long centuries of posterity their judgement on the Greek Sophists.

It was the great work of nineteenth-century scholarship to revise the verdicts passed by Antiquity upon itself; and since then the case of the Sophists, among others, has come up repeatedly for retrial. It was an English businessman, George Grote, who first seriously attempted to upset the verdict of Plato. But his special pleading did little to rehabilitate his clients. It happened to be peculiarly difficult for late-Victorian scholars, in England at any rate, to pass unbiased judgement on the Sophists. For they had met, or thought they had met, men very like the Sophists, and they did not find these men congenial. The Sophists wished to popularize knowledge: were they not the ancient equivalent

[1] This slight sketch of some aspects of a complex subject was delivered as a lecture to the Classical Association in 1937, and reflects the political and moral anxieties of the late thirties. To the professional scholar it will be chiefly of historical interest, especially since the publication of the splendid third volume of Guthrie's *History of Greek Philosophy*. But in the belief that it may still have something to say to a new generation of non-specialist students I print it here substantially as it stood in 1937, save for the omission of a couple of paragraphs used elsewhere and the addition of one or two footnotes in square brackets.

of journalists or, at best, extension lecturers? The Sophists professed to educate the young for citizenship: their counterparts were seeking to introduce pseudo-sciences like politics and sociology into the curricula of our universities. The Sophists made utility or even pleasure their standard, and based on it radical proposals for social change: surely they were no better than Benthamites? Finally, the Sophists were altogether blind to the value of tradition, religious, moral, social, political: could anything be more un-English (and *a fortiori* un-Greek)? With reflections like these in the background of their thoughts the verdict of the scholars could not be in doubt. Plato's battle was their battle: in condemning the Sophists they took the field, consciously or not, against forces that threatened the established order in their own day, and with Plato for an ally they were assured of easier victory in the historical conflict than in the contemporary one.

Are we better placed today for assessing the significance of those ancient controversies? In some respects I think we are. Thanks to Diels, the evidence is far easier to marshal and coordinate; and papyri have added something to our meagre collection of first-hand fragments. But even more important is the change in our own position as observers. Since the War of 1914 there has been a fresh twist of the Great Wheel, creating along with new contemporary problems a new backward perspective, though it may take us scholars some time to adjust our eyes to it. A generation which has come to manhood in a completely unstable world; which has witnessed in their nakedness class war and war between nations, and has grown accustomed to drastic theories and radical solutions; which has cut itself loose from traditional metaphysic, so that 'idealist' has become a common term of abuse; which cares passionately about man's relation to his society but hardly at all about his relation to the gods—a generation, in fact, to which the word 'justice' means a great deal, the word 'piety' very little—such a generation will look back on the fifth century, if not with clearer eyes than its grandparents, at least with very different eyes.

Having this new sort of jury in mind, I propose to speak mainly about the social and political theories of the Sophists and about their relationship to political action. But first I want to touch briefly on some other aspects of the movement.

In one of the most brilliantly perverse chapters of his *Thales to Plato* the late Professor Burnet maintained that 'the "age of the Sophists" is, above all, an age of reaction against science'. This generalization seems to me to have less truth in it than most. What characterizes the later fifth century is rather a reaction against dogmatism, combined with an attempt to apply the methods of science to a new object, man. The concept of *phusis* ('nature') with which the Ionian thinkers had operated was still the central concept, but it was extended to include human nature. The speculations of Protagoras and Hippias and Prodicus about the origin of society, the origin of religious belief, the validity of *nomos* (law or custom), and the rights of the individual no more constituted a reaction against science than the social and political studies of Bentham and Mill. The old and the new inquiries went on side by side, and the same man often pursued both: the fifth century drew, and could draw, no sharp line of distinction between *sophistai* and *phusikoi* (natural scientists), except in so far as the former word applied to professional teachers, the latter primarily to researchers. Hippias, for example, wrote and lectured not only on ethics, history, geography, and literature,[1] but also on astronomy and geometry;[2] Gorgias studied under Empedocles and shared his views on sensation;[3] Prodicus wrote on physiology;[4] Antiphon discussed a variety of scientific and mathematical questions.[5] On the other side we find the *phusikoi* concerning themselves increasingly with humane studies. Empedocles, Anaxagoras, Democritus, all had theories about the origins of culture. Democritus wrote with deep earnestness about the value of democracy, the moral basis of legal sanctions, the folly of civil war 'which involves victors and vanquished in a common ruin'.[6] So too Archelaus, Anaxagoras' pupil and Socrates' teacher, was accounted both a scientist and a moral philosopher (*ēthikos*); he had views both on the nature of matter and on the nature of moral obligation.[7]

In actual practice, then, there was no conflict between the old learning and the new. But the dogmatic character of the earlier physical speculations began to be recognized. Gorgias quoted the

[1] Diels–Kranz, *Die Fragmente der Vorsokratiker*[7] (cited henceforth as DK) 86 A 11, 12; B 6, 9.
[2] DK 86 A 11; B 12, 13, 21.   [3] DK 82 A 2, 3; B 4, 5.
[4] DK 84 B 4.   [5] DK 87 B 13, 26, etc.
[6] DK 68 B 249; cf. B 248, 251, etc.   [7] DK 60 A 1, 6.

arguments of the old cosmologists as an example not of science but of propaganda (the art of persuasion, *peithō*) : 'They robbed us of one fancy', he says, 'to inculcate another; they took things beyond belief and outside experience and made them manifest to the eye of faith.'[1] That is reaction, not against science, but against bad science. Gorgias himself did not profess to teach anything more than the art of propaganda. He would, I think, have been surprised and amused to hear himself described as a 'philosophical nihilist' on the strength of his famous 'proof' that everything is incommunicable, unknowable, and non-existent.[2] Surely what he was really trying to prove on that occasion was that an expert propagandist can make a case for any paradox, however fantastic, can in fact 'make it manifest to the eye of faith'. That is how Isocrates, our oldest witness, understood the argument.[3] It is a philosophical joke with the Eleatics as its especial victims— the same sort of thing as a modern writer's elaborate 'proof' that Napoleon never lived.

What of the still more famous proposition advanced by Protagoras, the statement that 'Man is the measure of all things'? There is no doubt that this was seriously meant, and it has often been interpreted in a sense which would cut away the ground from all scientific thinking by making reality simply a function of the observer, the work of the individual mind. Protagoras would thus be the inventor of Subjective Idealism, a doctrine of which Antiquity is otherwise innocent. But that is not how the proposition is understood by our two best authorities, Plato's *Theaetetus* and the account in Sextus Empiricus (which is independent of Plato and claims to be based on Protagoras' own statements). Far from taking Protagoras as a subjective idealist, Plato and Sextus agree in making him an extreme realist. They understand him as meaning, not that reality is merely my private world, but on the contrary that each man's private world corresponds to something in reality (that is why Protagoras denied that reality is one).[4] As Sextus puts it, 'Protagoras says that the causes of all perceptions are immanent in matter ... but men apprehend different characters of matter at different times, according to the varying states of the percipient. People in normal and in abnormal states, people of different ages, people awake

---

[1] *Helenes Encomium* 13 (DK 82 B 11). [2] DK 82 B 3.
[3] Isocrates, *Helena* 1–4. [4] DK 80 B 2.

and asleep, and so forth, each of them apprehend those characters of matter which are accessible to persons in their particular state.'[1] This must mean that just as sugar tastes sweet to the normal palate in virtue of some quality inherent in sugar, so if it tastes bitter to an abnormal palate there must be a quality in sugar, normally imperceptible but nevertheless present, to account for *that*. Every judgement thus corresponds to some truth. In its respect for individual experience that is typically fifth-century doctrine.

The opinion that all judgements are true might seem to be as inconvenient for science as the opinion that all are false. But it seems likely that Protagoras would have saved the possibility of science, just as Plato makes him do,[2] by pointing out that not all judgements are equally *useful*. The man to whom sugar tastes bitter is an eccentric person apprehending an eccentric aspect of reality; it is the doctor's business to bring him back to normal perception of normal reality. Similarly it is the business of the statesman to induce society to adopt, not truer views of right and wrong, but better or more useful ones, *chrēsta* as opposed to *ponēra*. For Protagoras, as for William James, the practical test of any theory was that it should work; but he differed from James in holding that what works is only a selection from the many-sided truth.[3]

On the whole, then, we should hesitate to call the Sophists anti-scientific even in theory, and certainly they were not as a class anti-scientific in practice. While Burnet thus overstated their conflict with science he was inclined to understate their conflict with religion. Protagoras' essay *On the Gods*, which he is reported to have read aloud at the house of Euripides, began with the words: 'About the gods I have no means of knowing either that they exist or that they do not exist or what they are like to look at; many things prevent my knowing—among others, the fact that they are never seen and the shortness of human life.'[4] Burnet remarked that from the Greek point of view there was nothing impious in this statement, since Greek religion 'consisted

---

[1] DK 80 A 14 (abbreviated).   [2] *Theaet.* 166 d ff.
[3] Cf. H. Gomperz, *Sophistik und Rhetorik* (1912), 200 ff.; F. M. Cornford, *Plato's Theory of Knowledge* (1935), 32 ff. [Controversy about Protagoras' meaning continues: for the sort of view here adopted see now von Fritz in Pauly–Wissowa s.v. 'Protagoras', 916f.; for the 'subjectivist' view, Guthrie, *A History of Greek Philosophy*, iii. 181 ff., 267 f.]   [4] DK 80 B 4.

entirely in worship and not in theological affirmations or negations'.[1] I find it difficult to agree. As Diogenes of Oenoanda put it,[2] to say that you have no means of knowing whether gods exist amounts in practice to saying that you know they do not exist; and 'worship' is hardly in the long run compatible with negation of what is worshipped. For Protagoras the belief in gods had *no* direct basis in sense experience, and thus lacked even the sort of limited validity which he would allow to the proposition 'Sugar is bitter'. Some people professed to detect in human history the workings of divine justice; but Protagoras, as I understand him, thought life too short for us to weigh the enormous mass of evidence involved. So, as Plato says,[3] he 'eliminated' the gods from discussion—an agnosticism which the ordinary man would not easily distinguish from atheism.

Others expressed themselves with less reserve. Plato's kinsman Critias—sophist, tragic dramatist, and unscrupulous political adventurer—set forth in a famous dramatic fragment the view that religion is an artificial moral sanction, deliberately invented to bolster up the laws.[4] And for the widespread breakdown of this sanction during the Peloponnesian War there is abundant and familiar evidence in Thucydides and Euripides. The belief in divine justice was subjected to Protagoras' pragmatic test—does it work?—and for all except the wilfully blind the answer was clearly 'No'. The gods were dead or asleep: how should the vacuum be filled? We must turn for an answer to sophistic social theory.

The problem, so familiar to us, of reconciling the claims of the individual with the interests of the community was for the first time consciously recognized as a problem in the fifth century B.C. But it presented itself to the Greeks in a peculiar way, as one aspect of a still wider issue, the issue between *nomos* and *phusis*, law and nature. We can see how that came about. When a Greek of the archaic period spoke of 'law', and even when he spoke of 'the laws' in the plural, he usually meant not the contents of a statute-book but the entire body of traditional usage which governed the whole of his civic conduct, political, social, and religious. He thought of it, not as something which was liable to be altered next year, but as an accepted inheritance which

---

[1] *Thales to Plato*, 117. [2] DK 80 A 23. [3] *Theaet.* 162 d–e.
[4] DK 88 B 25 (= frag. 1 Nauck).

formed the permanent background of his life. The laws represented the collective wisdom of the past; perhaps they had been codified by some great man, a Lycurgus or a Solon, but they were felt to rest ultimately on an authority higher than that of any individual statesman. Heraclitus made the feeling explicit when he declared that 'all human laws are sustained by one law, which is divine'.[1]

In the course of the fifth century two things happened which between them upset the unquestioned authority of *nomos*. One was the growing complexity of the social and economic structure, which compelled the introduction of a multitude of new laws. These had no sanction of antiquity, and at Athens at least they were continually being changed—a situation personified by Aristophanes in the figure of the 'Decree-merchant' who is so roughly handled in the *Birds*.[2] 'How', asks Hippias in the *Memorabilia*, 'can one take seriously laws which are constantly being repealed by the very same people who passed them?'[3] As early as 441 B.C. Sophocles could already contrast such ephemeral man-made laws, to their disadvantage, with the timeless prescriptions of tradition, 'the statutes of Heaven, unwritten and unshakeable'.[4]

That was one determining factor. The other was the widening of the Greek horizon which made possible the beginnings of a comparative anthropology. The inquisitive Greek traveller in foreign lands could not fail to observe that different peoples have different and mutually inconsistent laws and customs: the classic example is the symposium in Herodotus on the right way to dispose of a deceased parent, cannibalism versus cremation.[5] Herodotus' conclusion is that we ought not to laugh at any people for thinking their own laws the best—which is a confession of the relativity of *nomos*. In Greece as in nineteenth-century England anthropology acted as an acid solvent upon traditional beliefs. We can see why Plato, like the Nazis and the Russians, wished to restrict opportunities of foreign travel. (He would forbid it to persons under forty: an experience so unsettling is only safe when middle age has fortified the mind against the infiltration of new ideas; and even then he would put the returned traveller into a sort of intellectual quarantine until he has been pronounced free from germs of dangerous thought.)[6]

[1] DK 22 B 114.   [2] *Birds* 1035 ff.   [3] Xenophon, *Mem.* 4. 4. 14.
[4] *Antigone* 454 f.   [5] Hdt. 3. 38.6   [6] *Laws* 950 d, 952 b–d.

Against the old conception of law, thus stripped of its prestige, it was inevitable that men should set up the new conception of human nature, that they should contrast *nomos* as the variable with *phusis* as the constant. The antithesis was perhaps first made explicit in the special field of medicine: are health and sickness determined mainly by a man's *phusis*, his 'constitution' as we say, or mainly by his *nomos*, i.e. his customary regime of diet, exercise, and so forth? But very soon the problem assumed an ampler scope. When law and human nature conflict, which ought we to follow? Is the social restraint which law imposes on nature a good or a bad thing? For the Sophists that was the grand question.

They did not all answer it in the same way. Protagoras' view of the matter, as represented by Plato, is much like that of Herodotus (who may well have been influenced by him). There are better and worse laws, but the laws of any state are valid for that state for so long as the people believe in them. It is the business of a wise man to get the laws improved by peaceful propaganda.[1] But laws there must be: without *dikē* and *aidōs*, respect for the legal and moral rights of others, there can be no civilization; life in the state of nature is poor, nasty, brutish, and short.[2] Protagoras himself drafted a legal code for the new colony at Thurii, and since he did so as the trusted friend of Pericles we can infer that he was considered a sound democrat. He belonged to the optimistic generation which grew up immediately after the Persian Wars, the generation which gave currency to the idea of progress.

But the belief in progress had an even shorter run in Athens than it has had with us. We may observe its decline if we look at a little essay written by a man who may have been Protagoras' pupil, the unidentified Sophist known as Anonymus Iamblichi. He too is a firm supporter of *nomos*, and he anticipates Plato in holding that the reign of law and justice is rooted in *phusis* itself.[3] But he writes without optimism, as one who has watched the crumbling of the social and moral order. The lust for power, he says, should not be called manliness (*aretē*), nor obedience to the law be thought cowardice.[4] Such lawlessness brings with it an

---

[1] *Theaet.* 167 c. [2] *Prot.* 322 a–323 a. [See above, p. 10.]
[3] DK 89. 6, p. 402. 28 ff.; cf. Plato, *Laws* 890 d.
[4] DK 89. 6, p. 402. 21 f.

ever-present insecurity and anxiety for the individual; for the state it brings stagnation of trade, class warfare, and increased danger of foreign war. Above all, it is the root from which dictatorship (*turannis*) grows. If the people lose their freedom, he concludes, it is their own fault; dictatorship would be impossible if only the common man seriously cared for justice and constitutional government.¹ These reflections, which have to us a distressingly familiar ring, seem to be those of a serious-minded conservative democrat writing in the later years of the Peloponnesian War.

Parallel with this is a more radical trend of thought which apparently goes back to the sophist Hippias. For the school of Protagoras the law was the true king of a democratic society;² for Hippias the law is a tyrant.³ According to Xenophon⁴ he recognized as binding only those laws whose universality showed them to be of divine origin. Respect for parents, he thought, was such a law; the prohibition of incest was not, for some nations do not prohibit it. The notorious line quoted from the *Aeolus* of Euripides,⁵ 'There is nothing shocking but thinking makes it so', seems to belong to a similar argument: it formed part of a speech in defence of incest. And we may compare the view attributed to Archelaus, the earliest native Athenian philosopher, that the distinction between right and wrong had no basis at all in *phusis* but was purely a matter of custom.⁶

The political applications of this line of thought are interesting. Hippias is represented as drawing from it the consequence that nationalism, an artificial bond created by custom, should have less force than the international bond between intellectuals, who are natural fellow citizens in the kingdom of the intelligence.⁷ To the Sophists, wandering scholars whose profession denied them any fixed home, this must have been an attractive thought. They were the first internationalists. Gorgias in his great speech at Olympia preached pan-Hellenic unity against the barbarians; and in his funeral oration over Athenians killed in the war with Sparta he had the courage to say that victories gained over fellow Greeks were a matter for lamentation, not for hymns of

---

¹ DK 89. 7, p. 403. 32 ff.
² Hdt. 3. 38; Anon. Iamb. DK 89. 6, p. 402. 28.   ³ Plato, *Prot.* 337 d.
⁴ *Mem.* 4. 4. 14.   ⁵ Frag. 19 Nauck.
⁶ DK 60 A 1.   ⁷ Plato, *Prot.* 337 c–d.

the Failure of Greek Liberalism

thanksgiving.[1] Antiphon, in one of the papyrus fragments, goes beyond this and rejects as superficial even the distinction between Greeks and barbarians: 'By nature', he says, 'we all start with a like equipment, whether we are barbarians or Greeks; our natural wants are the same...We breathe a common air.' In the same passage[2] he condemns class distinctions: 'We feel', he observes, 'respect and awe for the nobly born, and for them only: in this matter we behave like barbarians to our own people.'

It is difficult to suppose, as some still do, that the author of these words is the man who planned the oligarchic revolution of 411.[3] If we are to judge him by the new fragments, he writes from the standpoint of a passionate individualism: 'The requirements of the laws', he says, 'are most of them at war with nature: they have made rules for our eyes, to tell them what to see; for our ears, to tell them what to hear; for our tongues, what to say; for our hands, what to do; for our feet, where to go; for our minds, what they shall desire.'[4] The same intense consciousness of the rights of the individual against society finds expression in many passages of Euripides, and with it the same feeling for the oppressed classes—for the peasant against the nobly born, for the bastard against the legitimate son, for women against men, and even for slaves against masters. Of all ancient institutions slavery seems to us the most manifestly contrary to 'nature'; but none of the major Greek thinkers dared to recognize the fact. Euripides hints at it more than once,[5] but the first explicit condemnation of slavery which has come down to us was uttered by a Sophist, Gorgias' pupil Alcidamas. 'God', said Alcidamas, 'has left all men free; Nature has made none a slave.'[6]

So far the movement of thought which we have been considering has appeared to us as a liberal movement. It shows the same typical traits as the liberal thought of the eighteenth and nineteenth centuries: the same individualism, the same humanitarianism, the same secularism, the same confident arraignment

---

[1] DK 82 A 1.
[2] DK 87 B 44 (= *P. Oxy.* 1364), frag. B. Aristotle (frag. 91 Rose) attributed a similar view to Lycophron.
[3] [Cf. E. Bignone, *Studi sul pensiero antico* (1938), 161–74; Guthrie, *Hist. of Greek Philosophy*, iii. 292 f.; and for a different argument against identifying the two, *C.R.* 68 (1954) 94 f.]
[4] DK 87 B 44, frag. A, pp. 347 f.   [5] [Cf. Guthrie, op. cit. iii. 157–9.]
[6] Schol. Aristotle, *Rhet.* 1373^b. His view is echoed by a character in Philemon, frag. 95 Kock.

of tradition at the bar of reason, the same robust faith in applied intelligence as the key to perpetual progress. It should have heralded a great age of intellectual, social, and political emancipation. But we know that it did not. What it in fact heralded was first an age of civil war and war between cities, waged with a conscious satisfaction in brutality that until recently had seldom been surpassed among peoples of high culture, and after that an age of dictatorships (the so-called 'second *turannis*') for which Dionysius of Syracuse set the model. That is broadly what happened in the world of action. In the world of thought, what emerged was first the 'superman' theory, the political immoralism so brilliantly presented by Callicles in Plato's *Gorgias*, and then Plato himself, whose philosophy has been rightly described by Mr. Crossman as 'the most savage and the most profound attack upon liberal ideas which history can show'. Within a century from the dawn of the sophistic movement Plato had reached the final phase of his thought: he was declaring that the true king should be above the laws, that heresy should be an offence punishable by death, and that not man but God was the measure of all things. With the first of these statements he announced the Hellenistic monarchies; with the second and third he announced the Middle Ages.

History does not repeat itself—fortunately, since life would be unendurable if it did. Nevertheless we can sometimes detect in its fabric recurring constellations of thought and action, particular sequences that recall earlier sequences, though they are never repeated identically. And for us, who have seen in our own time the sudden arrest and reversal of another liberal movement, it is of peculiar interest to try to understand the failure of the liberal movement in Greece and, in particular, to ask how far its promoters were responsible for its failure. This is too large a question to be canvassed adequately here, nor could it be answered fully and finally without a more intimate knowledge than we possess of the complex currents of thought in the last years of the fifth century. But certain things can be said.

In the first place, the great war which cut across the whole pan-Hellenic cultural movement initiated by the Sophists was in no sense itself a product of that movement. But it operated fatally not only to check but to distort it. I need not dwell on what happens to liberal movements of thought under war conditions: whether we have read our Thucydides or not, we have all of us watched a comparable pattern of distortion reproduce itself in the Europe of today. We should remember, however, that in the ancient situation war came into the pattern at a much earlier stage of its development than it did with us. Democracy's first line of defence, universal state education, had not yet been thought of, much less constructed. The first man to suggest it, so far as our information goes, was Phaleas of Chalcedon, who probably wrote in the fourth century, not the fifth.[1] Plato was to propose in the *Laws* that there should be compulsory universal education for both sexes at the public expense up to the age of sixteen.[2] But these voices went unheeded: for a state-supported system of education Athens had to wait until the time of Marcus Aurelius.[3] When the Peloponnesian War broke out the appetite for higher education was there[4] and the Sophists were there to supply it, but it was still a costly luxury available only to the rich; the masses were untouched by it.

This had its inevitable reaction on the character of the teaching. True, the Sophists were not required to teach a particular official doctrine, as many European professors are today; but neither were they free, like English professors, to inflict what they pleased on their pupils. They depended for a livelihood on their fees, as we do not; we can bore our pupils with impunity, they could not. Hence demand exercised a dangerous control over supply. What such men as Protagoras would have liked to teach, if I understand them rightly, was simply the art of citizenship; what the discontented young aristocrats of Athens required them to teach was something more specific—the art of acquiring personal power in a democratic society. If the seed of the new learning produced a strange crop, we must remember that Alcibiades was a pupil of Socrates, and blame the soil before we blame the seed.

Nevertheless there was, I think, a fault in the seed. A liberalism which is merely individualist, which does not take the community as its moral unit, is always in danger of giving birth to its opposite, an individualism which is the reverse of liberal. The idea of

---

[1] Aristotle, *Politics* 1266ᵇ31.   [2] *Laws* 804 d.
[3] Dio Cassius 72. 31: Marcus Aurelius 'provided teachers at Athens in every branch of education, paying them annual salaries'.
[4] Cf. Aristotle, *Politics* 1341ᵃ28 ff.

nature was a critical weapon with two edges. Nature assures us that distinctions of birth and blood rest on arbitrary convention—man was created free. And liberalism welcomes the assurance. But suppose nature whispers that democratic justice and obedience to the will of the people are also an arbitrary convention, that man was created free to be himself and push the weak to the wall? So long as it treats the individual as an ultimate moral unit liberalism has no effective answer to Callicles. And Callicles is in a sense its child. Certainly he was no Sophist: he represents himself as a practical man who despises Sophists.[1] And certainly Plato was right in making Gorgias shrink from Calliclean conclusions: the older Sophists were as anxious as Jeremy Bentham to fit their individualism into the framework of traditional ethical teaching. Yet it was they or their pupils who furnished Callicles with his intellectual weapons. *Phusis* became the slogan of the robber-individual and the robber-society, as 'the survival of the fittest' was in the later nineteenth century and as 'realism' is today.

It was from the *phusis*-men that Menon in the *Anabasis* learned to say that moral scruples were a sign of defective education.[2] From them were descended those fourth-century cliques of young intellectuals described in the *Laws*, who interpreted 'the natural life' to mean a life devoted to dominating other people.[3] It is the language of the *phusis*-men which we hear in the Melian dialogue: 'We think', says the Athenian spokesman, 'that mankind certainly, and the gods too so far as we know, always keep what they can conquer in obedience to a law of nature.'[4] This does not mean that but for the Sophists Melos would have been spared: in time of war brutality does not always wait on philosophical reasons. But conscious immoralism is a different thing from mere brutality, and much more formidable, because the immoralist believes himself to be doing what is 'natural' or 'realistic' and therefore right.

I can remember the legend current among simple folk in England during the war of 1914 that at the bottom of the whole mischief there were two mysterious figures of evil, two sinister and influential demons, called Nitch and Tritch. When the war ended

---

[1] Plato, *Gorg.* 520 a. [Cf. my edition of the dialogue, pp. 13–15.]
[2] Xenophon, *Anab.* 2. 6. 22.   [3] Plato, *Laws* 890 a.
[4] Thucydides 5. 105.

it was a disappointment to the British public to learn that Nitch and Tritch could not after all be hanged, as they had been dead a good many years. It seemed absurd at the time; but looking back today, when in many countries people of many political complexions profess and practise a more or less conscious immoralism under the name of realism, one feels that the popular judgement on Nitch and Tritch was perhaps not wholly mistaken. Nor in Antiquity was the popular condemnation of the Sophists wholly mistaken. Indeed, Nietzsche himself recognized the affiliation of his immoralism to the sophistic movement. 'The Sophists', he says in *The Will to Power*, 'are simply realists: they have the courage, which all strong spirits have, to recognize their own un-morality.'[1] He was thinking, no doubt, rather of Plato's Callicles than of the true Sophists. But his own doctrine, which is practically a restatement of Callicles' position, is in fact based, like it, on the radical Sophists' antithesis between the free individual and the herd-morality prescribed by *nomos*. In effect, if not in intention, the *phusis*-men harnessed the reason to the service of individual and national egotism. The intellectual who does that is a *faux clerc*, and he bears a heavy responsibility.

Nevertheless—and this is my last reflection—the abortive liberal movement left behind it certain seeds of genuinely liberal ideas which were to fructify in later Greek thought. Among those who claimed to live as Hippias advised, 'according to nature', were not only the immoralists but also the Stoics. And it seems likely that both the Stoic humanitarianism, the consciousness that we are all children of one mother, and also the Stoic ideal of the self-sufficient *sapiens*,[2] whose head is bloody but unbowed because he owes his allegiance to no earthly ruler but to the divine spark within his own breast—that both of these derive ultimately from the *phusis* doctrine of the Sophists. If so, the work of the Sophists was not entirely destructive. Stoic humanitarianism was destined to affect the world profoundly, through its influence on Roman law; and the ideal of self-sufficiency, inadequate though it is to the full human possibility, has throughout the centuries been a strong place of refuge for the spirit of freedom in bad times. It was in these things that the sophistic movement had its truest fulfilment.

[1] Para. 429. [See further the appendix to my edition of the *Gorgias*.]
[2] Cf. DK 86 A 1 and 12.

VII

Plato and the Irrational[1]

THE purpose of this paper is to inquire into Plato's attitude towards a group of related problems which at the present time have assumed an unusual importance. By 'the irrational' I mean that surd element in human experience, both in our experience of ourselves and in our experience of the world about us, which has exercised so powerful—and as some of us think, so perilous—a fascination on the philosophers, artists, and men of letters of our own day.[2]

That contemporary problems and interests should determine the questions which we address to the great thinkers of the past is entirely natural and proper. But he who uses this approach needs to be alive to its dangers. Such contemporary interests have very frequently determined not only the questions which scholars have asked, but also the answers which they have put into the mouths of the defenceless dead. Too often we unconsciously identify a past thinker with ourselves, and distort his thoughts to make him the mouthpiece of our own preconceptions; or else, unconsciously identifying him with our opponents, we belabour him with gusto, serene in the assured knowledge that

[1] A paper read to the Classical Association at its General Meeting, 9 April 1946, and published in the *Journal of Hellenic Studies*, 1947. The summary nature of the judgements which I have ventured to express on several disputed questions of Platonic scholarship is, I hope, sufficiently explained by the paper's purpose: if anything like a comprehensive picture was to be presented, drastic simplifications were unavoidable. Certain topics, such as the theory of Ἔρως, had to be omitted even so. I am indebted to Dr. Walzer for some useful comments and references. [Parts of this paper were incorporated in chapter vii of my *Greeks and the Irrational*; but since it deals with a wider range of problems than that chapter, and approaches them from a somewhat different angle, I reprint it here virtually without alteration.]

[2] Future historians will, I believe, recognize in this preoccupation with the surd element the governing impulse of our time, the δαίμων or Zeitgeist which in different guises has haunted minds as various as Nietzsche, Bergson, Heidegger in philosophy; Jung in psychology; Sorel, Pareto, Spengler in political theory; Yeats, Lawrence, Joyce, Kafka, Sartre in literature; Picasso and the surrealists in painting.

he cannot hit back. I think such distortion of the past in the interest of the present to be a kind of *trahison des clercs*—though it is a treachery which we can never be quite certain of avoiding, since we commit it for the most part without our own knowledge. Plato has at all periods been one of its principal victims: he was bound to be, his personality being so complex, his thought so richly various and yet, as we know it in his dialogues, so incomplete—so full of hesitations, restatements, fresh starts, of ideas that go underground for a time to reappear later in a new guise, of lines of argument that seem to converge, yet never quite meet to form a tidy system. Arm yourself with a stout pair of blinkers and a sufficient but not excessive amount of scholarship, and by making a suitable selection of texts you can prove Plato to be almost anything that you want him to be. By the skilful use of this method Plato has been revealed at various times as a complete sceptic and as a complete mystic, as a pupil of Hegel and as a pupil of Aquinas, as a Cambridge Platonist and as one of Nature's Balliol men, as an early Christian and as a very early Nazi. Each of these partisan Platos has his title-deeds, he can produce for you a nice little anthology of texts to prove his claim: for all these artificial *homunculi* have been constructed out of fragments of Plato himself. Let me therefore make it plain that my object in the present paper is neither to construct a fresh *homunculus* nor to resuscitate an old one, but rather, if possible, to get a clearer view of certain attitudes of the historical Plato—a person who lived at Athens in the fourth century B.C. and could not have lived at any other time or place, a person who was unaware of being an early anything, and who (being a man and not a *homunculus*) permitted himself on occasion to change his mind.

Let me begin by formulating my questions. The word 'rationalist' is used with several distinct meanings. In the theory of knowledge a rationalist is opposed to an empiricist: he is one who believes that reason and not the senses provides the ἀρχαί, the first principles on which scientific knowledge is built. That Plato was a rationalist in this sense is evident;[1] and I have no question to raise. Secondly, rationalism may be understood as the belief that both the life of man and the life of the universe are governed by, or are manifestations of, a rational plan. That Plato was on the

---

[1] *Phaedo* 65 b, 79 c–d, *Rep.* 509 d ff., etc.

whole a rationalist in this sense also no one is likely to dispute. But I shall raise the question how far Plato qualified his rationalism by recognizing the influence of irrational factors upon the behaviour both of men and of the world, and how he interpreted these factors. Thirdly, rationalism may signify, in the words of the Shorter Oxford Dictionary, 'the principle of regarding reason as the chief or only guide in matters of religion'. Here I shall ask whether Plato was in this sense a rationalist, and if he was not, how his religion is related to his philosophy.

First, then, did Plato realize the importance of irrational factors in determining human conduct? To this question most people, I think, would answer 'No'. When we speak of Platonic ethics, what comes first to our mind is the somewhat bleak pronouncement that 'virtue is knowledge', and that other naïve-sounding assertion that οὐδεὶς ἑκὼν ἁμαρτάνει, 'nobody does wrong if he can help it'. When we speak of Platonic politics, we think first of the Guardians in the *Republic*—those pitiable victims of a totalitarian system, warped by a narrowly scientific education which has no room for the humanities, deprived of most of the normal incentives to industry, cut off from most of the normal sources of human happiness, and yet expected to exercise with unerring wisdom unlimited power over the lives of their fellow citizens. We marvel that so great a philosopher should have had so little understanding of human nature.

In judging thus, I think we get the perspective wrong, and for that reason do Plato less than justice. In the first place, the intellectualist approach to ethics is not something perversely invented by Plato or even by Socrates:[1] it is part of the general inheritance which came down to Plato from the fifth century, and which he spent his life in criticizing and reshaping. Not Socrates only, but all the great sophists,[2] conceived moral goodness as a technique, a τέχνη of rational living, which, like other techniques, could be acquired by study, provided one applied

[1] In the popular sense of the term, at least, Socrates was far from being an unqualified 'rationalist': his attitude to his δαιμόνιον is sufficient proof of his respect for that intuitive wisdom whose sources escape the probe of the intelligence; and his intellectualism did not prevent him from being, in Festugière's words, 'un maître de vie intérieure' (*Contemplation et vie contemplative chez Platon* (1936), 73). Cf. also Jaeger, *Paideia*, ii. 65 ff.

[2] And, it would seem, Democritus. Cf. frag. 242 Diels-Kranz, πλέονες ἐξ ἀσκήσιος ἀγαθοὶ γίνονται ἢ ἀπὸ φύσιος: frag. 83, ἁμαρτίης αἰτίη ἡ ἀμαθίη τοῦ κρέσσονος.

sufficient intelligence to the problem. In this they were the counterparts of our Victorians. Like the Victorians, they had a vision of progress—of the perpetual onward march of civilization—and for the same cause: they had themselves in their formative years experienced progress, swift and indisputable, holding, as it seemed, the promise that human life could be lifted by the exercise of reason to always higher levels of material and intellectual achievement. Plato's starting-point was thus historically conditioned. It can be studied in Xenophon's *Memorabilia*, but much better, as I think, in his own *Protagoras*, which in my view still breathes the atmosphere of the fifth century, with its optimism, its genial worldliness, its simple-minded utilitarianism, and its Socrates who is still no more than life-size. To read it otherwise, in order to make Plato a 'consistent Platonist', seems to me a wilful falsification.[1]

To see what Plato did with this inherited rationalism, we naturally look first to dialogues like the *Phaedo* and the *Republic*, where we find a very different conception of the nature of that knowledge or wisdom (φρόνησις) which constitutes true virtue: it lies not in an enlightened calculation of future satisfactions, but in the intellectual vision of eternal Forms. It is this phase of Plato's thought about conduct which has earned him the reputation of grossly over-estimating human nature. But we are apt to forget that it is not the final phase, and to forget also that Plato never supposed 'true virtue' in this sense to be within the reach of the ordinary man. Even in the days of the *Phaedo* and the *Republic* he realized that only a very small number of exceptionally endowed persons were capable of achieving that goodness which derives from knowledge of the Forms: philosophic vision is the rarest of all gifts, confined to a φύσει ὀλίγιστον γένος.[2] For the rest—that is to say, the overwhelming majority of mankind—he seems to recognize at all stages of his thought that an intelligent hedonism provides the best practicable guide to a satisfactory life.[3] But in the dialogues of his middle period, preoccupied as he is with exceptional natures and their exceptional possibilities—those possibilities which, through the

[1] Cf. Hackforth, *C.Q.* 22 (1928), 39 ff., whose arguments appear to me unanswerable.
[2] *Rep.* 428 e–429 a, cf. *Phaedo* 69 c.
[3] *Phaedo* 82 a–b, *Rep.* 500 d, and the passages quoted below from *Philebus* and *Laws*.

foundation of the Academy, were to be developed systematically for the first time—he shows scant interest in the psychology of the ordinary man.

In his later work, however, after he had dismissed the philosopher-kings as an impossible dream, and had fallen back on the rule of law as a second-best,[1] he paid more attention to the motives which govern ordinary human conduct, and even the philosopher is seen not to be exempt from their influence. To the question whether any one of us would be content with a life in which he possessed wisdom, understanding, knowledge, and a complete memory of the whole of history, but experienced no pleasure or pain, great or small, the answer given in the *Philebus*[2] is an emphatic 'No': we are anchored in the life of feeling which is part of our humanity, and cannot surrender it even to become 'spectators of all time and all existence'[3] like the philosopher-kings. In the *Laws* we are told that the only practicable basis for public morals is the belief that honesty pays: 'for no one', says Plato, 'would consent, if he could help it, to a course of action which did not bring him more joy than sorrow.'[4] With that we seem to be back in the world of the *Protagoras* and of Jeremy Bentham. The legislator's position, however, is not identical with that of the common man. The common man wants to be happy; but Plato, who is legislating for him, wants him to be good. Plato therefore labours to persuade him that goodness and happiness go together. That this is true, Plato happens to believe; but did he not believe it, he would still pretend it true, as being 'the most salutary lie that was ever told'.[5] It is not Plato's own position that has changed: if anything has changed, it is his estimate of human nature. In the *Laws*, at any rate, the virtue of the common man is evidently not based on knowledge, or even on true opinion as such, but on a process of conditioning or habituation—ὀρθῶς εἰθίσθαι ὑπὸ τῶν προσηκόντων ἐθῶν (653 b) —by which he is induced to accept and act on certain 'salutary' beliefs. After all, says Plato, this is not too difficult: people who can believe in Cadmus and the dragon's teeth will believe anything (664 a). Far from supposing, as his master had done, that 'the unexamined life is no life for a human being',[6] Plato now

---

[1] *Politicus* 297 d-e, 301 d-e; cf. *Laws* 739 d-e. [2] 21 d-e.
[3] *Rep.* 486 a.   [4] 663 b, cf. 733 a.   [5] 663 d.
[6] *Apol.* 38 a. Prof. Hackforth has endeavoured (*C.R.* 59 (1945), 1 ff.) to convince

Plato and the Irrational

appears to hold that the majority of human beings can be kept in tolerable moral health only by a carefully chosen diet of 'incantations' or slogans (ἐπῳδαί)[1] and myths.

Another way in which Plato's later work shows an increased understanding of the part played by affective elements is in the account it gives of the causes of misconduct and unhappiness. Plato still believes that 'nobody does wrong if he can help it';[2] but he no longer makes ignorance the sole cause of wrongdoing, or increased knowledge its sole cure. Side by side with the intellectualist theory which he inherited from Socrates and the Sophists, he comes to recognize an irrational factor within the mind itself, and so gradually develops a deeper view of moral evil as being the result of psychological conflict (στάσις).[3] The germ of this is the Pythagorean conception of goodness as a ἁρμονία, and the first hint of it appears in the dialogue where the Pythagorean influence on Plato first shows itself—in the *Gorgias*.[4] There are occasional references to such internal στάσις in the *Republic*,[5] where freedom from it makes part of the philosopher's happiness.[6] But the theory is first worked out in the *Sophist*,[7] where στάσις is defined as a psychological maladjustment resulting from some sort of injury (τινὸς διαφθορᾶς), a kind of disease of

---

us that Plato remained loyal to this maxim throughout his life. But though he certainly paid lip-service to it as late as the *Sophist* (230 c–e), I see no escape from the conclusion that the educational policy of the *Republic*, and still more clearly that of the *Laws*, is in reality based on very different assumptions. Plato could never confess to himself that he had abandoned any Socratic principle; but that did not prevent him from doing it. Socrates' θεραπεία ψυχῆς surely implies respect for the human mind as such; the techniques of suggestion and other controls recommended in the *Laws* seem to me to imply just the opposite.

[1] In the *Laws* ἐπῳδή and its cognates are continually used in this metaphorical sense (659 e, 664 b, 665 c, 666 c, 670 e, 773 d, 812 c, 903 b, 944 b). Cf. Callicles' contemptuous use of the word, *Gorg.* 484 a. Its application in the early dialogue *Charmides* (157 a–c) is significantly different: there the 'incantation' turns out to be Socratic cross-examination. But in the *Phaedo*, where the myth is an ἐπῳδή (114 d, cf. 77 e–78 a), we already have a suggestion of the part which ἐπῳδαί were to play in the *Laws*.

[2] *Laws* 731 c, 860 d.

[3] Plato's recognition of an irrational element in the soul was seen in the Peripatetic School to mark an important advance beyond the intellectualism of Socrates (*Magna Moralia* 1. 1, 1182ª15 ff.); and his views on the training of the irrational soul, which will respond only to an irrational ἐθισμός, were later invoked by Posidonius in his polemic against the intellectualist Chrysippus (Galen, *de placitis Hippocratis et Platonis*, p. 466 f. Kühn, cf. 424 f.).

[4] 482 b–c.   [5] 351 d–e, 440 b, 554 d, 603 d.   [6] 586 e.

[7] 227 d–228 e.

the soul, and is said to be the cause of cowardice, intemperance, injustice, and (it would seem) moral evil in general, as distinct from ignorance or intellectual failure. With this one may connect the saying of the *Epinomis*, that man will attain unity, which is happiness and wisdom, only when he is dead; ἐκ πολλῶν ἕνα γεγονότα, εὐδαίμονά τε ἔσεσθαι καὶ σοφώτατον ἅμα καὶ μακάριον (992 b). If Plato did not write the *Epinomis*, I suspect that his literary executor found these words in one of his notebooks: they have the true Platonic ring. Finally, I would remind you of a striking passage in the *Timaeus*,[1] where a wide range of emotional disorders, including sexual excesses, irritability and despondency, rashness and cowardice, and even forgetfulness and stupidity, are attributed by Plato to bodily causes over which the victim has no control—very much as some physiological psychologists attribute them today to a failure of balance in the glandular secretions. Here surely Plato's thinking has swung to the opposite pole from the intellectualism with which he started. But I find nothing in it which is inconsistent with the rest of his later teaching. He recognizes similarly in *Laws* IV that the history of human societies is largely determined by physical catastrophes, so that one could say τύχας εἶναι σχεδὸν ἅπαντα τὰ ἀνθρώπινα πράγματα (709 b)—though he is careful to add that both providence and human intelligence also play a part.

Before leaving this topic, I am tempted to urge that, after all, Plato's error lay not merely in thinking too nobly of human nature, but also in thinking too meanly of it. There are in the *Laws* one or two very remarkable utterances on this subject. We are told in Book I that man is a puppet whom the gods have made, whether simply as a plaything or for some serious purpose we cannot tell: all we know is that the creature is on a string, and his hopes and fears, pleasures and pains, jerk him about and make him dance.[2] Further on, in Book VII, the Athenian observes that it is a pity we have to take human affairs seriously, and remarks that man is God's plaything, 'and that is really the best that can be said of him': men and women should accordingly make this play as charming as possible,

---

[1] 86 b–87 b. The passage is quoted by Galen (*Scripta Minora* 2. 49. 12 ff. Müller) as showing that Plato recognized the influence of body on mind.
[2] 644 d–e.

Plato and the Irrational

sacrificing to the gods with music and dancing; 'thus they will live out their lives in accordance with their nature, being puppets chiefly, and having in them only a small portion of reality.' 'You are making out our human race very mean', says the Spartan. And the Athenian apologizes: 'I thought of God, and I was moved to speak as I did just now. Well, if you will have it so, let us say that our race is not mean—that it is worth taking a little bit seriously (σπουδῆς τινος ἄξιον).'[1]

Plato suggests here a religious origin for this way of thinking; and we often meet it in later religious thinkers, from Marcus Aurelius to T. S. Eliot—who has said in almost the same words, 'Human nature is able to endure only a very little reality.' It agrees with the drift of much else in the *Laws*—with the view that men are as unfit to rule themselves as a flock of sheep,[2] that God, not man, is the measure of things,[3] that man is the gods' property (κτῆμα),[4] and that if he wishes to be happy, he should be ταπεινός, 'abject', before God[5]—a word which nearly all pagan writers, and Plato himself elsewhere, employ as a term of contempt. Ought we to discount all this as a senile aberration, the sour pessimism of a tired and irritable old man? It might seem so: for it contrasts oddly with the radiant picture of the soul's divine nature and destiny which Plato painted in his middle dialogues and certainly never abjured. But then I remember the philosopher of the *Republic*, to whom, as to Aristotle's megalopsych, human life cannot appear important (μέγα τι);[6] I remember that in the *Meno* the mass of men are likened to the shadows that flit in Homer's Hades, and that the conception of human beings as the κτήματα of a god appears already in the *Phaedo*.[7] I recall also another passage of the *Phaedo*, where Plato predicts with undisguised relish the future of his fellow men: in their next incarnation some of them will be donkeys, others wolves, while the μέτριοι, the respectable bourgeoisie, may look forward to becoming bees or ants.[8] No doubt this is partly Plato's fun; but it is the sort of fun which would have appealed to Jonathan Swift. It carries the implication that everybody except the philosopher is on the verge of becoming subhuman, which is

---

[1] 803 b–804 b.   [2] 713 c–d.   [3] 716 c.
[4] 902 b, 906 a; cf. *Critias* 109 b.
[5] 716 a: for the implication cf., for example, 774 c.
[6] 486 a, cf. *Theaet*. 173 c–e, Ar. *E.N.* 1123^{b}32.
[7] *Meno* 100 a, *Phaedo* 62 b.   [8] 81 e–82 b.

(as ancient Platonists saw)[1] hard to reconcile with the view that every human soul is essentially rational.

In the light of these and other passages I think we have to recognize two strains or tendencies in Plato's thinking about the status of man. There is the faith and pride in human reason which he inherited from the fifth century and for which he found religious sanction in the doctrine of the soul's immortality and likeness to God. And there is the bitter recognition of human worthlessness which was forced upon him by his experience of contemporary Athens and Syracuse (read the Seventh Letter). This, too, could be transposed into the language of religion, as a denial of all value to the activities and interests of this world in comparison with τὰ ἐκεῖ. A psychologist might say that the relation between the two tendencies was not one of simple opposition, but that the first became a compensation—or over-compensation —for the second: the less Plato cared for actual humanity, the more nobly he thought of the soul. The tension between the two was resolved for a time in the dream of a new Rule of the Saints, an élite of purified men who should unite the incompatible virtues of (to use Mr. Koestler's terms) the Yogi and the Commissar, and thereby save not only themselves, but also society. But when that illusion faded, Plato's underlying despair came more and more to the surface, translating itself into religious terms, until it found its logical expression in his final proposals for a Servile[2] State, to be ruled not by the illuminated reason, but (under God) by custom and religious law. The 'Yogi', with his faith in the possibility and necessity of intellectual conversion, did not wholly vanish even now, but he certainly retreated before the 'Commissar' whose problem is the conditioning of human cattle. On this interpretation the pessimism of the *Laws* is not a senile aberration: it is the fruit of Plato's personal experience of life, which in turn carried in it the seed of much later thought.[3]

---

[1] μεταλαβούσης δὲ θήρειον σῶμα θαυμάζεται πῶς, λόγος οὖσα ἀνθρώπου Plot. *Enn.* 6. 7. 6. Cf. ibid. 1. 1. 11; Porphyry *apud* Aug. *Civ. dei* 10. 30; Iamblichus *apud* Nemes. *nat. hom.* 2 (*P.G.* 40. 584 A); Proclus *in Tim.* iii. 294. 22 ff.

[2] *Laws* 942 a-b: 'The principal thing is that no man and no woman should ever be without an officer set over him, and that none should get the mental habit of taking any step, whether in earnest or in jest, on his individual responsibility: in peace as in war he must live always with his eye on his superior officer, following his lead and guided by him in his smallest actions... in a word, we must train the mind not even to consider acting as an individual or know how to do it.'

[3] On later developments of the theme of the unimportance of τὰ ἀνθρώπινα

I turn now from Plato's view of man to his view of Nature. Here, too, Plato's thinking is rooted in fifth-century rationalism and optimism; here, too, it grows away from its roots towards the recognition of an irreducible irrational factor. But the case is plainer here, and I can be correspondingly brief. We are told in the *Phaedo*, and modern research[1] has confirmed it, that the notion of teleology—of replacing a mechanistic explanation of Nature by an explanation in terms of purpose—is part of Plato's inheritance from the fifth century. But its systematic application is first envisaged in the *Phaedo*, and first carried out in the *Timaeus*. In the *Phaedo* no limit is set to its applicability: physical agencies are recognized as conditions *sine quibus non* of physical events, but they are denied the name of causes.[2] In the *Timaeus*, however, besides these physical συναίτια which are popularly but falsely described as causes,[3] we meet also with a real cause which is non-rational—the πλανωμένη αἰτία or Errant Cause, alias 'necessity', which shares with Mind the responsibility for the constitution of the universe. I shall excuse myself from saying much about the Errant Cause, since it has been discussed so fully and lucidly by Cornford (*Plato's Cosmology*, 162 ff.). I take it to represent that element of 'cussedness' in Nature which is familiar to every farmer and every engineer. This cussedness is something quite real, and the Errant Cause is quite real for Plato: we must reject the unconvincing subterfuges by which Archer-Hind and Taylor tried to force on him their own belief in divine omnipotence.

There are two places in the *Laws* which throw, I think, some further light on what Plato meant by the Errant Cause. One is the passage in Book IV[4] which I have already referred to, where pestilences and bad seasons are mentioned as effects of τύχη or of τύχη μετὰ θεοῦ. Since Cornford has shown that the 'Necessity' of the *Timaeus* is virtually synonymous with τύχη, and since similar calamities are attributed by the Egyptian priest of the *Timaeus* to deviations of the heavenly bodies, I think we may see in them examples of the work of the Errant Cause, whose misbehaviour God is powerless to prevent, though he tries to turn

---

see Festugière in *Eranos* 44 (1946), 376 ff. For man as a puppet cf. M. Ant. 7. 3, Plot. *Enn.* 3. 2. 15.

[1] W. Theiler, *Zur Geschichte der teleologischen Naturbetrachtung bis auf Aristoteles* (1925); A. S. Pease, 'Coeli Enarrant', *Harvard Theol. Rev.* 34 (1941), 163 ff.
[2] 98 b–99 c.   [3] 46 c–d.   [4] 709 a–b; cf. 677 a, *Tim.* 22 c–d.

it so far as possible to good account. The other place is the well-known passage in *Laws* X where at least two souls are said to be concerned with the governance of the οὐρανός, one which works good and one which is capable of working the opposite.[1] We should not, with Clement of Alexandria,[2] salute here the first emergence of the Devil in Greek thought: for the inferior soul has no more than a potentiality of evil, which it realizes, as we are told further on,[3] only when it 'associates with mindlessness'. But neither should we, with some modern interpreters,[4] suppose that the inferior soul in question is merely a bad human soul: for this sense can be obtained only (as it seems to me) by mistranslating,[5] and is in any case excluded by a later passage, where we learn that the οὐρανός is full of evil things as well as good.[6] The inferior soul seems to stand to the good one in the same relation as Necessity to Mind in the *Timaeus* myth: it is a sort of untrustworthy junior partner, liable to fits of unreasonable behaviour, in which it produces 'crazy and disorderly movements'[7]—a phrase that recalls both the 'scared and crazy movement' attributed to the souls of human infants elsewhere in the *Laws*[8] and the 'discordant and disorderly movement' of the mythical chaos that preceded the mythical creation in the *Timaeus*.[9] All these movements I take to be symbols, not of deliberate evil, but of irrationality, the element both in man and in the κόσμος which is incompletely mastered by a rational will. The reality and importance of this element are already recognized in a famous passage of the *Theaetetus*[10] which asserts, without explaining why, that there must always be something which is opposed to the Good, and that therefore evil things haunt our mortal nature and the visible world (τόνδε τὸν τόπον) as a result of necessity (ἐξ ἀνάγκης). In his later work, at any rate, Plato can certainly not be accused of yielding to a credulous optimism. We may guess that he has projected into his conception of Nature that stubborn irrationality which he was more and more compelled to admit in man.[11]

---

[1] 896 e.   [2] *Strom.* 5. 14. 92. 5 f.   [3] 897 b. Cf. *Politicus* 270 a.
[4] e.g. Grube, in his excellent book *Plato's Thought*, 146.
[5] Grube translates 'Is there only one soul, or are there more than one?' But the context surely requires us to supply, not εἶναι, but τὸν οὐρανὸν διοικεῖν.
[6] 906 a.   [7] 897 d.   [8] 791 a.   [9] 30 a.   [10] 176 a.
[11] For the relation between order in the human soul and order in Nature cf. esp. *Tim.* 90 c–d, *Epin.* 982 a–b.

Plato and the Irrational

In recent years several distinguished scholars have suggested a different explanation for this 'ethical dualism' of the later dialogues: they hold that Plato was influenced by Persian religious ideas. I shall postpone what little I have to say about this until I have attempted some reply to my final question: did Plato regard reason as the chief or only guide in matters of religion? This question is sometimes answered with an unqualified affirmative: thus one of our best Platonic scholars, Professor Field, has said that in Plato's view 'hard thinking was the only way to arrive at truth'.[1] I cannot myself accept this without considerable qualification. But to avoid misunderstanding I had better begin by mentioning some kinds of irrational faith which I do not attribute to Plato.

1. Plato unequivocally condemns, both in the *Republic*[2] and in the *Laws*,[3] what may be called the magical view of religion—the idea that the gods can be influenced by the performance of certain rituals. In the *Laws* he prohibits the introduction of unauthorized private cults (which were often orgiastic or superstitious, and seem, in fact, to have constituted a real social danger in the fourth century).[4] He also prescribes severe penalties for persons who practise necromancy or magical attack (κατάδεσις, *defixio*): this because of the harmful social results of these practices, not because he believed in their magical efficacy; he is one of the very few ancient writers who had the intellectual courage to express scepticism on that subject.[5]

2. Plato frequently, from the *Apology* to the *Laws*, speaks of 'inspiration' (ἐνθουσιασμός), but usually, I think, with recognizable irony, whether the inspiration be that of seers or of poets. Such mental processes certainly aroused his curiosity; but that he does not in general take them very seriously as a source of truth seems to be implied by the passage in the *Phaedrus*[6] about the rating of lives, where the μάντις or τελεστής and the poet are placed in the fifth and sixth classes respectively, below even the businessman

---

[1] *Philosophy* 9 (1934), 285.   [2] 364 b–e.   [3] 905 d–907 d.
[4] 909 d–910 e. Cf. *Harv. Theol. Rev.* 33 (1940), 174.
[5] 909 b, 933 a–e. He clearly disbelieves in necromancy; on magic his attitude is agnostic, but seems to incline towards scepticism.
[6] 248 d. For Plato's opinion of μάντεις cf. also *Politicus* 290 c, *Laws* 908 d. But he did not reject such people entirely: he gives them a function in his State (*Laws* 828 b), and we hear of a μάντις who had studied under him in the Academy (Plut. *Dion* 22).

and the athlete. Such persons are in any case unable to explain or justify their intuition:[1] for Plato holds, in opposition to earlier theory, that clairvoyance is a function of the irrational soul (as we should say, of the subconscious mind), and has its seat in the liver.[2] (I would add that the term 'Platonic (or Socratic) mysticism', if we use it at all, should be applied not to the theory of ἐνθουσιασμός, but to the practice of mental withdrawal and concentration which is recommended in the *Phaedo*.[3] Neither this practice nor the Plotinian mysticism which derives from it can, I think, fairly be called irrational.)

3. Thirdly, I see little reason, and certainly no necessity, to credit Plato with a serious belief in the personal gods of Greek mythology and Greek cult. Some scholars would disagree here: Wilamowitz, for example, believed that 'the memories of a pious childhood always lived in Plato', and even grew stronger with advancing years.[4] Unfortunately Plato has not told us about his childhood; we may, however, recall that the best-known member of his family, his mother's cousin Critias, was not remarkable for his piety. Any judgement on this matter is, indeed, apt to be rather subjective, for it must depend on the impression made on us by Plato's scattered references to mythological gods. He nowhere casts direct doubt on their existence, though he speaks of the traditional theogonies with transparent irony, and allows Socrates to remark in the *Phaedrus* that our conception of such gods is based on no reasoned principle: we imagine them without having seen them or intellectually grasped their nature.[5] They figure in the myth of the *Phaedrus*,[6] where they contemplate the Forms; they are allowed a subordinate place in the creation-myth of the *Timaeus*;[7] and their worship is prescribed both in the *Republic* and in the *Laws*[8]—for a Greek city was, as Wilamowitz says,[9] unthinkable without the Greek gods. But I find little

---

[1] *Apol.* 22 b–c, *Meno* 99 c–d.
[2] *Tim.* 71 d–72 b. Cornford contrasts Pindar frag. 131S. (116B.) and Ar. π. φιλοσ. frag. 10 Rose³ (12 Ross).
[3] 67 c, 80 e, 83 a–c. Cf. Festugière, *Contemplation et vie contemplative chez Platon*, 61 ff., 123 ff.
[4] *Glaube der Hellenen*, ii. 250.
[5] *Tim.* 40 d–e, *Phdr.* 246 c. Cf. *Epinomis* 984 d, where the tone seems definitely contemptuous.
[6] 247 a. But here one may suspect that they have an astral status: see below, p. 125.
[7] *Tim.* 41 a–d.   [8] *Rep.* 427 b; *Laws* 717 a–b.   [9] Loc. cit.

Plato and the Irrational

or no religious warmth in any of Plato's references to them: they are for him οἱ κατὰ νόμον ὄντες θεοί,[1] 'the Church of Hellas as by law established', and, I suspect, not much more. The traditional mythology he will expurgate so far as is morally needful,[2] but he is bored by the 'laboriously clever' persons who want to rationalize it: he prefers to accept 'the received opinion' (τὸ νομιζόμενον).[3] Similarly he will abstain from meddling with any cult that has been founded as the result of an oracle or a divine epiphany:[4] he will leave all that to Apollo, the πάτριος ἐξηγητής who sits on the ὀμφαλός of the world.[5] Does this mean that Plato personally believed in divine epiphanies, or held that infallible truth was communicated to man through the lips of an entranced medium at Delphi? We are not bound to think so: for we know that he authorized his legislator to lie to the citizens for their good and to forge oracles as required.[6] His own attitude to Delphi and to the supposed epiphanies may have been somewhat like that of the modern 'political Catholic' towards the Vatican and towards Lourdes: he may have seen in the former simply a great conservative force, in the latter a harmless means of maintaining popular faith.[7]

In any case these are surely not the deities whom Plato has in mind when he speaks, for example, of likeness to God, ὁμοίωσις θεῷ, as man's supreme aim.[8] Where then shall we look for the God of Plato's personal devotion? That we should have to look for him, and should differ about where he is to be found, is in itself surprising and suggestive. If the Second Letter is genuine, as some now maintain, the mystification was deliberate; but the fuss about secrecy in that letter, and especially the use of the Pythagorean term ἀκούσματα,[9] look to me much more like the work of a forger—part of the campaign to represent Plato as a Pythagorean initiate. I should be more inclined to explain

---

[1] *Laws* 904 a; cf. 885 b and (if the text is sound) 891 e.
[2] *Euthyphro* 6 a–c; *Rep.* 377 d ff.   [3] *Phdr.* 229 c–30 a.
[4] *Laws* 738 b–c.   [5] *Rep.* 427 b–c; cf. *Laws* 828 a.
[6] *Rep.* 414 b–15 d; *Laws* 663 d.
[7] On this attitude towards popular religion and its deplorable consequences cf. the remarks of F. W. Walbank, *JHS* 64 (1944), 14 f. It seems to me, however, misleading to suggest, as Professor Walbank does, that Plato's motive 'was unquestionably the maintenance of privilege'. Plato was not so simple a character as all that.
[8] *Rep.* 500 c–d, 613 a–b; *Theaet.* 176 b, Cf. *Tim.* 29 e.
[9] *Ep.* 2. 314 a.

Plato's lack of clarity on this subject by the cleavage between his mythical or religious thinking and his dialectical or philosophical thinking, and the fact that the former was not bound, in the same degree as the latter, by the requirement of logical consistency. Mythical thinking is thinking in images, and its logic is wholly or partly the logic of feeling, like the coherence of a dream or a work of art, not the logic of science or philosophy. Its conclusions are valid for those who share the feeling, but they cannot compel assent. In this Plato's myths resemble the intuitions of the poet or the seer.¹ Plato knew this, and has warned us of it more than once:² it is our own fault if we insist on ignoring the distinction, and the result is likely to be confusion.

Our confusion about Plato's God is, I think, an instance. His philosophical thinking about the nature of goodness and truth led him to posit an Absolute, which is the Form of the Good: this Absolute is hardly a possible object of worship, and he nowhere in fact calls it or any of the Forms a God.³ His religious feeling, on the other hand, created the figure of a benevolent and mighty (though not omnipotent) Father-god, father and maker of gods and men and of the world itself.⁴ If we try to identify the two, in the hope that they will add up to the equivalent of one Christian Deity, we make, as I think, nonsense.⁵ Yet as an independent figure the Father-god seems to have no function in the Platonic scheme of things save at the mythical level. If, as the best judges now agree, Plato did not believe in a creation in time, a divine creator seems otiose. Ought we, then, to regard him as a mere expository device? I cannot feel content with this, either: for, like Taylor, I feel that Plato's attitude to him 'is charged with a deep emotion of a kind that can only be called religious'.⁶ I incline to see in him the highest God of Plato's personal faith, whom we meet also at the end of the Sixth Letter,⁷

---

¹ Cf. Stöcklein, 'Über die philosophische Bedeutung von Platons Mythen', *Philol. Supp. Band.* 30, iii (1937).
² *Gorg.* 527 a, *Phaedo* 114 d, *Tim.* 29 c–d.
³ Unless they are to be identified with the ἀΐδιοι θεοί of *Tim.* 37 c. Cornford's interpretation of this disputed passage can hardly, I think, be right: it destroys the antithesis between ἀϊδίων and γεγονός. But θεῶν may be a gloss (Taylor).
⁴ Maker also of the Forms, if we are to generalize from the passage about the 'ideal bed' in the *Republic* (597 b–d).
⁵ Cf. Hackforth, *C.Q.* 30 (1936), 4 ff.; Festugière, *L'Idéal religieux des Grecs et l'Évangile* (1932), 187 ff.; Solmsen, *Plato's Theology* (1942), 113 f.
⁶ *Mind*, N.S. 47 (1938), 190.   ⁷ 323 d.

Plato and the Irrational

and whom I should suppose Plato commonly has in mind when he speaks of ὁ θεός in the singular without further explanation. But Plato could integrate him into a world-scheme only at the mythical level. I think he means to tell us as much in a famous sentence of the *Timaeus*: 'To find the maker and father of this universe is hard; when he is found, to declare him to all men is impossible.'[1]

Plato, then, if I am right in my general view, admits two types of belief or two levels of truth, which we may call respectively truths of religion and truths of reason. The former are, as such, indemonstrable, and he does not claim for them more than a probability that 'this or something like it'[2] is true. I find nothing surprising in this: most men—including, I suspect, most philosophers—believe in practice a good many things which they are incapable of proving. But since Plato preferred to convince his readers by reasoning, if possible, rather than by emotive eloquence, he continually tried to transpose his religious beliefs from the mythical to the philosophical level, thus transforming them into truths of reason. This has the curious result that his conclusions often emerge earlier than the philosophical arguments by which they are established: thus his doctrine of the soul appears in mythical guise in the *Gorgias* before it is presented as a truth of reason in the *Phaedo*; the divinity of the stars is casually mentioned in the *Republic*[3] and assumed in the *Timaeus* myth, but only in the *Laws* do we find an attempt to prove it. Now, it is psychologically understandable that an idea should be intuitively apprehended on the mythical level before its logical connections are fully grasped: we often seem to ourselves to know something before we know why we know it. But Plato does not conceal that the 'hard thinking' which he requires of us in the *Phaedo* or in the tenth Book of the *Laws* concerns an issue which for him is already prejudged; and it is difficult to resist the suspicion that his premisses are in fact determined by his conclusion rather than his conclusion by his premisses. The identification of the sources from which he originally derived his doctrine of the soul is a question which I cannot here discuss; but it seems clear from his own statements that he attributes to them some measure of

---

[1] 28 c. In this sense I cannot fully agree with Grube's remark (*Plato's Thought* (1935), 178) that there was never, for Plato, any antagonism between his religion and his philosophy. [2] *Phaedo* 114 d. [3] 508 a.

authority. It is particularly significant that many years after the *Phaedo*, when, apropos of Dion's death, he is moved to speak of immortality in the Seventh Letter (at present accepted as genuine by almost all the experts), he makes no reference to his own philosophical proofs, but says simply, 'We must always truly believe the old and sacred doctrines which *reveal* (μηνύουσιν) that the soul is immortal.'[1] If Plato the philosopher held that 'hard thinking' was the best way to arrive at truth, this passage shows that Plato the man was content to reach it by a different and shorter route: he rides that 'steadier raft' of 'divine' revelation which Simmias desired in the *Phaedo*.[2]

I take it, then, as undeniable that certain Greek religious traditions, which it is convenient though perhaps unscientific to label *en bloc* 'Orphic–Pythagorean', deeply influenced Plato's personal religious ideas, and through these his philosophical thought also; indeed, I believe with Wilamowitz[3] that about the period when he wrote the *Gorgias* Plato experienced something resembling religious conversion. Was this experience unique in his life? Or was a religious impetus communicated for a second time to his thought when at a later date he made the acquaintance of the Persian religion of Zoroaster? The latter thesis has been maintained by Jaeger,[4] Reitzenstein,[5] Bidez, and Cumont,[6] and although it has been little discussed in this country, the names of its sponsors forbid us to dismiss it as a mere whimsy. If they are right, we have here a second instance of a religious influence affecting Plato's thought from without, appearing at first, as did the 'Orphic–Pythagorean' influence, chiefly at the mythical level—in the myths of the *Republic*, *Phaedrus*, *Politicus*, and *Timaeus*—and finally transposed to the rational level in *Laws* X and the *Epinomis*. I cannot rule out such a possibility on *a priori* grounds, either psychological or historical. What has happened to a man once can happen to him twice; and as early as the *Phaedo*[7] Plato had hinted at his willingness to learn from barbarians as well as from Greeks. There is also good evidence

---

[1] 335 a. For the sense of μηνύουσιν cf. *Rep.* 366 b.
[2] 85 c–d.   [3] *Platon*, i. 234 ff.   [4] *Aristotle*, 131 ff. (English edition).
[5] 'Plato und Zarathustra', *Vorträge Bibliothek Warburg* 1924–5, 20 ff.
[6] J. Bidez, 'Platon, Eudoxe de Cnide, et l'Orient', *Bull. Acad. Belg.*, *Classe des Lettres* 1933, 195 ff., 273 ff.; 'Les couleurs des planètes dans le mythe d'Er', ibid. 1935, 257 ff.; Bidez–Cumont, *Les Mages hellénisés* (1938), i. 12 ff.
[7] 78 a.

Plato and the Irrational 123

that some information about Persian religion was available to Plato, both from a Chaldaean whose name appears in a list of pupils of the Academy,[1] apparently in Plato's later years, and from Plato's friend, the astronomer and geographer Eudoxus, who thought Zoroastrianism 'the most beneficial of the philosophical sects,' and may have thought Plato an 'avatar' of Zoroaster.[2] Zoroaster is mentioned in the *Alcibiades major*,[3] and we know that both Aristotle and others of Plato's pupils were interested in him.[4]

So far, so good. But we must note that whereas Plato habitually, if in annoyingly vague terms, makes acknowledgement to his Greek theological sources—to a παλαιὸς λόγος or to οἱ περὶ τὰς τελετάς—he nowhere attributes his doctrine to a Persian source: if we exclude the *Epinomis*, the nearest he gets to it is the Cretan's remark in *Laws* X that Greeks and barbarians alike believe in gods,[5] which does not take us far, and perhaps the fact, if it is a fact, that Er the son of Armenius has a Persian name (but why in that case does Plato call him a Pamphylian?). We are thus reduced to observing resemblances between Platonic and Zoroastrian doctrine and deciding, if we can, whether they are too close to be accidental.

I cannot attempt to give here a detailed list of such resemblances. The two major points of Platonic doctrine which prima facie might suggest Persian or Perso-Chaldaean influence are the dualism in his later account of man and Nature, and the high importance attached to the sun in *Rep.* VI and to the heavenly bodies generally in *Laws* X and the *Epinomis*. We saw, however, that Plato's dualism, unlike that of Persia, does not go the length of postulating a Devil, a principle which deliberately chooses evil, and that it seems capable of psychological explanation in terms of his personal experience. If it has roots in any earlier doctrine, I should be inclined to look for them, as did the ancients,[6] in Pythagoreanism rather than in Persia.

[1] *Index Acad. Herculan.*, col. iii, p. 13 Mekler.
[2] Pliny, *N.H.* 30. 3; cf. Jaeger, loc. cit. The avatar idea is a speculative inference from the 6,000-year interval said by Eudoxus to separate Zoroaster from Plato (cf. the cautious remarks of Nock, *J.H.S.* 49 (1929), 112). [3] 122 a.
[4] Aristotle, frags. 6, 8, 12, 19 Walzer, *Met.* 1091^b8; Hermodorus, Diog. L. *prooem.* 2; Heraclides Ponticus, Plut. *adv. Col.* 14, 1115 a.
[5] 886 a.
[6] Theophrastus attributed a dualism of this type to Plato and the Pythagoreans in common (*Metaph.* 33, p. 322. 14 Br.). Other passages in Ritter and Preller, §71.

As for the sun and stars, Plato asserted that these were the oldest Greek gods;[1] and though he was doubtless mistaken, their claim to veneration (as distinct from cult) was surely nothing novel. Sophocles knows of philosophers who call the sun γεννητὴν θεῶν καὶ πατέρα πάντων;[2] Socrates prays to him;[3] Anaxagoras is prosecuted for calling him a stone; to the homely Watchman in the *Agamemnon* certain constellations are λαμπροὶ δυνάσται, 'bringing winter and summer to mankind'; and, much more important for us, Alcmaeon of Croton had already argued, like Plato, that, being in perpetual motion, the stars must be alive, and, being alive, they must be gods.[4] Alcmaeon's argument was doubtless much strengthened for Plato by Eudoxus' discovery that the planetary movements conformed to a determinate law.[5] To us such uniform motion suggests a machine; to most Greeks it suggested a god—for the poor things had never seen a machine.[6] In the circumstances it seems unhistorical either to brand Plato's (and Aristotle's) astral theology as irrational,[7] or to assume that it necessarily had a foreign origin—even though it was to play an important, perhaps a decisive, part in the dehellenizing of the religious tradition in the following age.[8] What is certainly an importation, and is frankly presented as such, is the *public worship* of the planets recommended in the *Epinomis*:[9] the writer hopes the Greeks will borrow this cult from the barbarians but will adapt it, as they have adapted earlier borrowings, 'to nobler ends'. The latter hope was not fulfilled: Platonism had opened the door to astrology, and astrology came in.

Some of the details in Plato's later myths appear—so far as a non-orientalist can judge—to have an oriental colouring: for

---

[1] *Crat.* 397 c–d.   [2] Frag. 752 Pearson; cf. also *O.T.* 660.
[3] *Symp.* 220 d (a passage which will hardly be claimed as reflecting Persian influence).
[4] Diels–Kranz, *Vors.* 14 A 12.
[5] For the deep impression made on him by the new astronomy cf. *Laws* 821 a–e.
[6] Cf. *Laws* 967 b, Ar. π. φιλοσ. frag. 21 Walzer; and Cornford, *Plato's Cosmology* 173.
[7] Cumont has quoted Renan's remark that 'Avant que la religion fût arrivée à proclamer que Dieu doit être mis dans l'absolu et l'idéal, c'est à dire hors du monde, un seul culte fut raisonnable et scientifique, ce fut le culte du Soleil' (*Dialogues et fragments philosophiques* (1876), 168).
[8] Cf. Nilsson in *Harv. Theol. Rev.* 33 (1940), 1 ff., who concludes that between them 'Greek philosophy and popular belief paved the way for the lasting and dominating belief in the stars'.
[9] 987 d–988 a, cf. 986 e–987 a.

example, the 'astral influence' exerted upon the souls of the unborn by the twelve gods of the *Phaedrus*, who seem to be associated with the twelve signs of the zodiac.[1] And I am very willing to believe that in his talks with Eudoxus Plato picked up this or that bit of Oriental symbolism and wove it into the rich web of his fantasies about the unseen world. This, however, does not make Plato in any important sense a Zoroastrian; and beyond this, unless the *Epinomis* is taken as representing his views, we do not at present seem justified in going. I do not rule the plea of the orientalizers out of court; but pending the production of further evidence I think the provisional verdict should be 'Not proven'.

[1] 252 c–253 c, 247 a; cf. Bidez, *Bull. Acad. Belg.* 1933, 287 ff.

VIII

Tradition and Personal Achievement in the Philosophy of Plotinus[1]

I

THE collected philosophical essays of Plotinus—to which we still unfortunately give the senseless and non-Plotinian title *Enneads*—constitute a nodal point in the evolution of Western ideas. In this book converge almost all the main currents of thought that come down from 800 years of Greek speculation; out of it there issues a new current, destined to fertilize minds as different as those of Augustine and Boethius, Dante and Meister Eckhart, Coleridge, Bergson, and T. S. Eliot. And the historian cannot but ask himself what is the secret of this transmutation by which the old is taken up in the new and given a fresh direction and significance. Such a question admits of no complete answer and none is offered here. The present paper seeks merely to illustrate a few aspects of the problem for the benefit of readers who are not deeply versed in Plotinus. It omits much that a Plotinian specialist would rightly think important; and it uses broad terms where an expert might well insist on the need for qualification.

It is natural to begin by asking what Plotinus thought of his own work and how he conceived his historical function. To this the answer is easy, but disappointing. Plotinus apparently did not know that he was a Neoplatonist; he thinks of himself as a Platonist *tout court*. 'These doctrines', he says (5. 1. 8. 10), speaking of his own system, 'are no novelties, no inventions of today; they were stated, though not elaborated, long ago; our present teaching is simply an exposition of them—we can prove the antiquity of these opinions by Plato's own testimony.' This is not the language of a creative thinker acknowledging his debt

---

[1] A paper read at the Third International Congress of Classical Studies, September 1959, and published in the *Journal of Roman Studies* 50 (1960).

to a great predecessor; it is the language of a schoolman defending himself against a charge of unorthodoxy (καινοτομία). And indeed Plotinus avoids as a rule making any claim to originality; the rare exceptions have reference only to details of his system. At first sight this is disconcerting. But we must accept the fact that Plotinus *was* a schoolman. He was born into a world where for almost half a millennium no one had ventured to found a new philosophical school, or even to present a new idea as something genuinely and entirely new. Naturally this does not mean that men *had* no new ideas. On the contrary, between the third century before Christ and the third century after, not only Platonism but also Pythagoreanism, Stoicism, and even Aristotelianism underwent major changes of doctrine and, above all, a radical shift of interest: the questions most keenly debated in these schools when Plotinus was a boy were no longer those which had preoccupied the founders: Epicureanism alone remained frozen in a dogmatic rigidity. But the new ideas continued to sail under the old flags. The climate had changed; and philosophers, like other men, felt the change in their bones. But they could not admit the change, even to themselves—wisdom was timeless. Even Antiochus—that most elastic and elusive of Platonists— even he, we are told, had somehow to read back his Stoic theories into Plato and claim that his eclectic doctrine was a return to the teaching of the Old Academy.[1] The same thing happens with Numenius two centuries later: preaching his own very personal amalgam of Platonic, Pythagorean, and Gnostic elements, he professes that what he is really doing is to restore the true teaching of Plato, purged of all Aristotelian and Stoic accretions.[2] These examples may warn us not to take too literally Plotinus' claim to be an unoriginal thinker. Originality, as such, was not in demand in the third century.

Formally, but only formally, the philosophy of Plotinus is an interpretation of Plato; substantially, I should call it an attempt to solve the spiritual problems of his own day in terms of traditional Greek rationalism. He nowhere openly disagrees with his Master, though he recognizes that Plato sometimes speaks in riddles (6. 2. 22), leaving us to work out his meaning for ourselves (5. 8. 4), and also that his teaching is not always consistent, at

[1] Sext. Emp., *Pyrrh. Hyp.* 1. 235.
[2] Numenius, frag. 1 Leemans, *apud* Eus., *Prep. Evang.* 14. 5, 728 d.

any rate on the surface (4. 4. 22; 4. 8. 1). For each of the major features of his own system he can produce, and feels obliged to produce, certain Platonic texts as 'authority'. Thus he finds his three Divine Principles in the πρῶτον ἕν, the ἓν πολλά, and the ἓν καὶ πολλά of the *Parmenides* and in the three 'Kings' of the *Second Letter* (which like all his contemporaries he accepted as genuine). For the transcendence of the Good he can appeal to *Rep.* 509 b; for his dynamic conception of the Forms and their equation with Nous, to *Soph.* 247 e and 248 e, and to *Tim.* 39 e; his doctrine of Matter he rediscovers in the Platonic ὑποδοχή (*Tim.* 49 a). Some of his interpretations can be regarded as legitimate prolongations of Plato's thought; others are plainly distortions. Some of them, like the interpretation of the *Parmenides*, are known to have been current before his day;[1] others may be the outcome of his own thinking—for example, in an early essay (3. 9. 1) he toys with Numenius' interpretation of a crucial passage in the *Timaeus*,[2] but later, having rethought the problem, he explicitly rejects the Numenian view of it (2. 9. 6. 14).

But these Platonic texts are not the true *starting-points* of his philosophy: he does not believe in the One because he has found it in the *Parmenides*; on the contrary, he finds it in the *Parmenides* because he already believes in it. Nor does his exposition normally start from Plato: his more usual method is to state a problem and try out various ways of solving it until he arrives at something which he finds logically satisfying (εὔλογον); then, and most often only then, he will cite for confirmation a text from Plato. In fact, he quotes Plato pretty much in the same spirit in which some seventeenth-century philosophers quote Scripture—not as part of his logical argument but as evidence of orthodoxy. His basic question is not the historical one, 'What did Plato think about this?', but the philosophical one, 'What is the truth about this?' Respect for the Great Founder required, indeed, that both questions should have the same answer. But where violence had to be used to achieve this agreement it is generally Plato who is wrenched into concordance with the truth; so far as I can judge, the truth is seldom distorted to make it agree with Plato. Had Plato never lived, Plotinus would have had to formulate his

[1] Cf. *C.Q.* 22 (1928), 129 ff.
[2] Numenius *apud* Procl. *in Tim.* 3. 103. 28 (= test. 25 Leemans). Cf. my paper in *Les Sources de Plotin* (Entretiens Hardt, tome 5, 1960).

in the Philosophy of Plotinus 129

thought in some entirely different way, but I am tempted to guess that its general structure and direction would still have been recognizably what they are. What spoke to him in Plato's name was his own daemon, even when it used the very words of Plato.

Plato is not, of course, Plotinus' only source—if 'source' is the right term to apply in this connection. That Stoic and Peripatetic elements are to be found in his writings was already remarked by Porphyry (*vit. Plot.* 14). In itself, this was no novelty: eclecticism had long been modish in the Platonic School. But Porphyry adds a qualification to his remark: in Plotinus these alien elements were λανθάνοντα, which I take to mean that their alien origin passed unobserved by readers, since they were fused and transmuted in a new intellectual context. Here he puts his finger on the essential difference between Plotinus and his eclectic predecessors. It is true that if you pull Plotinus' system to bits you can usually find for each bit, if not anything that can strictly be called a 'source', at any rate some more or less closely related model or antecedent or stimulus, whether the stimulus came from within the Platonic School or from outside it. Plotinus built his structure very largely out of used pieces, the materials that Greek philosophical tradition presented to him. But the essence of the Plotinian system lies in the new meaning which the whole imposed on the parts; its true originality is not in the materials but in the design (as, indeed, I suspect is the case with every great philosophical system). And this, I take it, is what Longinus meant by the ἴδιος τρόπος θεωρίας that he found in Plotinus' writings (*vit. Plot.* 20. 70). To appreciate this kind of originality you must read your author *in extenso*; it is not enough to be familiar with a few catchwords and a few purple passages. But I shall attempt in the remainder of this paper to indicate some aspects of the Plotinian design which are both novel and historically important.

II

Like most systematic thinkers, Plotinus is centrally concerned with two concepts, Being and Value, and with the relationship between them. But his way of picturing the relationship is essentially his own. He sees the map of reality as a complex field of forces (ποικιλία δυνάμεων, 4. 4. 36. 9), kept in equilibrium by the everlasting interplay of two impulses, which he calls the Outgoing (πρόοδος) and the Return (ἐπιστροφή). For the Outgoing his favourite image is that of an expanding circle, whose radii all take their rise in the pure simplicity of an unextended and indivisible point and carry outwards towards the circumference a trace of that potent simplicity, which fades gradually as the circle expands, but is never wholly lost (4. 2. 1, etc.) We may think of the continuously expanding and continuously weakening circles of ripples that you get when you throw a stone into still water—save that here there is no stone-thrower, and no water either: reality *is the ripples* and there is nothing else. The unitary source and the weakening of its influence in successive emanations was the common assumption of the time. But there are three distinctive marks which differentiate this Plotinian Outgoing from other ancient theories of substance.

(i) It is a dynamic conception. For Plotinus all Being derives from the overspill of a single infinite reservoir of force, a reservoir which is, in Blake's language, not a cistern but a fountain, a δύναμις βυσσόθεν ἄπειρος (6. 5. 12. 5). And this initial dynamism communicates itself to all the subsequent levels of existence. The Platonic Forms are no mere static archetypes, as Aristotle mistakenly supposed (*Met.* 991^{b}4); δύναμις, creative potency, is the very stuff of their being (6. 4. 9). And the overspill continues in the sensible world: Nature, in Plotinus' homely metaphor, 'boils over with life' (ὑπερζεῖ ζωῇ, 6. 5. 12. 9); and life is at all levels a transmission of power.

(ii) The Plotinian theory is not a historical or mythological account of the *origin* of the universe. For Plotinus, the universe had no origin: there was never a time when the fountain did not overflow, just as there will never be a time when it runs dry. Causation is not an event: it is a relationship of timeless dependence by which the intelligible world is sustained in eternal being, the sensible world in a perpetual becoming comparable to the 'continuous creation' in which some astronomers now believe. This differentiates Plotinism from Jewish or Gnostic creation-myths, as well as from the kind of Platonism which took the *Timaeus* literally. It follows that creation is not for Plotinus the result of an act of will (5. 1. 6). The fountain overflows simply because it is its nature to do so, and all subsequent creation is similarly automatic and involuntary; the higher produces the lower as an incidental consequence of its own being.

(iii) This brings me to the third of my distinctive marks: the relationship between cause and effect is for Plotinus *non-reciprocating*: that is to say, the higher determines the lower without itself being determined or modified by its own causative activity; it communicates its own force, in a diminished degree, to its product, but itself suffers thereby no diminution of force, or change of any kind, any more than a man suffers change or diminution through casting a shadow. This doctrine perhaps originated in the Middle Stoa, which was concerned to give God a real place in the Stoic system over against the Cosmos. But it is in any case the essential feature which differentiates Plotinism from any kind of pantheism or pampsychism. Without it, the cause must eventually be exhausted by dissipation among its effects, the creative Unity swallowed up in the creation.

If this Outgoing, this timeless outward and downward impulse, stood alone in the system of Plotinus, with no inward and upward impulse to balance it, his universe would be a domain of rigid determinism—a mentalist determinism, it is true, and not a materialist one, but none the less crushing to the individual for that. Such a doctrine could have little appeal to a world that craved above all for 'salvation', that is, for the escape of the individual from the paralysing power of Heimarmenē. But the individual for Plotinus is more than the helpless product of a cosmic overflow: he is a creature possessed of will, and it is open to him to realize his true self—not by the assertion of an illusory independence, but by a voluntary self-identification with his source, a deliberate reversal of the Outgoing, in a word, by a Return. This possibility is not, in theory, confined to man: we are told that it is eternally exercised by the Divine Intelligence in relation to the One and by the World Soul in relation to the Intelligence. But it is plain that the only model for such a conception is to be found in human experience. Its germ appears in the *Phaedrus* myth, and in the well-known passage of the *Republic* about the 'turning round' of the eye of the soul; and it may have more immediate antecedents in Middle Stoicism, to judge by sayings like Seneca's 'sursum illum vocant initia sua' (*Epist.* 79. 12; cf. 65. 16). But for Plotinus it is the linchpin of the whole system: the value which Reality necessarily lost in the process of expansion or unfolding is restored to it again by the voluntary act of Return, without thereby annihilating the individuality which the expansive process is perpetually creating. He is thus enabled to reconcile freedom with necessity, and the reality and worth of the part with the unity of the whole.

Two distinctive marks are worth noticing, since they establish the difference between the Plotinian Return and the analogous doctrines of what has lately been called 'proletarian Platonism'[1] —the sort of thing that we find in the *Hermetica*, the *Chaldaean Oracles*, and many Gnostic systems. In the first place, the Plotinian Return of the soul, whether accomplished in this life or after death, is nothing but a turning inward, a recovery of the true self: it involves no spatial movement, no 'flight of the soul through the universe'; the soul's journey is a journey into the interior—ἥξει οὐκ εἰς ἄλλο, ἀλλ' εἰς ἑαυτήν (6. 9. 11. 38). And secondly, it depends neither on any secret knowledge (γνῶσις) nor on any specific act of divine grace, but simply on the soul's choice: as M. de Gandillac has put it, 'salvation is the work of the saved'.[2] The antithesis between Plotinian self-dependence and Gnostic or Christian 'grace' has indeed been attenuated, if not denied, by one of the subtlest of Plotinian scholars, M. Jean Trouillard,[3] but his argument leaves me unconvinced. No doubt the *capacity* to return is given in the Outgoing; and no doubt the One, like Aristotle's God, κινεῖ ὡς ἐρώμενον (6. 7. 31). But Plotinus assures us that the One does not need its products and would not care if it had *no* products (5. 5. 12); I have yet to find a text which suggests that it is interested in the salvation of the individual, or even aware of it.

III

I propose next to illustrate the way in which Plotinus' personal vision gives a new life and a new meaning to old concepts; and I shall choose as my example his treatment of the two Platonic worlds, the κόσμος νοητός and the κόσμος αἰσθητός. They are not,

[1] W. Theiler in *Recherches sur la tradition platonicienne* (Entretiens Hardt, tome 3), 78.
[2] M. de Gandillac, *La Sagesse de Plotin* (1952), 27.
[3] J. Trouillard, *La Purification plotinienne* (1955), 11, 125 ff.; cf. A. H. Armstrong, 'Salvation, Plotinian and Christian', *Downside Review* 1957, 126 ff., and H. Crouzel, *Bull. de litt. ecclés.* (Toulouse), 1956.

of course, locally distinct, since the κόσμος νοητός is not in space. I think we should not be wrong in saying with Bréhier[1] that for Plotinus the intelligible world *is* the sensible world minus its materiality (which includes its spatiality and its temporality). But this higher world is not to him an abstraction from the lower; it is more like what Bradley was to call a concrete universal, a totality of pure relations existing in its own right, of which the spatio-temporal κόσμος yields only a distorted image. To Plotinus this world was intensely real and he succeeds far better than Plato does in making it real to his readers.

He shows how temporal sequence is in such a world replaced by a timeless *totum simul*, in his own words 'a life whose every event is concentrated as it were in a single point, without fluxion' (3. 7. 3. 16–20), in fact, the ἐνέργεια ἀκινησίας which Aristotle attributed to his God (*E.N.* 1154^{b}27). And he also shows how the mutual exclusiveness of spatial relations is replaced by a system where the whole is implicitly present in each part and each part is potentially the whole, yet without loss of identity (5. 8. 4, etc.). We have, as he points out, a small-scale approximation to such a system in any well-articulated body of knowledge (5. 9. 6, cf. 4. 9. 5) and a still better one in a living organism, where each part implies the whole and the whole actuates each part (6. 7. 14). He owes something here to Plato's κοινωνία γενῶν; something to Aristotle's conception of organic unity; and something, finally, to the Stoics, who applied that conception to the sensible world as a whole. But he goes much beyond his 'sources' in forcing the reader to contemplate what such a world-picture would involve. Completely to think away the spatio-temporal vesture demands a sustained imaginative effort, and one which Plotinus insists on our making. We should begin, he says, by picturing a transparent luminous sphere, in which all the phenomena of the universe are visible simultaneously, yet without confusion or loss of identity. Keeping this before the mind's eye, we are then to construct a second sphere from which we must 'think away the extension and the spatial relations' (ἀφελεῖν τὸν ὄγκον καὶ τοὺς τόπους). And we must not yield to the temptation to make this second sphere merely a smaller copy of the first; if the effort defeats us, we are to invoke the help of that god who created the original (namely Nous)—and he will come,

---

[1] E. Bréhier, *La Philosophie de Plotin* (1928), 91.

says Plotinus, bringing his own world with him (5. 8. 9). This is very like the exercises in meditation prescribed by Indian and Christian mystics, and seems to indicate that in passing from διάνοια to νόησις we are really passing from scientific or logical to religious thought—that is, to pre-logical or post-logical thought.

The same highly personal quality may be seen in a celebrated passage (3. 8. 4) which deals with the origin of the sensible world. Plotinus imagines the philosopher interrogating Nature (φύσις) and asking her why she creates. She explains in reply that the sensible world is her θέαμα, her vision: 'For I inherit', says She, 'a taste for vision, and that which contemplates in me creates its own object of contemplation, as geometers when they contemplate draw lines. Only, I *draw* no lines: I merely contemplate, and the outlines of bodies take substance, as though they had fallen from my lap.' Plotinus goes on to say that Nature's contemplation is feeble and dreamlike, as compared with the contemplation of Nous or Psyche: that is why her product is the *last* product, incapable of reproducing itself in further worlds. With her, θεωρία, the characteristic activity of all Reality, has become so weak that it can express itself only in πρᾶξις, the making of something physical. 'In the same way', he adds, 'there are men too weak to contemplate, who find in action a shadow of contemplation . . . that with their eyes they may see what with their intelligence they could not.' The statesman and the artist, in fact, are philosophers *manqués*, who project their dream precisely because they cannot live it. And Nature, too, is a philosopher *manqué*, whose dream takes shape as an extended corporeal world just because it is not intense enough to exist otherwise. The degradation of πρᾶξις to an inferior substitute for θεωρία was, of course, in principle no novelty in the third century; it is the culmination of a long development which we can trace from the Pre-Socratics to Epicurus and beyond. What is distinctively Plotinian is the bold way in which this idea is transferred from man to the κόσμος, and used to furnish an answer to a characteristic third-century question, 'Why must there be a corporeal world?' In this as in other respects Plotinus' theory of the Real is a kind of Brocken spectre—the enlarged shadow cast on the screen of the universe by his theory of man. πάντα εἴσω, he says (3. 8. 6. 40), 'the sum of things is within us': if we wish to know the Real, we have only to look in ourselves.

IV

This self-exploration is the heart of Plotinism, and it is in the analysis of the Self that he made his most original discoveries, one or two of which I must briefly mention. He was apparently the first to make the vital distinction between the total personality (ψυχή) and the ego-consciousness (ἡμεῖς); in the *Enneads*, as Stenzel observed, 'the ego' becomes for the first time a philosophical term.[1] On this distinction between Psyche and ego his whole psychology hinges. For him the Psyche is, as Plato put it (*Tim.* 90 a), like a tree growing upside down, whose roots are in Heaven, but whose branches extend downwards into a physical body; its experience ranges through the entire gamut of Being, from the negative darkness of Matter to the divine darkness of the One. Man's personality is a continuum: there is not one part which is natural, another which is divine and comes from outside, like Aristotle's νοῦς θύραθεν; there is no sharp line between Psyche and Nous. But the ego-consciousness never covers the whole of this continuum: it fluctuates like a spotlight, embracing now a higher and now a lower sector; and as it fluctuates it creates an apparent, but not a real, break between the part of the continuum which is within the circle of consciousness and the part which is outside it. In ordinary life there fall below it the functions of the physiological life-principle which directly controls the body: not only are processes like breathing and digestion outside of conscious control and, normally, of conscious awareness, but Plotinus recognizes (anticipating Leibniz) that there are sensations which do not reach consciousness unless we specially direct attention to them (4. 4. 8; 5. 1. 12), and also (anticipating Freud) that there are desires which 'remain in the appetitive part and are unknown to us' (4. 8. 8. 9). The same is true of the permanent dispositions which result from past experiences or mental acts. Such dispositions, he says, can exert the strongest pull when we are least conscious of them: for when we know we have a disposition, we are aware of our distinctness from it; but when we have it without knowing it, we are apt, he observes, 'to be what we have' (4. 4. 4). This recognition that consciousness and mental life are not coextensive is

[1] J. Stenzel, *Metaphysik des Altertums* (1934), 191 (quoted by H. C. Puech, *Bull. de l'Assoc. Budé*, no. 61, 46).

surely one of his most important psychological insights, although for many centuries it was virtually ignored and its validity was eventually established through a quite different approach.¹

Plotinus is also, with Alexander of Aphrodisias, the first writer to formulate clearly the general idea of *self*-consciousness (συναίσθησις or παρακολούθησις ἑαυτῷ), the ego's awareness of its own activity.² Such awareness is not the same thing as self-knowledge, and Plotinus does not rate it very highly. He points out, correctly, that it is not necessary to effective action and is indeed often a hindrance to it. 'There is no need', he says, 'for one who is reading aloud to be aware that he is reading aloud, particularly when he reads with concentration; or for the doer of a gallant deed to know that he is acting gallantly.' Self-consciousness, he concludes, may easily weaken an activity: there is more intensity of life, because there is greater concentration, when we are not aware of what we are doing (1. 4. 10).

But neither the subconscious nor the self-conscious is so important to Plotinus as that tract of personality which lies *above* the ego-consciousness and beyond its everyday reach. Just as the self has a downward prolongation in the subconscious life-principle, so it has an upward prolongation in a higher form of mental life which is also for the most part outside our consciousness. In each of us, he believes, there is a secret 'inner man' who is timelessly engaged in νόησις (4. 8. 8; 5. 1. 12). The time-bound ego can by an effort of will identify itself with this inner man, and thus see things 'sub specie aeternitatis'; but since its normal life and function are in time, to time it must return. This doctrine was *not* traditional in the Platonic school: Plotinus says it was παρὰ δόξαν τῶν ἄλλων (4. 8. 8). It may have been suggested partly by personal experience, partly by the 'active Nous' of the *de anima*, which leads an unexplained existence somewhere in the depths of our being. But Plotinus has worked out the implications which Aristotle left so provokingly vague; and thanks

---

¹ Freud in fact recognized that knowledge of the Unconscious might be gained through mystical experience. 'Certain practices of the mystics may succeed in upsetting the normal relations between the different regions of the mind, so that, for example, the perceptual system becomes able to grasp relations in the deeper layers of the ego and in the id which would otherwise be inaccessible to it' (*New Introductory Lectures on Psychoanalysis*, trans. Sprott (1933), 106).

² On the history of these terms see the important paper by H.-R. Schwyzer in *Les Sources de Plotin* (1960).

to his distinction between psyche and ego he can do so without breaking the human mind in two, as Aristotle has been accused of doing. It is also this distinction which enables the Return to be achieved without the intervention of extraneous mediators (as in Philo, or in Gnosticism). The ego can apprehend the Platonic Forms because the Forms are already present in the structure of the psyche (ἐσμὲν ἕκαστος κόσμος νοητός, 3. 4. 3. 22). And because the hidden centre from which that structure springs coincides with the Centre of all things, the ego may hope at rare moments to achieve total unification, that is, to become God—'or rather', says Plotinus, 'to *be* God' (6. 9. 9. 50). The Pindaric γένοιο οἷος ἔσσι might be Plotinus' motto: for him ecstasy is but the momentary revelation of an eternal datum.[1]

I have kept to the last this doctrine of mystical union, though it is the first which every one associates with the name of Plotinus; for I thought it better to illustrate his originality from examples which may be less familiar to the non-specialist. And in fact this topic does not bulk very large in his collected writings: out of more than 800 Teubner pages, perhaps twenty or thirty touch on it. Nevertheless they are, of course, important pages. That they have their source in personal experience no reader could doubt, even if we lacked the explicit testimony of Porphyry (*vit. Plot.* 23. 14 ff.) and, indeed, of Plotinus himself (4. 8. 1). And it is legitimate to ask what influence Plotinus' experience had on his philosophy, even if we can give no confident answer. There is, I think, some danger of conceiving this influence in too specific a way. Plotinus did not invent the One because he had experienced unification. The *term* τὸ ἕν was given in the tradition; the *concept* can be reached, and by Plotinus most often *is* reached, through a purely philosophical argument, an argument from the existence of the relative to the necessity of an Absolute which has often been repeated since—it is, for example, much like Bradley's contention that 'the relational form implies a substantial totality beyond relations and above them'.[2] What the experience of unification seems to do is to give the assurance that the outcome of this regressive dialectic is no hollow abstraction, that the minus signs of the *via negativa* are in reality plus signs, since this

---

[1] Cf. Puech, op. cit. 45.
[2] F. H. Bradley, *Appearance and Reality* (1893), 160.

experience, as Professor Armstrong has said, 'carries with it an implied judgment of value, which is instantaneous, without deliberation, and impersonal'.[1] It is, as it were, the experimental verification of the abstract proposition that the One is the Good; for to experience unification is to experience the highest of all forms of life, ζωὴν ἀρίστην ἐνεργεῖν (4. 8. 1. 4).

But if the experience in this sense confirmed the system, it is also likely that the system in turn influenced the interpretation of the experience. I am reminded of a sensible remark which Joyce Cary put in the mouth of one of his characters: 'Mysticism is not a religion; it is a temperament.'[2] It is a temperament which has appeared, sporadically, in many different cultures and has proved compatible with a wide variety of beliefs. It is no doubt 'un-Hellenic' in the simple sense that most Greeks (like most Englishmen) did not have it; but Plotinus, who did have it, has subjected it to the discipline of Hellenic rationalism. The technique of attainment is not for him physiological or magical, but intellectual. He prescribes no breathing exercises, no navel-brooding, no hypnotic repetition of sacred syllables. Nor would he have agreed with the view expressed by Aldous Huxley that 'the habit of analytical thought is fatal to the intuitions of integral thinking'.[3] On the contrary, the habit of analytical thought is to Plotinus a necessary and valuable discipline, a κάθαρσις in which the mind must be exercised before it attempts what Huxley calls 'integral thinking' (1. 3. 4). Mystical union is not a substitute for intellectual effort, but its crown and goal. Nor is it a substitute for moral effort. It is the presence of ἀρετή and φρόνησις, he says, that reveals God to us; 'without true virtue all talk of God is but words' (2. 9. 15. 38). And finally, the unitive experience is in his system a *natural* event, not a supernatural grace as in Christian mysticism. The human spirit is not replaced by another, as in Philo or in Montanism, where ecstasy is a kind of possession. In Plotinus, the self is not obliterated but regained; he sees the experience as an 'awakening to myself' (4. 8. 1. 1). Nor does this divine self await *liberation*, as in Gnosticism; it awaits only discovery—there is no 'drama of redemption'. In all

[1] A. H. Armstrong, *Architecture of the Intelligible Universe in the Philosophy of Plotinus* (1940), 46.
[2] Joyce Cary, *An American Visitor* (1933), 151 [Carfax edition].
[3] Aldous Huxley, *The Perennial Philosophy* (1946), 27.

these ways Plotinus remains a genuine Hellenist.¹ His account of mystical union is the most intimately personal of his achievements; but it is the achievement of a mind nourished in the classical Greek tradition and determined to preserve the integrity of that tradition against the intrusion of alien modes of thought.

¹ Paul Friedländer has overlooked this in the contrast which he draws between 'Platonism' and 'mysticism' (*Plato* i. 77 ff., English ed.) and is thus led to exaggerate the difference of outlook between Plotinus and Plato.

IX

The Religion of the Ordinary Man in Classical Greece[1]

WHAT I propose to talk about is the place of religion in the daily life of the ordinary Greek. I remember that when I was in the sixth form myself, and indeed for years after that, my notions on this subject were extremely vague and confused, and I suspect that many young students today are not much clearer about it. This is no accident—there are reasons for it. One reason is that very few Englishmen, and scarcely any schoolboys, have personal experience of any form of religion other than the contemporary version of Christianity; and whoever tries to measure ancient religion by Christian yardsticks will either deceive himself or retire baffled. There are large areas of Christian experience which have no true counterpart in the classical age of Greece. For example, the concepts of sin and redemption, central in Christianity, are simply missing from the vocabulary of that age: there are plenty of words for guilt and wrongdoing, but if we translate them 'sin' we nearly always import a false implication. Or take the love of God. Aristotle denies that there can be such a thing as *philia* between man and God, the disparity being too great; and in the *Magna Moralia* one of his pupils remarks that it would be eccentric (*atopon*) for anyone to claim that he loved Zeus.[2] Classical Greece had in fact no word for such an emotion: *philotheos* makes its appearance

---

[1] A talk addressed to the sixth form at Marlborough College, 1965.

[2] Aristotle, *E.N.* 1159ª4; *M.M.* 1208ᵇ30. Personal or group devotion to a particular deity, like the devotion of Odysseus to Athene or Hippolytus to Artemis, certainly existed; but I can find little evidence that 'Zeus' or 'the gods' or 'the Divine' evoked feelings of affection. The formal invocation 'Dear Zeus' does occasionally occur, e.g. in the seemingly ancient ritual prayer for rain quoted by Marcus Aurelius (5. 7). But was it a mark of personal devotion? Theognis uses it once (373), but the tone there is hardly devout: it politely introduces a protest, as 'My dear Sir' so often does in English.

[3] Despite L.S.J., the much commoner *theophiles* seems never to have an active sense.

for the first time at the end of the fourth century and remains a rarity in pagan authors.

This then is one difficulty: to try to understand Greek religion is to enter a world of alien experience; the price of entry is that we should unthink twenty centuries of Christian thinking. But there is another, an even more fundamental obstacle. Every religion has two aspects, an outward aspect and an inward one. Its outward aspect is ritual—a series of traditionally prescribed actions and utterances such as prayer, sacrifice, thanksgiving, the recital or re-enactment of sacred stories. or the repetition of sacred formulas. Most rituals are collective, performed by a family, a local community, or an entire society; some of them are for special occasions such as birth, death, marriage, others recur at fixed intervals like Christmas and Easter. About some though not all of the ancient Greek rituals we happen to be relatively well informed, thanks in part to inscriptions, in part to the zealous antiquarianism of the Alexandrine scholars. But what did these ritual acts *mean* to those who took part in them? Viewed from within, religion is a state of mind, a complex of beliefs and feelings about the forces which govern man's life and situate it in the world. Such states of mind are personal and infinitely various. The same ritual behaviour can mean very different things to different people, as we see in the practice of Christianity today; and if it persists unchanged in outward form through many generations, its inner meaning may sometimes change almost beyond recognition. But how then shall we recover the beliefs and feelings of persons long dead, the vast majority of whom have left us no report of what they thought and felt? We find in extant Greek literature plenty of theological speculation, but hardly anything which reads like a direct record of personal religious experience: the Classical age has left us no counterpart of Augustine or of Kierkegaard. In this sense the inner side of Greek religion escapes us; we can study it only in its external, collective aspect, as a social phenomenon. And even about the beliefs implied in collective acts it is hard to speak with any confidence.

The citizen of a Greek state was required by custom to perform certain minimum religious duties; but he was not required to subscribe to a specific creed, and could not be, since no such creed existed in the sense of having been formulated and written down. A collective creed can be formulated only where you have a recognized religious authority—either a body of traditional writings believed to be divinely inspired, in other words a Bible, or else an organized professional priesthood, in other words a Church. But the Greeks had neither a Bible nor a Church. The familiar saying that Homer was 'the Bible of the Greeks' is true only in the sense that Homer's influence on the development of Greek literature and of Greek education may be compared to the influence of the Authorized Version on English literature and on English education. The Homeric poems were never regarded as a Sacred Book: you could think as you pleased about what Pindar so frankly called 'Homer's lies';[1] no one ever went to the stake or suffered, so far as I know, even the mildest social disapproval for disbelieving Homer. The nearest thing to a Sacred Book that classical Greece knew was the Orphic poems; but these were not canonical, and there is no evidence that they were in fact taken seriously at any period by more than a small minority of the population.

Priests, of course, they did have. But the priests were not organized into anything that we should call a Church, nor were they bound together by a common training, a common rule of life, or common professional interests. To hold a priesthood was seldom a full-time occupation, and no special preparation was required for it: 'Any man', says the orator Isocrates, 'is thought qualified to be a priest.'[2] Nor does it seem to have been a matter of vocation, of an inward call: some priesthoods were hereditary in particular families; others were filled by election, or even by drawing lots (which was considered a way of leaving the choice to God); and in many places, even as early as the fifth century B.C., you could *buy* a priesthood, just as an English doctor used to be able to buy a practice. Finally, many priesthoods were tenable only for a year—which is a sure proof of amateur status. Evidently the motley collection of people who acquired in these various ways the honourable title of 'priest' would have no common doctrine or common policy.

There was thus no authority in Greece capable of formulating the articles of a national creed, and no authoritative Scripture

---

[1] *Nem.* 7. 23.
[2] *Ad Nic.* 6. Plato, *Laws* 759 c–d, would require only that a priest should be a legitimate member of an unpolluted family and aged over sixty.

on which to base it. There was not even any clear line, such as Christian culture drew, between 'religious' and 'profane' literature. All that Greek literature offers us is the opinions of *individuals*, and in particular the opinions of a long line of highly individual poets and philosophers, from Hesiod to Plotinus, about the nature of the Divine and man's relationship to it. Most of the older books on Greek religion were mainly devoted to listing and examining these opinions. But we must not think that to study the theological views of great men is the same thing as studying Greek religion. And we must beware especially of attributing to a timeless and unlocated phantom, called '*the* Greek', what were in fact the highly personal judgements of some man of genius, an Aeschylus or a Plato. Consider what a fantastic caricature would result if some future historian set out to reconstruct the religion of *the* Englishman from a comparative study of *Paradise Lost*, the philosophy of Berkeley, and the poems of William Blake.

With no Church or Bible to impose even superficial uniformity, the gap between the beliefs of the thinking minority and the beliefs of the people must have been a pretty wide one. Ancient Greece had no system of universal education, and even in fifth-century Athens there must have been a great mass of illiterate or semi-literate people who got their religious ideas mainly from oral tradition. The educated class, on the other hand, would naturally be affected by the traditional poetry which they read at school, and especially by Homer, even though they were not bound to believe all they read. But what Homer transmitted to them was in the main a soldier's creed, the religious beliefs of a fighting aristocracy. The court of Zeus on Olympus is a sort of Brocken spectre, a magnified reflection or 'projection' of the court of an Achaean High King on earth, and the gods who matter in Homer are the gods who can protect your vitals from the impact of an enemy spear. The Homeric picture of the gods has caught the imagination of the world, but it bears no close relation to the actual practice of religion as we know it in the Classical age. Homer ignored—it would seem deliberately—a whole body of ritual behaviour and religious or magical ideas which we have reason to think are very old, probably much older than Homer. He ignored them, but he did not succeed in killing them. They lived on in the actions and thoughts of the people, and they keep cropping up in later literature: in Hesiod, in the dramatists, in the orators, even in Plutarch and Pausanias, we find reference to many religious acts and beliefs which almost certainly antedate Homer. For these reasons the Homeric poems are on the whole a bad place to look for the basic elements of Greek religion as it affected the everyday life of the masses.

We seem thus to be driven back upon the study of Greek ritual, external as this is. Much of our evidence about it comes from late writers and late inscriptions, but that is less of a drawback than one might suppose. While myths are liable to change their form every time they are retold, the astonishing thing about ritual is its fixity, its stubborn conservatism. Although the Aegean world has passed through two great religious changes, from Minoan to Classical Greek religion and from Classical Greek religion to Christianity, there are actually cult practices which have survived *both* these changes. Let me give you a small instance. At harvest festivals in the Greek Church today they use a peculiar type of vessel consisting of a set of little cups and candle-holders attached to a common base like a modern cruet, the cups being filled with corn, wine, olive oil, and other country produce. This same vessel and its use for the same purpose, to contain harvest offerings, was described in the Hellenistic age by the antiquarian Polemon, who calls it a *kernos*.[1] And now actual examples of *kernoi* have been dug up, not only in the *agora* at Athens and elsewhere in Mainland Greece, but in Cretan graves some of which date back to the Early Minoan age. One could not wish for a better instance of the timelessness of ritual usage. And this particular usage is associated with such a simple and natural and almost universal religious act—the offering of first-fruits to the Powers that gave them—that in this case at least we can make a guess at the feelings of the countryman who carried the *kernos* in Minoan or in Classical times; we may suppose that they were not so very different from the feelings of the man who cultivates the same fields today and celebrates his harvest-home with the same ritual act.

Another example of this conservatism is the continuity of holy ground. The Minoans and Mycenaeans built no temples to their gods. Their places of worship seem to have been of two types: on the one hand palace shrines like the one at Knossos,

[1] Quoted by Athenaeus, 11. 476 f.

which appear to be the private chapels of Minoan kings; on the other, caves in the mountains and walled enclosures on mountain tops. Both these types have left descendants in the Classical world. The Hall of the Mysteries at Eleusis was built on the site of a Mycenaean palace and went by the name of 'the King's House'; it is a fair inference that the first Mysteries were the private mysteries of a Mycenaean royal family. The sacredness of caves continued too: one need only recall the cave of the Nymphs in the *Odyssey* and the Corycian cave on Mount Parnassus. And the holiness of mountain tops has lasted to this day, though they have twice changed ownership: they were taken over first by Zeus the Cloud-gatherer, the Indo-European weather god, and then by the Christian weather god, the prophet Elijah who gives his name to so many Greek mountains. In England we speak of *consecrated* ground: the place is holy because a church has been built on it. In Greece it was, and is, the other way round: you build a temple, or a church, because the place is holy. Both Delos and Delphi, for example, were holy ground before ever Apollo came there. And only recently I came across a pleasing minor instance. There was a holy spring near Nauplia in which the goddess Hera used to bathe once a year in order to renew her virginity. That spring still exists, and it appears that its waters still keep their miraculous power—for it stands today in the garden of a nunnery.

These continuities in Greek religious life rest ultimately, I suppose, on the continuity of their economic and social life. The majority of Greeks have always got their living directly or indirectly from the land, as they still do, and their religious outlook is conditioned by that fact. The Greek towns of the Classical age were very small by modern standards (many an independent 'city' was no bigger than Salisbury or even Stratford) and to a large extent their inhabitants retained the customs and interests and ways of thinking which belong to the countryside. It was only in post-Classical times, with the growth of great cities like Alexandria and Antioch, that real urbanization set in; where that happened, it did fundamentally alter the basis of social life and therefore of religious life too. But in the Classical age the pattern of communal religion everywhere was still mainly set by the pattern of the farmer's year, which has gone on with little change through the centuries all over the Mediterranean world.

It is a pattern of anxiety punctuated by relief, and it repeats itself every year in much the same form. The anxiety is always there, but every year it mounts to a crisis at certain crucial periods: at seedtime, when the precious grain is committed to the earth (the Greeks do their main sowing in autumn, about the end of October); and again in the spring, when the farmer measures the dwindling store in his barns and worries about the yield of the coming harvest—for spring, as the poet Alcman unpoetically defined it, is the season when 'things are growing but there is not enough to eat'.[1] Then follow the stages of the harvest: cutting in most parts of Greece is at the end of May, threshing in June, vintage in late September. If it is a good harvest the farmer's year ends in relief and thanksgiving, only to begin again with the October sowing and a fresh crisis of anxiety. It is a pattern of endless recurrence, unchanging through the generations of men.

This pattern was the foundation of the Greek religious calendar: the annually recurrent alternations of anxiety and relief found expression in annually recurrent collective religious acts, carried out by the whole of the local community. The detail of the ritual varied somewhat in different parts of Greece; the examples I shall give are taken from Attica. There the anxiety of seedtime had its outlet in the linked festivals of the Skira in late June and the Thesmophoria in late October, whose central rite was an attempt to reinforce the Earth's creative power at a critical period. On the former occasion certain objects symbolic of fertility, including some live pigs, were thrown into a pit; on the latter their decayed remains were ceremoniously fetched up again, 'and people believe', says our informant, 'that if you mix these remains with your seedcorn you will have a good harvest'.[2] It sounds like compost-making, but actually it is sympathetic magic of the simplest kind. The rite was performed by women only. That *could* be a survival from the Stone Age, before the invention of the plough, when agriculture is thought to have been exclusively women's work. But an easier explanation is suggested by the well-known answer the bishop gave to the feminist lady who demanded to know what difference there was between the sexes—'Madam, I cannot conceive.' Women can, in which,

[1] Frag. 76 Bergk.   [2] Schol. Lucian, pp. 275 f. Rabe.
[3] *Menexenus* 238 a.

as Plato says, 'they imitate the Earth'.³ At the Thesmophoria they tried to persuade the Earth to imitate *them*.

To relieve the spring anxiety the Athenians had the Anthesteria in February, when the new wine was solemnly opened and every one, slaves as well as hired men, had a good drink. It was an occasion for gaiety and social relaxation after the strain and isolation of winter on the farm. But it seems to have included also a sort of spiritual spring-cleaning, a purging away of the evil influences which had accumulated during the winter and might endanger the coming harvest if not suitably dealt with. It was thought prudent at this time to chew buckthorn, a plant both medically and magically purgative, just as the modern Greek peasant on Clean Monday, the first day of the eastern Lent, chews garlic and onion 'to blow the Devil out of his body'.¹ It was also customary to smear the doorway with pitch, to catch any evil spirits who might try to slip into the house; for evil spirits, as we see them in the vase paintings, were mostly pictured as nasty little flying things, somewhat like mosquitoes to look at. Furthermore, the Anthesteria included a sort of All Souls' Day: it was the occasion when the dead were allowed to revisit their old homes for one day and were entertained with a *panspermia*, a dish of gruel made from all the crops of the year. That too was, in part at least, fertility magic: 'From the dead', says a fourth-century writer, 'come growth and increase and seeds.'² The custom is still alive today; the *panspermia* is still offered in churchyards at the beginning of Lent.

Then there were the summer meetings for thanksgiving after harvest. There were several of these, for the several different harvests; as Aristotle remarked,³ the summer was the favourite time for farmer's festivals, because there was then most leisure on the farm. As you would expect, they included a dedication of firstfruits. They also included something almost as familiar to us—processions of children carrying a ritual object from door to door, wishing good luck to the household in return for small donations. In this worldwide custom all that varies is the ritual object. With us it is 'a penny for the Guy'; when I saw it done in China it was 'a penny for the dragon'; in ancient Greece it was 'a penny for Eiresione'. Eiresione was an olive or laurel

---

¹ Kevin Andrews, *The Flight of Ikaros* (1959), 211.
² [Hipp.] *de victu* 4. 92.   ³ *E.N.* 1160ª25.

branch, hung with cakes and figs and other firstfruits, and also with woollen threads to show its sacredness. But Eiresione was at the same time an old woman, as we see from the song the children sang, which Plutarch[1] has recorded:

> Eiresione brings
> All good things,
> Figs and rich cakes to eat,
> Oil for your toilet and a pint of honey sweet,
> And a cup of wine, strong and deep,
> That she may get tipsy and go to sleep.

'She' means Eiresione, the green branch which is also the harvest spirit. And when the festival is over, Eiresione stands at the door of the farmhouse until next year's festival comes round and a fresh one is made.

The reader may very well ask what all this elementary farmers' magic has to do with real religion. My answer would be that simple people are commonly unaware of any distinction in principle between religion and magic, and that in fact their religion very often grows out of their magic; the magical act becomes religious when it is incorporated in an order of divine service and interpreted as a symbolic aid to prayer. So it was in ancient Greece. The pitching of pigs into a pit was doubtless originally intended not as a sacrifice to a personal goddess but as a piece of magical direct action; it was raised, however, to the religious level when it became part of an earnest supplication addressed to the goddess Demeter, who gives us our daily bread. Similarly the Greek All Souls' Day with its ghosts and gruel may once have been independent of any god, but in historical times it was attached to a festival of Dionysus and thus acquired a religious character. But the clearest case of such development from magic to religion is the Eleusinian Mysteries, which were rooted in agricultural magic yet undoubtedly aroused deep and sincere feelings of a kind that we can only call religious.

The Mysteries were celebrated at the beginning of October, just before the autumn sowing, when the seedcorn is brought up from the underground silos in which it has lain hidden through the summer (that seems to be what is meant by the *anodos* of Kore, the 'resurrection' of the Corn-maiden). And although

---

[1] *Theseus* 22. My version is adapted with a few changes from Jane Harrison's *Prolegomena to the Study of Greek Religion* (2nd edn., 1908), 80.

the agricultural magic has been overlaid with other things, traces survive which show the original purpose of the rite. ὗε, the worshippers cried, looking up at the sky, and then κύε, looking down to the earth:[1] it was a prayer in two words for rain to swell the seed. And if we can believe Hippolytus[2] the final vision granted to the initiates was even simpler: it consisted in nothing more than 'an ear of corn reaped in silence'. (Hippolytus is a suspect witness, being a Christian Father. But the very simplicity of his statement suggests that it may perhaps be correct; invention would surely have hit on something more sensational.) The rebirth of the corn, however, was linked with a divine rebirth, possibly preceded by a sacred marriage: every year at Eleusis a god was born, and Hippolytus preserves the archaic formula in which the hierophant announced the event—ἱερὸν ἔτεκε πότνια κοῦρον Βριμὼ Βριμόν, 'A Holy Child is born to Our Lady, Brimos to Brimo.' We do not know who Brimo and Brimos were,[3] but we may guess them to be primitive titles or counterparts of Demeter and her child Ploutos, the Wealth that springs from Corn.

Here magic already leads over into religion. But there is more than that. There is the famous promise to the initiates: 'Blessed is he, whoever of men upon earth has seen these things; but whoever is uninitiated in these rites, he has always a different portion down in the murky darkness when he is dead.'[4] Here, in language discreetly vague, we have the earliest European statement of a religious dogma which has had a long though not very creditable history—the dogma that salvation in the next world depends on taking part in certain rituals in this one. It goes back at least to the seventh century, how much further we do not at present know (it could be Mycenaean, it could also be a product of the Greek Archaic Age). In any case it made Eleusis one of the world's greatest religious centres throughout Classical and post-Classical times.

I have talked so far about festivals, which were *collective* acts of worship. But there was also, of course, private and family worship. In most Greek homes you would find a small altar where little offerings were made for the protection of the house-

---

[1] Proclus, *in Tim*. 3. 176. 28. The ritual of the πλημοχόαι (Athen. 496 a) had presumably a like purpose.   [2] *Ref*. omn. *haer*. 5. 8. 39.
[3] The equation of Brimo with Hecate (schol. Apoll. Rhod. 3. 861) looks to be late and secondary.   [4] [Hom.] *Hymn. ad Dem*. 480 ff.

hold. It might be dedicated to Hestia, the hearth goddess, or to Zeus Ktesios, the protector of property, or just to Agathos Daimon, a sort of general guardian angel. It was the centre of family worship, the humble successor of the Minoan palace shrines; its own successor today is the holy ikon which is to be seen in every Greek cottage. Hesiod prescribes the equivalent of morning and evening prayers at such an altar: at sunrise, and again at bedtime, the farmer must offer wine and incense to the undying gods, 'that their hearts and feelings may be gracious towards you, so that you shall buy another man's land and not another man yours'.[1] Observe the strictly personal and practical motive. When man begins to reflect on his own religious behaviour he usually rationalizes it in terms of economic advantage—*do ut des*, as the Latin formula puts it. And he is of course partly right, but I think only partly, for no religion is quite so simple and quite so rational as that.

Besides these small daily offerings the farmer should, when he can afford it, offer the gods their traditional dinner of thigh-bones burnt with fat. It was a poor sort of dinner, as the Greeks knew very well: a god in a Greek comedy complains that he gets a helping suitable only for a dog.[2] There had to be a story to explain it, the story of the trick Prometheus played on Zeus. But it satisfied the essential: it was a sharing of what you had, and no one thought of killing an animal for food without offering the gods their bit. Hesiod also recommends prayers for special occasions. The autumn ploughing should not begin without a prayer to Demeter and 'the underworld Zeus'[3] (not the Indo-European weather god but the old earth god, who is called 'Zeus' by analogy because he is King among the dead). Again, you must not cross a river 'with your badness and your hands unwashed':[4] before traversing the ford you must wash your hands and pray, just as the Greek peasant today will cross himself before he fords a stream. Greek rivers are not tame things like our sluggish English ones; they are savage, violent, incalculable, and must be treated with respect. And rivers were only one of the hazards. Much of Greece is frightening country even today,

---

[1] *Works and Days* 338 ff. Cf. Plato, *Laws* 887 e.
[2] Pherecrates, frag. 23 Kock.   [3] *Works and Days* 465.
[4] Ibid. 740. The text is odd and disputed, but the requirement of clean hands is certain.

Man in Classical Greece

because Nature is so much stronger in it than Man; the isolated farms are such tiny patches in an almost trackless wilderness of stone and scrub. It is easy to lose your way there, and the ancient farmer would not venture far from home without a prayer to Hermes the Waygod, who perhaps gets his name from the *hermata*, the cairns that serve to mark a trail in wild country.

In such places there were also other, less material dangers. You might meet something half-bestial, half-daemonic, a centaur or a satyr. You might meet Pan himself, as Philippides did the day he ran from Athens to Sparta;[1] and although Pan has his uses as a promoter of fertility, he also has his unpleasant side, as our English word 'panic' still testifies. Worst of all, you might meet a nymph and so become *numpholēptos*, 'nymph-struck', crazy. If that happened, your only hope of recovery was to make a handsome offering at the local nymph-cavern (for the nymphs have always lived in caves since the days of Odysseus). There is a cave in Attica which shows evidence of a continuous worship of Pan and the nymphs over something like 2,000 years, from Mycenaean down to Christian times. Indeed, in some places the cult has lasted almost to our own day: in Corfu the nymphs were still getting offerings of milk and honey late in the nineteenth century, exactly as they did in the days of Theocritus, and perhaps they still are. Country habits are tenacious—the nymphs have long outlived Zeus and Apollo. And they still have a Queen, as they already had in Homer's time. Nowadays she is called only the Great Lady, or the Lady Fair, but once her name was Artemis, and many centuries earlier still, in Crete, men may have known her as Britomart.[2] She is the Queen of the untamed wilderness and the mistress of animals; her earliest portraits show her standing posed between two great heraldic beasts.

In addition to the dangers of the farm and the dangers of the wilderness our ancient Greek had of course to face the great critical moments of the individual life—birth, puberty, marriage, death. And for each of these he had ceremonies which gave them dignity and provided a measure of reassurance by placing them in the framework of traditional religion. To examine these in detail would be too long a task; but something must be said about Greek attitudes to the dead. There are several sorts of

---

[1] Herodotus 6. 105.   [2] Hesychius s.v. Βριτόμαρτις.

dead people. There are in the first place the dead of one's own family. To these one has a duty: they expect to be fed at regular intervals; neglect may cause the crops to fail. This custom has gone on since Neolithic times and still goes on today. It is not 'ancestor worship'; it is simply a way of feeling that the dead are not quite dead, since they still need our care. They are fed in fact for much the same reasons that cause a little girl to feed her doll, but the fantasy is taken seriously because it is psychologically useful—it eases the pain of bereavement. In Classical times the family dead lived on *choai*, a mixture of oil, honey, and water, which was poured on the grave or even into a feeding-tube placed in the dead man's mouth. Such tubes can still be seen in cemeteries in Turkey and parts of the Balkans; fantasy can be very literal-minded. This sort of behaviour was unaffected by the Homeric belief that the dead are in Hades, just as it is unaffected today by the belief that they are in Heaven.

Besides the family dead there is also the nameless general host of the dead. As we saw, these had their annual outing at the Anthesteria; and once a month loaves of bread were put out for them at the cross-roads. But still the poor souls were hungry: Aristophanes; mentions the belief that you should not sweep up the crumbs that fall under the table, you should leave them for the souls. In general, people's feelings about the dead seem to have held more of compassion than of fear, though no doubt there was something of both. One kind of ghost, however, was definitely dangerous—the ghosts of those who had met a violent and/or untimely end. Such ghosts had been cheated of their proper portion of life, and therefore bore a grudge against the living. Hence the practice in such cases of mutilating or chaining the corpse to keep it from walking, just as down to 1823 English law prescribed that a stake be driven through the body of a suicide. That explains why Agamemnon's corpse was mutilated, and why chained skeletons are sometimes found in Early Bronze Age graves. As late as the nineteenth century such things were occasionally done: Lawson[2] described the mutilation said to have been practised upon the victim of a ritual murder on the island of Thera at the time of the Greek War of Independence.

[1] Frag. 305 Kock.
[2] J. C. Lawson, *Modern Greek Folklore and Ancient Greek Religion* (1910), 340 f., 435 f.

Finally, there were the 'Heroes', whom the Greeks believed—rightly in the main—to be a special class of dead men. The Heroes were the ghosts of the *mighty* dead, princes of old, who because they had been powerful in life were powerful still. 'Hero tombs', that is to say, the conspicuous graves of Mycenaean chieftains, were scattered up and down the Greek countryside, and at some of them offerings were continuously made from Mycenaean down into Classical times. It was probably from the cult at these tombs, aided by a dim popular memory of the Mycenaean greatness, that the peculiar Greek notion of the Hero developed, though some fully historical persons were also later 'heroized'. The cult of the Hero differed from the ordinary tendance of the family dead only in its greater lavishness and in its communal character: a Hero belonged to the whole local community, and he got a hot meat dinner in place of the usual slops. In return, he protected the community in peace and war, as the local saint does today. But his territory was restricted: he could operate only where his bones were; they acted as a sort of talisman. Hence several amusing cases of public bone-snatching, like the translation of the relics of medieval saints. A Hero was usually friendly to his own people, but if annoyed he could turn dangerous: he could haunt; he could cause epilepsy or madness; you were advised to pass his tomb very quietly, lest trouble come of it.

It may surprise the reader that I have talked about nymphs and Heroes, and have mentioned some of the gods of the countryside, but have said little or nothing about Zeus and Apollo and Athena. These are in an especial sense the gods of the cities, the gods of the State cult, to whom great temples were built as monuments of civic pride and patriotism. They were of course honoured in the countryside as well. Yet I have a feeling that a picnic at the local shrine of Pan, like the one represented by Menander in the *Dyskolos*, probably meant more to the average countryman, even in Attica,[1] than the grand ceremonies of the official religion. The ordinary Greek, like the ordinary Italian, has inclined throughout history to regard the High Gods as too

[1] It is significant that in the recently discovered calendar of annual sacrifices at the Attic village of Erchia (G. Daux, *Bulletin de Correspondance Hellénique*, 87 (1963), 603 ff.) nearly half of those listed are offered to no Olympian deity but to a menagerie of heroes, daemons, and obscure godlings like the Kourotrophos and the Tritopatores.

remote and too awe-inspiring to be the object of direct appeal in the petty troubles of human life. He needs a more intimate and more accessible Divine Helper. In time of doubt or danger his thoughts are likely to turn not to any member of the Christian Trinity but to the Panagia, the Blessed Virgin, or to some well-tried and reliable saint—preferably a local saint, who can be trusted to protect his own, or else his personal name-saint, whose picture hangs in a little shrine in his house.

It was not otherwise in Antiquity. The Classical Greek for 'God save us!' is not ὦ Ζεῦ, it is 'Ἡράκλεις. That was the standard reaction to any alarming or startling piece of news. Heracles was the most immediately accessible of Helpers. You could count on his sympathy, for he had once been a man himself and had plenty of human weaknesses. But you could also count on his strength: no monster or bogey had ever been able to stand up to Heracles. That is why when a Greek built himself a house he would, at least in later times, put up a warning to spiritual trespassers: 'Heracles the invincible, the son of Zeus, lives in this house: let no wicked thing enter it.' It was like saying to the demons 'Beware of the bull!' The practice was taken over, with the necessary changes, by nervous Christian householders. A Christian amulet of the sixth century A.D. has the formula: 'Let no wicked reptile or uncanny thing enter this house: holy Phocas lives here.' The Christian saint has taken over the police duties of the pagan Hero.[1]

There were many other Divine Helpers, for whom I can find no room in this brief talk. Every trade and profession had its own tutelary god or half-god—Hephaestus for smiths, Prometheus for potters, the Dioscuri for sailors, Asclepius for physicians, and so on—who received special cult from the members of their guild and in return stood ready to intervene at need on their behalf. Cities also had their own protecting deities, towards whom their people felt a relationship of special devotion and special trust. Despite what I said just now about the remoteness of the greater gods, for many Athenians their city goddess must have been an exception; indeed, it is perhaps in the religion of Athena that faith in God comes nearest to replacing fear of God as the strongest emotional component. Solon believed that

[1] For other examples see L. Robert, 'Échec au Mal', *Hellenica*, 13 (1965), 265-71.

while the protecting hands of Athena were stretched above her city, Athens could not perish save by the fault and folly of her citizens.[1] Aeschylus had the same faith, as we see in the last scene of the *Eumenides*: 'Whom the wings of Pallas shelter, her Father cherishes.'[2] Athena was both a powerful protectress in her own right and a powerful intercessor with the still greater deity from whom she sprang.

What of that greater deity, who stands at the apex of the polytheist pyramid? The development of the religion of Zeus is no part of my present subject; it belongs to the history of Greek thought. It was the intellectuals and not the people who took the old loose-living weather god, himself as fickle as the weather, and attempted to transform him, first of all into an embodiment of divine justice, and then into a symbol of that ultimate Maker and Father of All Things who, as Plato said, is hard to know and if known impossible to explain to all and sundry. Our debt to the Greek intellectuals is very great: it is to them, almost as much as to the Jews, that we owe our own partial emergence from the magical phase of religion. But they and their ideas are outside the scope of this talk. All I have tried to do is to convey by a few examples some notion of the place religion occupied in the daily life and thoughts of ordinary unintellectual men in the centuries between Homer and Menander.

[1] Frag. 4. 1 ff. Bergk.   [2] *Eum.* 1001 f. Cf. above, p. 62.

X

Supernormal Phenomena in Classical Antiquity[1]

THIS paper is concerned with the point of intersection of two interests which have been with me through most of my working life—curiosity about the religious ideas of Classical Antiquity and curiosity about those oddities of human experience which form the subject-matter of psychical research or, to use a more pretentious word, 'parapsychology'. I am not the first to combine these two interests. Among the pioneers who in 1882 founded the Society for Psychical Research the leading spirit was a classical scholar, Frederic Myers; and important contributions were made to the new studies by scholars like Andrew Lang, Mrs. A. W. Verrall, and Professor Gilbert Murray. In these circumstances a question naturally presented itself: did the contemporary phenomena which were now for the first time subjected to serious examination reflect any fresh light upon the field of ancient religious beliefs and practices? The question was raised by Myers in his essay on Greek Oracles[2] and by Lang in a paper on 'Ancient Spiritualism';[3] both writers answered it with a confident—perhaps too confident—affirmative. But since their day there has been little scholarly attempt to approach the problems of ancient religion from this particular angle. Jejune and obviously second-hand ancient material, torn from its context of thought and interpreted in the light of the author's prepossessions, continues to figure in the various popular and semipopular 'histories of occultism' and the like. On the other hand serious students of ancient beliefs about the super-

---

[1] Reprinted with a few additions from *Proceedings of the Society for Psychical Research* 55 (1971). Part I incorporates and expands an essay on 'Telepathy and Clairvoyance in Classical Antiquity' published in *Greek Poetry and Life, Essays presented to Gilbert Murray* (1936). Parts II and III are substantially new. I am indebted for helpful suggestions to David Lewis and Nicholas Richardson.

[2] In *Hellenica*, ed. Evelyn Abbott (1880); reprinted in Myers's *Classical Essays* (1883).

[3] In his *Cock Lane and Common Sense* (1894).

normal rarely[1] betray any knowledge of, or interest in, their modern counterparts.

Yet the Myers–Lang method may perhaps have a modest utility both for the classical scholar and for the psychical researcher. By comparing certain ancient beliefs with their present-day analogues the classical scholar can, I think, hope to understand better the underlying experience out of which the beliefs grew. Some similarities—for example, in the popular tales about haunted houses[2]—may be due to the influence of literary or oral tradition; but there are other cases where one seems driven to assume the independent occurrence of the same type of psychological event. And the differences can be no less instructive than the similarities: they illustrate the way in which the interpretation of such events is coloured by the belief-patterns current in a particular society.

For the psychical researcher too there is in my opinion something to be learnt from this sort of inquiry. I do not mean that it can directly confirm the authenticity of phenomena whose occurrence today is a matter of dispute. The scientific study of the preconceptions, illusions, false memories, and other factors which tend to vitiate testimony, and the insistence upon such documentation as shall minimize their influence, hardly began before the latter half of the nineteenth century. In Antiquity the importance of first-hand documents in any branch of history was notoriously little appreciated; and first-hand ancient accounts of supernormal experiences are of extreme rarity. Indirectly, however, something can be gained by the application of two critical principles which I will now state.

[1] There are exceptions. A. Delatte in *La Catoptromancie grecque et ses dérivés* (1932) made legitimate and convincing use of modern experiments in 'scrying' to elucidate certain features of the ancient mantic practice (see below, pp. 186 ff.). And Martin Nilsson wrote to me in 1945: 'I am persuaded that the so-called parapsychical phenomena played a very great part in late Greek paganism and are essential for understanding it rightly.' Cf. also the just remarks of Friedrich Pfister, *Bursians Jahresbericht*, Supp.-Band 229 (1930), 307 f.

[2] The tradition that earthbound spirits haunt their place of death or of burial is as old as Plato (*Phaedo* 81 c–d) and doubtless far older. It persisted throughout Antiquity and survived the advent of Christianity (cf., e.g., Origen, *c. Cels.* 7. 5; Lactantius, *div. inst.* 2. 2. 6). The prototypical tale is that told by the younger Pliny (*Epist.* 7. 27. 4 ff.) of a haunted house at Athens and reproduced by Lucian (*Philopseudes* 30 f.) with a different location and a few additional horrors. For other haunted houses see Plutarch *apud* schol. Eur. *Alc.* 1128 (the Brazen House at Sparta); Plutarch, *Cimon* 1 (house at Chaeronea, said still to produce 'alarming sights and sounds' in Plutarch's day); and Suetonius, *Caligula* 59.

The first is a negative principle: namely, that if a particular supernormal phenomenon, alleged to occur spontaneously among civilized people in recent times, is *not* attested at any other time and place of which we have adequate knowledge, the presumption is thereby increased that it does not occur as alleged, unless clear reason can be shown why it remained so long unnoticed. Thus, if no case of telepathy had ever been recorded before (let us say) 1850, this would, I suggest, throw very considerable doubt on the actuality of its occurrence since that date. This is of course a principle to be applied with due caution, since it involves an argument from silence, whose strength will vary with the completeness of our documentation and also with the nature of the phenomenon. But it has some force as applied, for example, to 'poltergeist' phenomena. Disturbances of the sort popularly attributed to these rowdy, plate-throwing spirits are something not easily overlooked. Yet I have never come across a recognizable pre-Christian tale of a poltergeist, as distinct from the traditional 'haunt'.[1]

My second canon might be called the principle of variation. Suppose a phenomenon X to be accepted as occurring in modern Europe and America under conditions ABC and only under these; if it be recorded as occurring at another time or place under conditions BCD, then there is a presumption that neither the presence of A nor the absence of D is necessary to its occurrence. In such a case, since the conditions are partially identical, we have some assurance that the earlier report is not just a piece of free invention. And if that is so, the element of difference can be

---

[1] The ability to move objects without contact ('psychokinesis' in the modern jargon) is in certain hagiographical legends attributed to demons (see below, pp. 205 f.); but they can scarcely qualify as poltergeists, since their feats are provoked by an exorcist and are non-recurrent. Non-recurrence seems also to disqualify such cases as Suetonius' tale of the man who slept in a holy place and found himself ejected bed and all 'by a sudden occult force' (*vit. Augusti* 6). More interesting, though indirect and inconclusive, is the evidence of Andocides 1. 130, to which Mr. G. J. Toomer first called my attention: 'Hipponicus keeps an evil spirit (*aliterion*) in his house, who upsets his table (*trapeza*).' Nothing supernormal is intended here: the 'evil spirit' in question is Hipponicus' spendthrift son, and the word *trapeza* is introduced for the sake of a pun on its secondary meaning 'bank' (Hipponicus was a wealthy financier). But the joke would have additional point if the speaker's audience were familiar with stories of real poltergeists. The walking statue which upset the doctor's pharmacy in Lucian, *Philops.* 21, looks like an instance; but the parody is aimed at the belief in animated images rather than in poltergeists.

highly instructive. For it can show us which of the conditions are causally connected with the phenomenon and which are merely reflections of a contemporary pattern of belief.

I must, however, emphasize the need for especial caution in applying these critical principles to Classical Antiquity. In the first place, although the surviving ancient literature on the subject is in the sum total fairly considerable, we know that it is only a fraction of what once existed. The Stoic school, in particular, accumulated extensive case-books: Chrysippus wrote two books on divination, another on oracles—in which, says Cicero, he collected innumerable responses, 'all with ample authority and testimony'—and yet another on dreams; Diogenes of Seleucia, Antipater, and Posidonius all wrote on similar topics.[1] All these works are lost. In these circumstances the argument from silence is more than usually perilous. And secondly, it is a commonplace of psychical research that supernormal or quasi-supernormal experiences, more than any other class of human happenings, have the chameleon quality: from the background of belief against which they emerge they take so deep a colour, not only in tradition but in the experient consciousness itself, that their identity is hard to isolate. Consider, for example, the difficulty of making anything intelligible out of the seventeenth-century witch trials, relatively recent and relatively well documented as these are: seen through the medium of a universally accepted belief-pattern, the underlying psychological and objective data are consistently distorted, often beyond recognition. The ancient belief-patterns, though less blindingly uniform, carry similar possibilities of distortion; and their influence is the harder to allow for in proportion as they are less familiar to the modern imagination.

I. TELEPATHY AND CLAIRVOYANCE

I begin my inquiry with the two classes of phenomena which are today most widely accepted as genuine by critical students, viz. telepathy, defined as 'the communication of impressions of any kind from one mind to another, independently of the recognized channels of sense', and clairvoyance, defined as 'the faculty or act

[1] Cicero, *de div.* 1. 6; 1. 37; 1. 39. Other references in Zeller, *Philosophie der Griechen*[5], III. i. 345 ff.

of perceiving, as though visually, with some coincidental truth, some distant scene'.[1] It must be said at the outset that these are modern, not ancient categories. There is no ancient word for telepathy or clairvoyance. So far as they were recognized at all, they were embraced in the comprehensive notion of 'divination' (*mantikē*) along with retrocognition and precognition. The typical diviner is Homer's Kalchas, 'who knew things past, present, and to come'.[2] (In practice, as we shall see, the stress fell overwhelmingly on the last,[3] since divination was popularly valued for its utility, not for its theoretical interest, and his own future usually concerned the inquirer more nearly than other people's present or past.) The ancients subdivided divination, not according to the content supernormally apprehended, but according to the method of apprehension. They distinguished 'technical' or ominal from 'natural' or intuitive divination.[4] Cicero quotes as examples of the former class divining from entrails, the interpretation of prodigies and of lightning, augury, astrology, and divination by lots; to the latter he assigns divination in dreams and in ecstatic states.

In general the ominal species of divination are of little concern to the psychical researcher. But he will examine with interest the doctrine of intuitive divination, since some of the best modern evidence for extrasensory perception has been obtained with percipients in abnormal states (hypnosis and 'mediumistic' trance), and well-authenticated cases of coincidental dreams are abundant in modern records. What he will chiefly find, however, will be not a theory but a religious belief-pattern—or rather, perhaps, one belief-pattern superimposed on the remains of another. Halliday[5] may have been right in regarding the Greek diviner as a shrunken medicine-man, whose gift must at one time have been considered innate, as an element or aspect of his *mana*. But already

---

[1] I take these definitions from the glossary to F. W. H. Myers's *Human Personality* (1906).
[2] *Iliad* 1. 70. So too the dreams bestowed by the original Earth oracle at Delphi revealed 'the first things and the things thereafter and all that was to be' (Eur. *I.T.* 1264). But 'divination' is often used in a narrower sense, with exclusive reference to the future.
[3] Legendary seers sometimes exhibit supernormal knowledge of past events as evidence that their visions of the future will prove true (Prometheus, Aesch. *P.V.* 824-6; Cassandra, Aesch. *Ag.* 1194 ff.; Iarchas, Philostratus, *vit. Apollonii* 3. 16; cf. Gospel of John 4: 17-19). The implied assumption is that retrocognition and precognition are manifestations of the same power.
[4] Cicero, *de div.* 1. 12. The distinction is as old as Plato (*Phaedrus* 244 b ff.).
[5] W. R. Halliday, *Greek Divination* (1913), chap. 5.

by Homer's day ominal divination has passed under the control of religion. The diviner, in Halliday's phrase, 'holds his gift from God': Kalchas practises an art 'granted him by Apollo',[1] and all the great diviners of legend have a comparable status. Later, we find the two branches of intuitive divination similarly organized in the interests of the Olympians: in the main, Apollo takes over the patronage of trance mediumship and his son Asclepius that of the veridical dream, although older powers like Hecate and the Corybantes are still held responsible in popular belief for the more alarming and disorderly sort of manifestations. The supernormal, canalized and controlled, becomes the sensible evidence of the supernatural, and its authenticity is in turn guaranteed by its divine patrons: the Stoics spoke for the mass of men when they proclaimed the mutual interdependence of belief in the gods and belief in divination.[2]

So close an association with religious orthodoxy was naturally unfavourable to the growth of anything like critical study: it explains in particular the paucity of attempts at experimental investigation—what was of God was felt to be better left alone. Nevertheless, it is hardly correct to say, as Edwyn Bevan did,[3] that 'the theory of telepathy and thought transference had not occurred to antiquity'. At least one ancient account of divination—that of Democritus, about 400 B.C.—is founded on the notion of a physically mediated telepathy; and there are approaches to the idea in later writers.

Democritus' treatise *On images*[4] is lost, but an outline of the doctrine which concerns us is preserved by Plutarch.[5] We learn that Democritus, like his successor Epicurus, explained dreams in general by the penetration through the pores of the dreamer's body of the 'images' which are continually emitted by objects of all sorts and especially by living persons; he also held (and in this, says Plutarch, Epicurus did not follow him) that the images carry representations of the mental activities, the thoughts, characters,

---

[1] *Iliad* 1. 172. Dreams too, in Homer as in later belief, are often though not always sent to the dreamer by a god.
[2] Cicero, *de div.* 1. 10.
[3] *Sibyls and Seers* (1928), 163.
[4] Diels–Kranz, *Fragmente der Vorsokratiker*, 68 B 10.
[5] *Q. Conv.* 8. 10. 2, 734 f (= Diels–Kranz, *Vors.* 68 A 77). For discussion cf. A. Delatte, *Les Conceptions de l'enthousiasme chez les philosophes présocratiques* (1934), 46 ff.; W. K. C. Guthrie, *A History of Greek Philosophy*, ii (1965), 482.

and emotions of the persons who originated them, 'and thus charged, they have the effect of living agents: by their impact they communicate and transmit to the recipients the opinions, thoughts, and impulses of their senders, when they reach their goal with the images intact and undistorted.' The degree of distortion which the images suffer in transit depends partly on the weather, partly on the frequency of emission and on their initial velocity: 'those which leap out from persons in an excited and inflamed condition yield, owing to their high frequency and rapid transit, especially vivid and significant representations.' This is definitely a theory of telepathy (and clairvoyance, if we extend it to inanimate 'senders'), distinct from the complementary doctrine of *divine* images which served to explain precognition.[1] The remark that people in a state of excitement make, to use the modern term, the best telepathic 'agents' is deserving of notice, since it is confirmed by modern observations: a strikingly large proportion of telepathic dreams, hallucinations, and impressions are reported as having occurred when the assumed agent was experiencing some physical or mental crisis.[2]

The theory as presented in this passage is concerned only with dreams, but it is probable that its scope was actually wider. Plutarch tells us elsewhere[3] that Democritus explained 'the evil eye' on the same principle: the action at a distance is mediated by these same images, charged with a hostile mental content, which 'remain persistently attached to the person victimized, and thus disturb and injure both body and mind'. These effects are apparently produced continuously, and not merely in sleep. And Democritus is also credited with the belief that 'animals, wise men, and gods' possess a sixth sense—not further defined, but apparently linked with the apprehension of impinging images.[4] Moreover, if we are to believe Antisthenes,[5] Democritus actually undertook an experimental study of images (whether divine or ghostly in origin), sometimes isolating himself for the purpose in desert places and cemeteries. Was his choice of desert places

---

[1] Sextus Emp. *adv. math.* 9. 19 (= *Vors.* 68 B 166).
[2] Cf. Gurney, Myers and Podmore, *Phantasms of the Living* (1886), I. 229; Ian Stevenson, *Proc. Amer. Soc. for Psychical Research*, 29 (1970), 17–22.
[3] *Q. Conv.* 5. 7. 6 (= *Vors.* 68 A 77).
[4] Aetius 4. 10. 4 (= *Vors.* 68 A 116, cf. A 79.) Discussed by Guthrie, op. cit. ii. 449–51.
[5] Diog. Laert. 9. 38.

dictated by a realization of the difficulty which still confronts the student of 'spirit' phenomena—the difficulty of *excluding* telepathy from the living?

An important further step towards the naturalization of the supernatural was taken by Aristotle, who rejected ominal divination altogether[1] and ascribed the intuitive variety not to divine intervention but (in his youth at least) to an innate capacity of the human mind. In his early work *On philosophy* (now lost) he is reported as saying that 'the mind recovers its true nature during sleep';[2] in his *Eudemian Ethics* he associates the capacity for veridical dreaming with the 'melancholic' temperament which enables certain individuals to perceive, intuitively and irrationally, 'both the future and the present'.[3] But with advancing years he grew more cautious, though not less interested, as appears from his later essay *On divination in sleep*. Since, however, in that essay he was primarily[4] concerned with precognition, it will be more convenient to consider it under that heading.

The connection between divination and religion, which Aristotle had endeavoured to dispense with, was reaffirmed by the Stoics. Posidonius (about 135–50 B.C.) held that veridical dreams were due, if not to direct intercourse with the gods, then to the community of human with divine reason, or to reading the thoughts of the 'immortal souls' who throng the air beneath the moon.[5] For the existence of a common reason in God and man

[1] Plutarch, *Plac. phil.* 5. 1; cf. Cicero, *de div.* 1. 72.
[2] Frag. 10 Rose³ = 12a Ross. Here Aristotle is still under the influence of Plato (cf. *Rep.* 572a).
[3] *Eth. Eud.* 8. 2. 23, 1248ᵃ38 ff. The 'melancholic' is a person who suffers from an excess of black bile in his system, according to the teaching of the Coan school of medicine, and for that reason tends to be emotionally unstable. We should call him a 'manic-depressive'. The view that such people have an especial gift of divination appears in later medical writers (Aretaeus, *morb. chron.* 1. 5; Alexander of Tralles 1. 511, 591 Puschmann), but this pathological explanation was indignantly rejected by the Stoics (Cicero, *de div.* 1. 81). Aristotle mentions it again in his essay 'On Divination in Sleep' (*de div. p. somn.* 464ᵃ32), but his tone there is more sceptical. Cf. W. Jaeger, *Aristotle* (Eng. trans. 1934), 240 f., 333 f.
[4] Primarily but not exclusively. Like other ancient writers Aristotle treats telepathy and precognition as manifestations of the same faculty. Cf. the reference at 463ᵇ1 to dreams about 'a naval battle or (other) *distant* events' and at 464ᵃ1 to dreams of events which are 'outside the limits (of normal explanation) in respect of time, *place*, or importance'. (The category of 'importance' covers, I suppose, public events like battles, of which the dreamer could have no normal knowledge.)
[5] Posidonius in Cicero, *de div.* 1. 64. How far the theory of 'souls in the air' originated with Posidonius   uncertain. Something rather like it appears in

the Stoics could claim the authority of Heraclitus (about 500 B.C.), and Calcidius[1] seems to say that Heraclitus explained in this way 'visions of unknown places and apparitions of the living and the dead'; but it is hard to tell how much of this passage is genuine Heraclitus and how much is Stoic amplification. Among such bold speculations the humbler psycho-physical problem of telepathy, which Democritus had stated and attempted to solve, naturally enough fell into the background. But there are some indications that Posidonius' theory of divination (which has come down to us only in a confused and fragmentary form) included, along with much else, the notion of a physically mediated telepathy, if not between the living, at least between the living and the 'souls in the air'. Plutarch,[2] discussing the 'daemonion' of Socrates, propounds the view that spiritual beings in the act of thinking set up vibrations in the air which enable other spiritual beings, and also certain abnormally sensitive men, to apprehend their thoughts. Such vibrations impinge upon us continually, but they can reach consciousness only when the mind is sufficiently calm to detect them, that is, as a rule only in sleep. Reinhardt[3] was probably right in thinking that Plutarch is here making use of Posidonian ideas. A similar contrast between normal human perception on the one hand and daemonic and mediumistic intuition on the other was found by Cicero in Posidonius: 'as the minds of gods have community of feeling without eyes, ears, or tongue ... so human minds when set free by sleep, or in detached states of excited derangement, perceive things which minds involved with the body cannot see.'[4]

Like the modern vibration theories of telepathy, the speculations we have been considering postulate a physical carrier for the mental content communicated. The plausible analogy of wireless telephony was not yet available; but experience offered other

Alexander Polyhistor's summary of Pythagorean doctrine (Diog. Laert. 8. 32), but his reliability as a witness to early Pythagorean teaching is open to much doubt (cf. Festugière, *R.E.G.* 58 (1945), 1 ff.; W. Burkert, *Weisheit und Wissenschaft* (1962), 46 f.).

[1] Calcidius, *in Tim.* cap. 251 (= *Vors.* 22 A 20). The theory of divination which he attributes to Heraclitus appears to be in fact that of Posidonius (K. Reinhardt, *Kosmos und Sympathie* (1926), 401).

[2] *Gen. Socr.* 20, 589 b.

[3] *Poseidonios*, 464 ff.; *Kosmos u. Sympathie*, 288 f.; Pauly–Wissowa s.v. 'Poseidonios', 802 f.

[4] *de div.* 1. 129.

Supernormal Phenomena in Classical Antiquity 165

seeming analogues. In popular belief every kind of action at a distance was explained by occult emanations proceeding from persons or objects. The most striking and indisputable case of such action was the influence of the magnet upon iron,[1] which had impressed the imagination of Thales, had aroused the scientific interest of Democritus, and had been used by Plato to illustrate the communication of poetic inspiration.[2] Quintus Cicero argues that it is no less mysterious and no less certain than divination.[3] And there were other generally accepted examples: do not the phases of the moon work tidal changes in our blood and affect the growth of all living things?[4] and does not 'the evil eye' imply a secret emanation from the human eye?[5] Such reflections were generalized in the Stoic and Neoplatonic doctrine of occult 'sympathies', which when combined with the notion of a world-soul issued in something like a reinstatement, on a higher philosophical level, of the primitive conception of the world as a magical unity.

For the Neoplatonist the linkage has become non-physical.[6] The world, says Plotinus,[7] is like one great animal, and its 'sympathy' abolishes distance; distant members may affect each other while the intervening portions of the organism are unaffected, 'for like parts may be discontinuous yet have sympathy in virtue of their likeness, so that the action of an element spatially isolated cannot fail to reach its remote counterpart'. This principle provides a rationale both of prayer and of telergic magic, as Plotinus did not fail to point out (*Enn.* 4. 4. 40–1; 4. 9. 3). It provides also a rationale of what we call telepathy; but to this, so far as I can see, Plotinus nowhere makes an explicit allusion, though certain passages have been interpreted in this sense: he gets no nearer than the remark that *discarnate* souls may be supposed to communicate mutually without speech.[8] Nor did his

---

[1] Pliny, *N.H.* 36. 126.
[2] Aristotle, *de anima* 405ª19; *Vors.* 68 A 165 (cf. Delatte, *Conceptions de l'enthousiasme*, 59 ff.); Plato, *Ion* 533 d ff. Other passages about magnetism will be found in J. Röhr, *Philol. Supp.* 17, 1. 92–5.
[3] Cicero, *de div.* 1. 86. [4] Pliny, *N.H.* 2. 102.
[5] Plut. *Q. Conv.* 5. 7. 2.
[6] On the difference between the Neoplatonic and the Posidonian conception of 'sympathy' see Reinhardt, *Kosmos u. Sympathie*, 248 f., 252 ff.
[7] *Enn.* 4. 4. 32.
[8] *Enn.* 4. 3. 18. The statement at 4. 9. 3 that 'a word softly spoken can influence a distant object and obtain a hearing from what is vastly remote in space'

successors, for all their interest in occult phenomena and in the relationship between mind and body, bestow much attention on telepathy. Outside metaphysics, Neoplatonism created few new patterns of belief: its concern was to defend old ones by giving them a metaphysical justification.

As the ancients had no name for telepathy or clairvoyance, so they practised no systematic observation of cases. The scattered examples which have come down to us are for the most part casually recorded and exceedingly ill evidenced. I propose briefly to review some of them, taking first those associated with oracles.

The most familiar of these is the famous story of the test applied by Croesus, King of Lydia in the sixth century B.C., to Delphi and other oracles—the earliest example of what would today be called an experiment in long-distance telepathy. If Herodotus[1] is to be believed, Croesus sent messengers to seven of the best oracles, who on the same day were to put the same question to each oracle—'What is the King of Lydia doing today?' The messengers themselves did not know the answer. Five of the oracles failed the test; a sixth, that of Amphiaraos, was highly commended for a near miss; but Delphi alone came up with the correct reply, that the King of Lydia was doing a bit of cooking—he was boiling a lamb and a tortoise in a copper pot. The story may be apocryphal—as rationalist historians have naturally assumed[2]—but the experiment as described was well devised: Croesus had taken adequate precautions to exclude both normal leakage and chance coincidence. The point to notice, however, is that neither he nor Herodotus knew that it was a *telepathic* experiment: they thought he was testing the alleged omniscience of various foreign gods or heroes.

Croesus' example was not followed for many centuries: the pious Xenophon considered it blasphemous,[3] and no doubt that

looks at first sight like a reference to telepathy (G. W. Lambert, *Proc. S.P.R.* 36 (1927), 398). But the wording suggests rather the persuasive power of prayer or the telergic magic which in Plotinus' day was taken seriously. See now Harder's note on the passage.

[1] I. 47.
[2] But see H. Klees, *Eigenart des griechischen Glaubens an Orakel und Seher* (Tübinger Beitr. 43 (1965), 91. 8), who argues from the un-Hellenic behaviour attributed throughout to Croesus that the stories of his dealings with Delphi must have a historical foundation. As W. G. Forrest puts it (*Gnomon*, 38 (1966), 629), 'parts may have been distorted or overlaid by Delphic propaganda, but the framework is Lydian'.
[3] *Cyrop.* 7. 2. 17.

view was widely shared. But it does not stand quite alone. We have Macrobius' story[1] about the Emperor Trajan, who sealed up a blank set of tablets and sent it to the oracle of Jupiter Heliopolitanus at Baalbek, an oracle which specialized in reading sealed letters without opening them. Trajan's missive was returned to him with the seal intact, accompanied by a second letter containing the god's answer. When the latter was opened, it in turn proved to contain a blank sheet of papyrus. The sceptic need not hesitate to believe this story, for the useful art of reading sealed letters appears to have been as closely studied in Antiquity as in our own day. While Greco-Egyptian magic provided specialist spells for the purpose,[2] simpler ways of performing the feat were likewise known. The third-century Christian writer Hippolytus includes in his curious collection of recipes for parlour tricks (derived, as Wellmann[3] has shown, from earlier pagan sources) several methods of taking a cast of a seal, which when set constitutes a duplicate die; and Alexander of Abonuteichus is accused by Lucian of 'working an oracle' by duplicating seals in this fashion. Lucian also knows of the still simpler plan of removing the seal intact with hot needles and later replacing it, and he mentions that yet other devices to the same end have been described by his friend Celsus in his treatise against the magicians.[4] We have here the most obvious explanation both of the Baalbek performance and of the obscure procedure involving a sealed vessel (analogous to modern 'slate-writing'?) which appears to have been practised at the Apolline oracle of Korope in Thessaly about 100 B.C.[5] Hence also, perhaps, if it ever took place, the successful experiment of that Governor of Cilicia who wrote privily on his tablets the question 'Shall I sacrifice to thee a white bull or a black?', sealed them, and sent them by a freedman to the

---

[1] *Saturn.* 1. 23. 14 f.
[2] *Papyri Graecae Magicae* (henceforth referred to as *P.G.M.*) iii. 371; v. 301.
[3] *Die Φυσικά des Bolos Demokritos* (Abh. Preuss. Akad. 1928), 64 ff.
[4] Lucian, *Alex.* 21.
[5] *S.I.G.* 1157. The inscription is unfortunately illegible at a critical point. For other interpretations see Louis Robert, *Hellenica*, 5 (1948), 16 ff., and H. W. Parke, *The Oracles of Zeus* (1967), 104 ff. Against the view adopted in the text the latter argues that it makes the Koropeans too naïvely credulous. But what was thought good enough for (if not by) the Emperor Trajan may well have satisfied the local patriotism of the city fathers in a small Greek country town. Cruder 'miracles' still command the implicit faith of thousands in the Mediterranean lands.

oracle of Mopsus; the freedman, sleeping in the temple, claimed to have heard in a dream the one word 'black'.[1]

The occasion of Croesus' test is apparently not the only one on which the Pythia succeeded in 'understanding the dumb and hearing the unspoken word': Plutarch, whose evidence has special weight in relation to Delphi,[2] says that 'she is accustomed to deliver certain oracles instantly, even before the question is put'.[3] A like claim is made by Tacitus for Claros: the priest on consultation days would merely inquire the names of the clients present and then, after retiring to a sacred grotto and there drinking the water of a certain fountain, would give appropriate replies in verse to their unspoken questions.[4] To assess the evidential value of such general statements is hardly possible, but it is unnecessary either to dismiss them as pure fabrications[5] or to assume that the managers of the oracles employed an army of private-inquiry agents. If we may judge by the number of living persons who claim to have received relevant 'messages' at anonymous sittings with 'mediums' previously unknown to them, there is nothing impossible about the feat, whether we explain it by thought-reading, by the will to believe, or by some blend of the two.

Oracles were occasionally consulted, as clairvoyants are today, concerning the whereabouts of missing objects: thus at Dodona one Agis 'consults Zeus Naos and Dione about the rugs and pillows which he has lost: did some outside person steal them?'[6] At oracles where 'incubation' (sleeping in the temple) was practised such questions might be answered in dreams.[7] Three narratives of clairvoyant dreams of this type are included in the Epidaurian temple record. In the first case (no. 24 Herzog) a boy named Aristocritus, from Halieis, has dived (or fallen) into the sea from a

[1] Plut. *def. orac.* 45. The story seems to be a temple legend: the speaker in Plutarch's dialogue says he heard it when he visited the oracle in question. Cf. Lucian, *Philops.* 38.
[2] Plutarch held a priesthood for life at the oracle.
[3] *De garrulitate* 20. Herodotus claims the oracles given to Lycurgus and Eëtion as instances of this (1. 65. 2; 5. 92 β).
[4] *Annals* 2. 54.
[5] This is what Farnell does (*Cults*, iv. 225). But the passage which he quotes from Ovid (*Fasti* 1. 19) does not disprove Tacitus' statement: it merely shows that consultation by letter was admissible in lieu of personal attendance. On the Pythia as 'medium' see below, pp. 196 ff.
[6] H. W. Parke, *The Oracles of Zeus*, 272.
[7] Cf. the dream of Sophocles in which Heracles revealed the name of the thief who had stolen some of the temple plate (Cicero, *de div.* 1. 54).

Supernormal Phenomena in Classical Antiquity 169

cliff, failed to effect a landing, and disappeared. His father sleeps in the temple, and in a dream Asclepius leads him to a certain spot and shows him that his son is there. Returning home, he identifies the spot, cuts a passage through the rock, and finds the boy on the seventh day (presumably dead, though the record refrains from saying so). In the second story (no. 46) a woman is looking for a treasure concealed by her late husband: the god tells her in a dream that 'the treasure will be lying within the lion at noon in the month of Thargelion,' and the hoard is eventually found to be buried at the spot where the shadow of a certain stone lion falls at noon at the date mentioned. No. 63 also concerns a missing sum of money, a deposit at Leucas which there is difficulty in tracing: Asclepius in a dream introduces the depositor to the ghost of the deceased trustee, 'who revealed the spot, and told him that if he came to Leucas he would get the gold from his (the trustee's) sons'. To these may be added a case of a different kind, no. 21, where the same (medical) dream is independently dreamt about the same time by a woman at Epidaurus and her daughter (the patient) at Sparta.

Probably few persons today would be satisfied with the crude view that the Epidaurian record is a wholesale forgery deliberately produced by the priests, or would assume with some of the earlier commentators that the patients were drugged, or hypnotized, or mistook waking for sleeping and a priest in fancy dress for the divine Healer: an explanation is to be sought rather in the analogy of medieval and modern religious faith-healing and the so-called 'medical clairvoyance' of hysterical subjects.[1] But the record is not a first-hand document: Herzog has shown in an admirable study[2] that it is based partly on genuine votive tablets dedicated by patients—which might be elaborated and expanded in the process of incorporation[3]—partly on a temple tradition which had attracted to itself miracle-stories from many sources.

[1] On medical clairvoyance see Myers, *Human Personality*, Appendix Va. Augustine records an interesting and typical case, *de Gen. ad litt.* 12. 17. On faith-healing in modern Greece see J. C. Lawson, *Modern Greek Folklore and Ancient Greek Religion*, 60 ff. Text and translation of the Epidaurian record will be found in Emma and Ludwig Edelstein, *Asclepius* (1945), 1. 221 ff.

[2] *Die Wunderheilungen von Epidauros* (*Philologus*, Supplementband 22, Heft iii, 1931). See also Edelstein, *Asclepius*, ii. 139–80; and my *Greeks and the Irrational*, 110–16, 127–30. Artemidorus thought that no man of sense would put faith in such records (4. 22, p. 255. 13 ff. Pack).

[3] No. 1 is a clear case of this (Herzog, p. 71).

Of the stories quoted in the previous paragraph, no. 46 is, as Blinkenberg and Herzog have pointed out, a widely diffused folk-tale which has attached itself to the tradition. On the other hand no. 24 looks like a genuine case: the names and local details are precise, and in fiction the boy would have been found alive. Herzog produces medieval German parallels, and one may add that the employment of clairvoyants to discover missing corpses is common today on the Continent. It is not necessary to regard the incident as supernormal: a subconscious inference from indications observed during the earlier search might well emerge in the symbolic form of the veridical dream. No. 21 has a parallel in *P. Oxy.* 1381[1] (second century A.D.), where the Egyptian healing god Imouthes appears simultaneously to the patient's mother in a waking vision and to the patient in a dream. In both stories the narrator's intention is evidently to exclude an interpretation of the appearance as merely subjective; in both, if we take them as fact, the operation of a common will to healing in parent and child may provide a normal explanation.

Finally, no. 63 is explained by Herzog as a folk-tale of the Honest Dead, which must originally have been associated with a necromantic dream-oracle, the mediation of Asclepius being a later addition. He brings it into connection with the story of Periander and Melissa (Hdt. 5. 92); with a somewhat similar legend about the Christian Bishop Spyridon (Sozomen 1. 12; Photius, *Bibl.* cod. 256, etc.); with Varro's[2] story of his uncle Corfidius, who when lying in a state of coma became aware supernormally of his brother's death, at or near the moment of its occurrence, and also of the place where the latter had secretly buried some gold; and lastly with Augustine's[3] story of the young man to whom his father revealed in a dream the whereabouts of a missing receipt. It may, I think, be doubted whether all these tales stand on the same footing. The story of Periander belongs unmistakably to folklore, and that of Spyridon to hagiology; but one's uncle is a less likely hero for a purely fictitious romance. We may suspect the 'buried gold' as a secondary elaboration

---

[1] Re-edited by Manteuffel, *de opusculis graecis Aegypti... collectis* (1930); translated and discussed by Nock, *Conversion*, 86 ff. For another story of a dream experienced simultaneously by two persons see Livy 8. 6; for modern cases, *Journ. S.P.R.* 4. 220 f.; 7. 104 ff.; 9. 331 f., etc.

[2] *Apud* Pliny, *N.H.* 7. 177; reproduced in Granius Licinianus 28, p. 7 Flemisch.

[3] *De cura pro mortuis* 11 (13).

derived from a folk-motive, but the remainder of Varro's narrative belongs to a type for which abundant first-hand modern evidence exists, the dream or vision (usually of a near relative) coinciding with the death of the person seen. The experience of Corfidius is curiously like that attributed to the eighteenth-century American Quaker Thomas Say, who when lying comatose and supposedly dead had a clairvoyant apprehension of the deaths of no less than three other persons and of the circumstances attending the end of one of them.[1] In the Epidaurian case, too, secondary elaboration may have been at work on a real dream: that the depositor should dream of finding the trustee dead and recovering his money from the sons is entirely natural; the only supernormal element lies in the vague words 'he revealed the spot', and one must remember that the instability of dream-memories renders them peculiarly liable to unconscious distortion in the light of waking belief. As for Augustine's story, it is second-hand and anonymous, though related to Augustine *pro certo*. It has, however, a striking modern parallel in the 'Chaffin Will case' (*Proc. S.P.R.* 36. 517 ff.), which has figured in an American court of law and is certainly not a folk-tale. It may be added that Augustine, with characteristic caution and acumen, warns us against assuming too hastily that the source of the supernormal apprehension in such cases is necessarily the deceased person.

If the anecdotes which circulated in the waiting-rooms of oracles carry as a group no very strong conviction of authenticity, it would be futile to seek a possible basis of fact for the stories of extrasensory perception which appear in hagiographical romances. We need not linger over the strange powers which already in Aristotle's day were attributed to Pythagoras, the prototype of Greek miracle-workers;[2] or over the claim of Hermotimus of Clazomenae to be regarded as the first practitioner of 'travelling clairvoyance';[3] or over the sensational feats ascribed to Apollonius of Tyana[4] and St. Benedict[5] by their respective

[1] *Journ. S.P.R.* 13. 87 ff. The story was written down many years later by Say's son. For this and some other parallels I am indebted to an unpublished thesis by Mr. F. T. Walton.
[2] Aristotle, frag. 191 Rose³ (Ross, *Fragmenta Selecta*, pp. 130 ff.). Most recently discussed by W. Burkert, *Weisheit und Wissenschaft*, 117 ff.
[3] Pliny, *N.H.* 7. 53; Plut. *gen. Socr.* 22; Tert. *de anima* 44; etc. Lucian, *Musc. Enc.* 7, calls his story a fable.
[4] Philostratus, *vit. Apoll.* 4. 12; 5. 24; 8. 26 f.
[5] Gregory the Great, *Dialogues*, Book 2 *passim*.

biographers. When material of this kind is excluded, the remaining evidence of telepathy or clairvoyance by private individuals is curiously scanty.[1] And apart from the tradition about Democritus there is very little trace, save at the crude level of the magical papyri, of any attempt at experiment.

In particular, the type of spontaneous case which is most abundant in modern records, viz. dreams or hallucinations coinciding with the death or physical peril of the person seen, is rare in Antiquity, though not unknown. If we exclude such things as Apollonius' highly questionable vision of the death of Domitian,[2] it is represented, so far as my knowledge goes, only or chiefly by the above-mentioned Corfidius story, by the vision of Sosipatra in Eunapius,[3] and by the well-known tale of the wicked innkeeper.[4] In that tale two travellers arrive at Megara, where one puts up at an inn while the other lodges with an acquaintance. The second man dreams that his fellow traveller is in danger of being assassinated by the innkeeper. He springs up to help him, but on realizing that it was a dream goes back to bed. He then has a second dream in which his friend tells him that he has been murdered and bids him go at dawn to one of the town gates and intercept a dung-cart, concealed in which he will find the corpse. He does so, the corpse is found, and the innkeeper is brought to justice. Here the first dream can plausibly be explained by telepathy from the dying man. Whether the second should be explained by telepathy from the murderer, by clairvoyance on the part of the dreamer, by the continued action of the murdered man's spirit, or by the tendency to make a good story better, I will not attempt to decide.[5] It is perhaps enough to say that it is one of those nameless and dateless incidents, painfully familiar to the modern investigator, which are copied, with improvements, from

[1] Among the 95 allegedly veridical dreams personally collected by Artemidorus from his contemporaries and reported in his Fifth Book I can find only two (5. 17 and 5. 50) which lend themselves to a telepathic explanation. But of course he was looking for instances of precognition, not of telepathy.
[2] Dio Cassius 67. 18; Philostratus, *vit. Apoll.* 8. 26 ff. Suetonius knows nothing of the story.
[3] *Vitae sophistarum*, p. 470 Boissonade, 6. 9. 11 ff. Giangrande.
[4] Chrysippus, frag. 1205 Arnim, *apud* Suid. s.v. τιμωροῦντος; Cicero, *de div.* 1. 57; Val. Max. 1. 7. ext. 3. The case of Hippothoös' housekeeper, [Hipp.] *Epidem.* 6. 8. 10 (v. 348 Littré), may be a further instance, but detail is lacking.
[5] The question is gravely discussed by de Boismont, *On Hallucinations* (Eng. tr. 1859), 176 f.; Flammarion, *Haunted Houses*, (1924), 44 ff.; de Vesme, *Hist. du spiritualisme expérimental*, i. 349 f.; etc.

Supernormal Phenomena in Classical Antiquity 173

one textbook into another;[1] the version quoted by Suidas from Chrysippus differs widely from Cicero's, to which in turn Valerius Maximus adds a few finishing touches.

More impressive is the case of Sosipatra, a Neoplatonist bluestocking, who in the midst of addressing a meeting of philosophers abruptly fell silent, and then proceeded to describe an accident which was happening somewhere in the country (we must assume, at the same moment) to a relative and admirer of hers. 'What is this? My kinsman Philometor riding in a carriage! The carriage has been overturned in a rough place! His legs are in danger! Oh, the servants have got him out unharmed, except for cuts on the elbows and hands—not dangerous ones. And now he is being carried on a stretcher while he makes a lot of fuss.' That is what she said, and it was so. And so everybody knew that Sosipatra was omnipresent and, as the philosophers say about the gods, a witness of all that happens.

It is a pity that this incident rests solely on the authority of Eunapius,[2] a notorious amateur of the miraculous.

There are also a few cases where the issue of a battle is said to have been supernormally apprehended by a distant person before the news could travel by ordinary means: besides the rumour at Mycale of the victory at Plataea (Hdt. 9. 100), we have the augural divination reported by Livy[3] to have been performed by his friend Gaius Cornelius at Patavium on the day of the battle of Pharsalus (this is transformed by Aulus Gellius[4] into an impressive case of visual clairvoyance); and the auditory hallucination by which John Hyrcanus was apprised of his sons' victory over Antiochus Cyzicenus.[5] The type seems to have been a recognized one by Aristotle's day: his example of an external event apprehended in a veridical dream is a sea-fight.[6]

The most careful and sober descriptions of supernormal occurrences which have come down to us from Antiquity are those furnished by Augustine, who deserves a more honourable place

---

[1] According to Cicero it was 'continually quoted by the Stoics'.
[2] *Vitae sophistarum*, p. 470 Boissonade. This was not the only occasion when Sosipatra (whom Eunapius may have known in his youth) displayed her telepathic powers: at the age of nine she described to her father the incidents of a journey he had just taken 'as though she had been in the driver's seat with him' (ibid., p. 468).
[3] *Apud* Plut. *Caesar* 47.
[4] *Noct. Att.* 15. 18.
[5] Josephus, *Ant. Jud.* 13. 282 f.
[6] *De div. per somn.* 463ª2.

in the history of psychical research than any other thinker between Aristotle and Kant.[1] One of his cases has already been quoted. Extrasensory perception may be involved in the following also:[2]

1. A case of apparent telepathic 'rapport' between a hysterical patient and a priest who was in the habit of visiting him, being the only person who could keep him quiet during his attacks and persuade him to take nourishment.[3] The priest's home was twelve miles distant from the patient's, and the latter would habitually recognize the moment at which the priest was setting out to visit him, and would describe exactly all the stages of his journey, saying 'Now he has got so far! now he has reached the farm! now he is coming up to the house!' The hysteric was naturally supposed by his friends to be possessed by an unclean spirit, and the spirit got the credit for these 'monitions of approach'; but Augustine prudently observes that 'he may have been merely mad, and the possession an inference from the powers which he displayed'. He eventually recovered, and his uncanny intuitions then ceased. The account has a genuine ring; but in Augustine's day it would not be easy to measure time-coincidences closely, and we do not know how far normal inference might enable the subject to forecast the priest's visits.

2. An unnamed person, whose truthfulness Augustine guarantees, told him that one night before going to rest he thought he saw

---

[1] Cf. W. Montgomery, 'St. Augustine's attitude to psychic phenomena', *Hibbert Journal* 25. 92 ff.; J. de Vooght, 'Les miracles dans la vie de S. Augustin', *Recherches de Théol. ancienne et médiévale*, 11 (1939), 5 ff.; Peter Brown, *Augustine of Hippo*, 413–18.

[2] I have not included the celebrated story of the two Curmas, *de cura pro mortuis* 12 (15). Although Augustine obtained the percipient's own story in this case, as well as corroborative testimony from other people, he must have been hoaxed by his informants; for the same tale appears a couple of centuries earlier in Lucian, *Philopseudes* 25 (and a couple of centuries later in Pope Gregory, *Dialogues* 4. 36). The names are different in each version, but the central incident is the same in all, and in all *the victim is a smith*. (A variant which makes him a cobbler occurs still earlier, Plut. *de anima*, frag. 1 *apud* Eus. *Praep. Evang.* 11. 36.) I can agree neither with Reitzenstein (*Hell. Wundererzählungen* (1906), 6), who thinks that Augustine made the story contemporary by a 'literary artifice', nor with Rose (*Proc. Camb. Philol. Soc.* (1926), 13 f.), who defends its genuineness.

[3] *De Genesi ad litteram* 12. 17 (Migne 34. 467 ff.). Augustine calls the patient's malady 'fever' as well as 'insanity'. But the special influence which the priest exercised over him during the attacks points to an illness of mental rather than physical character. For modern parallels see *Phantasms of the Living*, i. 251 ff. and J. L. Nevius, *Demon Possession and Allied Themes* (1897), 33 ff.

a philosopher of his acquaintance come in and expound certain questions about Plato which on a previous occasion he had refused to answer. It appeared later that the philosopher had *dreamed* that night that he came to his friend's house and answered the questions.[1] A few well-authenticated cases of this 'reciprocal' type have been recorded in modern times;[2] but modern phantasms are not reported as holding lengthy conversations with their hosts.

3. Finally, we have some interesting cases of extrasensory perception by a Carthaginian diviner named Albicerius which were witnessed by Augustine and his friends.[3] Augustine, while disapproving of Albicerius as a man of abandoned life, claims that he has demonstrated his supernormal powers in numberless instances extending over many years, though there have also been some failures. The following examples are given. (*a*) On an occasion when a spoon was missed, Augustine caused Albicerius to be informed simply that some one had lost something. The clairvoyant identified the missing object as a spoon, gave the owner's name, and correctly described the place where it would be found. It is not clear whether the spoon had been mislaid or stolen: on the former supposition the knowledge of its whereabouts might be in the subconscious memory of its owner, and it would be possible to explain the whole incident by telepathy. The sceptic will doubtless assume collusion with servants. We may compare Varro's story[4] of Fabius' consultation of Nigidius Figulus on a similar occasion, when with the aid of certain boys placed under a spell ('carmine instincti') Nigidius was able to describe what had happened to a number of missing coins. The employment of professional clairvoyants to discover stolen money is referred to in a fragment of an Atellane by Pomponius.[5] (*b*) On an occasion when Augustine's friend Licentius was consulting him on another matter, the clairvoyant became mysteriously aware that part of his fee, which was being brought him by a slave, had been abstracted *en route*. The details given are hardly sufficient to establish

---

[1] *Civ. Dei* 18. 18.
[2] *Phantasms of the Living*, chap. xvii; F. Podmore, *Apparitions and Thought-transference* (1894), 298 ff.; Mrs. Henry Sidgwick, *Proc. S.P.R.* 33 (1923), 419.
[3] *Contra Academicos* 1. 6 f. (Migne 32. 914 f.).
[4] *Apud* Apul. *Apol.* 42. See below, p. 189.
[5] Ribbeck, *Com. Rom. frag.*[3] v. 109. Pomponius may be gibing at Nigidius (Reitzenstein, *Hell. Mysterienreligionen*[3] (1927), 236 ff.).

the supernormal character of this incident. (*c*) Another friend of Augustine's, one Flaccianus, asked Albicerius as a test question what business he, Flaccianus, had been discussing lately. The clairvoyant told him correctly that he had been discussing the purchase of an estate, and to his great astonishment gave the name of the estate in question, 'although,' says Augustine, 'the name was so out-of-the-way that Flaccianus could hardly remember it himself'. The possibility of normal sources of information can scarcely be excluded here. (*d*) The fourth and last case is the strongest. A pupil of Augustine's asked Albicerius to tell him of what he (the pupil) was thinking. Albicerius replied correctly that he was thinking of a line of Virgil, and proceeded promptly and confidently, although he was a man of very slight education, to quote the verse. If this is accurately reported, the sceptic will, I suppose, fall back on the hypothesis of unconscious whispering. It does not appear what methods Albicerius used, or what explanation he himself gave of his remarkable powers. Flaccianus, we are told, used to put them down to the admonition of some 'low-grade spirit', *abiectissima animula*.

II. PRECOGNITION

Of all ostensibly supernormal phenomena precognition—defined by Myers as 'knowledge of impending events supernormally acquired'[1]—has been in virtually all societies, from the most primitive to the most sophisticated, the most widely accepted in popular belief, and often also in the belief of educated men. Yet of all such phenomena it is probably the one of which it is hardest to give any rational account. The paradox of the situation was recognized in Antiquity: Aristotle opens his discussion of the subject with the remark that it is difficult either to ignore the evidence or to believe it.[2] Ostensible precognitions formed part of the accepted matter of history: the pages of nearly all ancient historians, from Herodotus to Ammianus Marcellinus, are full of omens, oracles, or precognitive dreams or visions. Yet how can an event in an as yet non-existent future causally determine an event in the present? This was already for Cicero, and even for

[1] Glossary to *Human Personality*. On the difficulties of exact definition see C. D. Broad, 'The nature of "precognition"', in *Science and ESP*, ed. J. R. Smythies (1967), 180–6.
[2] *De div. p. somn.* 462^{b}12.

his credulous brother Quintus, the *magna quaestio*,[1] as it still is today. Modern theories of precognition mostly fall into one or other of three broad categories. They attempt to evade or attenuate the paradox either (*a*) by juggling with the concept of time (Dunne, Saltmarsh, etc.); or (*b*) by trying where possible to reinterpret the phenomenon in terms of unconscious inference from supernormally acquired knowledge of the present (Broad, Dobbs, Stevenson, etc.); or (*c*) by reversing the ostensible causal relationship and treating the precognitive experience as in some normal or supernormal ('psychokinetic') manner the cause of the subsequent event (Tanagras, Roll).[2] Theories of types (*b*) and (*c*) had, as we shall see, their counterparts in Antiquity. But the majority of men were content with a simpler and more comprehensive explanation: divination in all its forms was the gift of the gods, whom, as Aristotle says (*Poetics* 1454^{b}5), men assume to be omniscient. This assumption was encouraged by two deeply rooted religious traditions. One was the tradition of Delphi and other oracles where, as we have seen, a god spoke in his own person to men, using the vocal organs of an entranced medium, and advised[3] them on their future conduct in the light of divine foreknowledge. The other was the even older tradition of the oracular god-sent dream, essentially a theophany in sleep, which the Greeks had taken over very early from their eastern neighbours. The dream is, as Plutarch said, 'the oldest oracle'.[4] Here too men saw a direct message from the divine world, to be recognized 'when in sleep the dreamer's parent, or some other respected or impressive personage, perhaps a priest or even a god, reveals without symbolism what will or will not happen, or should or should not be done'.[5] These special messages, most often

---

[1] *De div.* I. 117.
[2] On these speculations see Broad, op. cit., 165–96, and more briefly Ian Stevenson, 'Precognition of Disasters', *Journ. Amer. S.P.R.* 64 (1970), 194–6.
[3] The primary function of a Greek oracle was to *advise*, not to predict: Apollo was not a fortune-teller. The questions asked of Delphi in Plutarch's day, 'Should I marry?' 'Should I make the voyage?' 'Should I invest the money?' are probably typical of the average inquirer at all periods, though Plutarch prefers not to think so (*Pyth. orac.* 28). Cf. the extant collection of questions addressed to the oracle at Dodona, mostly datable between 500 and 250 B.C., of which a representative sample are printed and translated by Parke, *The Oracles of Zeus*, Appendix I. [4] *Sept. sap.* 15.
[5] Macrobius, *in Somn. Scip.* I. 3. 8. I have discussed such dreams in my *Greeks and the Irrational*, 107–10.

vouchsafed to kings, priests, wise men, or other peculiarly qualified dreamers,[1] were *en clair*. But side by side with them there were the much commoner symbolic dreams whose prophetic significance could be discovered only with the help of a professional interpreter, an *oneirocrit*, as well as the ordinary non-significant[2] dream which merely reflected daytime residues.

In Egypt such *oneirocrits* had long been part of the official establishment, functioning as priests in the 'House of Life'; so high was their reputation that Esarhaddon in the seventh century B.C. thought it worth while to kidnap some of them and transport them to Assyria,[3] very much as the Russians kidnapped German scientists in 1945. We have parts of an Egyptian dreambook whose contents may go back to a date early in the second millennium;[4] and Esarhaddon's successor Assurbanipal had in his library a dreambook which has recently been published and translated by Oppenheim.[5] In Greece we have testimony to the existence of *oneirocrits* both in the world described by Homer and in fifth-century Athens,[6] and the earliest known Greek dreambook, that of Antiphon, dates from the fifth or the fourth century B.C.[7] His book is lost, as are most of the many which followed it, but we

---

[1] In early Mesopotamia only priests were thus privileged (A. L. Oppenheim, 'The Interpretation of Dreams in the Ancient Near East', *Trans. Amer. Philos. Soc.*, N.S. 46 (1956), 222, 224, 240). For the privileged position of kings cf. *Iliad* 2. 80–2; for wise men, the oracular dreams granted to Socrates (and the Stoic theory that only the dreams of the *sapiens* always come true). In later times such divine message-dreams are more commonly claimed by private persons: see Plato, *Laws* 909 e–910 a; *Epin.* 985 c; and for the abundant inscriptional evidence A. D. Nock, *J.H.S.* 45 (1925), 96 ff. The 95 contemporary dreams harvested in Artemidorus' Fifth Book include 9 in which gods (mostly healing deities) appear to the dreamer. Both Epicurus (frag. 353) and Lucretius (5. 1169 ff.) refer to visions of the gods in sleep.

[2] The distinction between veridical and non-veridical dreams is as old as Homer (*Odyssey* 19. 560 ff.); that the latter are echoes of daylight residues was commonly recognized from Herodotus (7. 16 β 2) onwards. One school of experts, however, claimed that *all* dreams would prove meaningful if only we could interpret them (Tert. *de anima* 46. 3; cf. Cicero, *de div.* 1. 60).

[3] Oppenheim, op. cit. 238. For the importance of capturing seers cf. also 2 Kings 6: 8–13.

[4] A. H. Gardiner, *Hieratic Papyri in the British Museum* I.   [5] Op. cit.

[6] *Iliad* 5. 149 f.; Magnes, frag. 4 Kock; Aristoph. *Vesp.* 52 f.; Xen. *Anab.* 7. 8. 1; Demetrius of Phaleron *apud* Plut. *Aristides*, 27.

[7] Diog. Laert. 2. 46 dates him somewhere between Socrates' time and Aristotle's. Against identifying him with the sophist of the same name see *The Greeks and the Irrational*, 132 n. 100, and *C.R.* 68 (1954), 94 f. The testimonia to no fewer than thirty-three lost works on dreams have been collected and edited by D. del Corno, *Graecorum de re onirocritica scriptorum reliquiae* (1969).

still have the *Oneirocritica* of Artemidorus (second century A.D.), not to mention the Byzantine dreambook of Achmes. Their 'science' rested largely on a gradual accumulation of alleged cases which were copied from one textbook into the next, usually without names, dates, or other distinguishing details, thus eventually building up a vast body of 'case law'. But this empirical case law was supplemented by some genuine though limited understanding of the nature of dream symbolism: Artemidorus appreciates, for example, the part played in it by punning associations.[1] Such books necessarily depend on the assumption (which Freud was to share) that dream symbols have in general a standard meaning common to all or most members of a given society[2] or even to the whole of mankind: see for example Artemidorus' list of symbols for women,[3] most of which would be acceptable to present-day analysts. But in order to account for variations in the eventual outcome the Greek interpreters (and already to some extent the Assyrian) found themselves forced increasingly to qualify this assumption by allowing the symbols to have different meanings for members of different professions or persons in different situations. Artemidorus carries this device so far that for a dream of being struck by lightning he admits at least fifteen different interpretations.[4] Casuistry of this sort enabled the expert to explain away false predictions—some vital qualification had been overlooked. Artemidorus warns his son against attempting to interpret any dream unless he knows the dreamer's character and circumstances.[5]

While the *oneirocrits* were thus building up their system for the masses, a few men were trying to make some logical sense of the precognitive dream. The initial impulse to this seems to have come from the doctors. 'The best medical opinion', says Aristotle,

[1] See 3. 38 on the role of significant proper names; 4. 80 on the two senses of *tokos*; and for other examples 1. 22 (p. 29. 9 Pack); 4. 22 (p. 257. 13); 5. 70 (p. 318. 8). Punning associations also play a part in the Egyptian and Assyrian dream interpretations (Oppenheim, op. cit., 241).

[2] That dream symbolism varies from culture to culture is recognized by Artemidorus (1. 9). Synesius, who was Bishop of Cyrene in the fifth century A.D., went further, holding that it varies from person to person: dreambooks were therefore useless—only by keeping careful records of all one's own dreams could one learn their predictive value (*de insomn.* 12).

[3] Preface to Book iv (p. 240. 6 Pack). His list is 'horse, mirror, ship, sea, female animal, articles of female dress, or anything else that symbolizes a woman.'

[4] 2. 9. [5] 4. 59 (p. 283. 4); cf. 1. 9.

'takes dreams seriously'; and we have confirmation in the Hippocratic writings, where dreams are frequently mentioned as clinical symptoms.[1] One fourth-century writer devoted a whole section of his treatise *On Regimen* (Περὶ διαίτης) to a discussion of precognitive dreams,[2] though he does not attempt to cover the entire field; he leaves 'god-sent' dreams to the *oneirocrits*, and he also recognizes that most dreams are merely wish-fulfilments.[3] The dreams which interest him as a doctor are those which express in symbolic form morbid physiological states, and thus have predictive value for the physician. These he attributes to a kind of medical clairvoyance exercised by the soul during sleep, when it is able to survey its bodily dwelling without distraction. And on this basis he proceeds to justify many of the traditional interpretations with the help of more or less fanciful analogies between the external world and the human body, macrocosm and microcosm.

Aristotle's interest in the precognition problem was both deeper and wider. His views about it changed considerably in the course of his lifetime.[4] In surviving fragments of early works which are now lost he accepts precognition and follows Plato in attributing it to an innate capacity of the soul itself, exercised either when withdrawn from the body in sleep or, more especially, when about to abandon the body in death.[5] In the slightly later *Eudemian Ethics* he traces success in divination to an irrational source which is 'superior to mind and deliberation'; hence the special powers in

[1] Aristotle, *de div. per somn.* 463ᵃ4. For examples see *Epidem.* 1. 10 (ii. 670 Littré); *Hum.* 4 (v. 480); *Hebd.* 45 (ix. 460). In particular, anxiety dreams were rightly seen to be significant symptoms of mental trouble, *Morb.* 2. 72 (vii. 110); *Int.* 48 (vii. 286).

[2] Text and French translation in Littré, *Œuvres d'Hippocrate*, vi. 640-63. For the date see W. Jaeger, *Paideia*, iii. 33 ff.

[3] Godsent dreams, chap. 87 (p. 640); wish-fulfilment, chap. 93 (p. 660), 'dreams about familiar persons or objects express a desire of the soul'.

[4] Cf. W. Jaeger, *Aristotle* (Eng. trans. 1934), 333 f.

[5] Frag. 10 Rose³ (= 12a Ross), from the dialogue *On Philosophy*, quoted above, p. 163. Premonitions of the sick were discussed in the still earlier dialogue *Eudemus*. In frag. 37 Rose³ (= 1 Ross) Aristotle tells how his friend Eudemus when lying gravely ill predicted not only his own recovery and survival for the following five years but the imminent death of Alexander, tyrant of Pherae, who was murdered within the next few days. And another fragment of the same work, recently recovered in an Arabic version, describes how a certain Greek king, lying 'in a rapt state betwixt life and death', predicted with accuracy a number of external events: see R. Walzer, 'Un frammento nuovo di Aristotele', *Stud. ital. di Filol. Class.* N.S. 14 (1937), 125 ff. For the popular belief in the mantic powers of the dying cf. Plato, *Apol.* 39 c; Xen. *Cyr.* 8. 7. 21; and the many passages from all periods collected by Pease on Cic. *de div.* 1. 63.

this direction which, as we have seen, he attributes to 'melancholics'.[1] But when he came to write his short essay *On divination in sleep* he took a more cautious view. He no longer talks of the soul's innate power of divination, and the notion of god-sent dreams he explicitly rejects: if the gods wished to communicate knowledge to men they would do it in the daytime, and they would choose the recipients more carefully.[2] Dreams are natural (even animals dream), and nature is not divine, though both nature and dreams may be called 'daemonic'.[3] Two classes of dream he accepts as having intelligible predictive value: those predictive of the dreamer's state of health, which can be reasonably explained (as the medical writers had already seen) by the penetration to consciousness of existing symptoms ignored in waking hours; and those which bring about their own fulfilment by suggesting a course of action to the dreamer.[4] Such dreams are internally generated and present no serious problem. There remain, however, veridical dreams about matters too remote in space or time, or too complex, to admit of explanation on these lines, and, in general, those whose fulfilment is completely independent of the dreamer.[5] Here Aristotle becomes hesitant. 'Melancholics' are mentioned again but are no longer assumed to be specially gifted; they are merely persons in whom nature is exceptionally 'talkative', prompting all manner of visions, some of which are likely at times to come true. And he proceeds to quote a proverb to the effect that if you shoot often enough you will sometimes make a hit.[6] Yet he is not satisfied that coincidence is a sufficient explanation for all cases. He rejects Democritus' atomist hypothesis, but tentatively suggests a non-atomist theory of wave-borne external stimuli, based on the analogy of disturbances propagated in water or air.[7] (This might account for telepathic or clairvoyant dreams, but seems ill suited to explain precognition, since wave disturbances require an existing agent to initiate them. It looks like a half-hearted adaptation of

[1] *Eth. Eud.* 1248ª29–ᵇ4; see above, p. 163. Plato had already associated divination with the irrational soul, *Tim.* 71 d–e.
[2] *De div. per somn.* 464ª20. These objections are taken over and elaborated by Cicero, *de div.* 2. 126, 129.
[3] 463ᵇ12 ff. As Freud remarked, the observation has deep truth if correctly understood (*The Interpretation of Dreams*, chap. 1).
[4] 463ª4 ff., 27 ff. These reductive explanations anticipate respectively the modern types (*b*) and (*c*).
[5] 464ª1 ff. See above, p. 163 n. 4.   [6] 463ᵇ15–22.   [7] 464ª4 ff.

Democritus' telepathic theory with the atomist presuppositions left out.)

Inconclusive though Aristotle's discussion is, it at least removed the topic firmly from the sphere of religion and attempted to apply to it the criteria of common sense. But with the rise of Stoicism a reaction set in. The Stoics defended the reality of precognition both on empirical and on religious grounds. Holding as they did that the course of events (though not men's subjective attitude towards events) is completely determined, and holding at the same time a resolute belief in divine providence (*pronoia*), they argued on the ground of the former assumption that precognition was possible, and on the ground of the latter that it must occur.[1] These *a priori* conclusions they supported, as I have already mentioned,[2] by extensive collections of cases (now lost, but utilized by Cicero in the first book of his work *On divination*).

How, then, should precognition be explained? Ominal divination, they held, had an empirical basis: certain causal sequences had been observed in the past and might be expected (though not with certainty) to occur again in the future. Intuitive divination was another matter: certain persons, in sleep or in abnormal states of consciousness, might with divine help supernormally apprehend, not the future event itself, but the nexus of existing causes from which that event will spring, and from this (unconscious?) apprehension might (unconsciously?) infer the event.[3] This is a reductive theory of what I have called type (*b*) : it reduces precognition to clairvoyance. It was the more acceptable in Antiquity because the ancients believed themselves to live in a finite universe of quite modest dimensions: hence the nexus of present conditions on which the future was thought to depend was for them finite and therefore theoretically knowable in its totality, at least by a god. 'If there were an infinity of worlds,' says Plutarch, 'divination would be impossible.'[4]

A problem which troubled ancient theorists, as it still exercises modern ones,[5] is the possibility of 'intervention', that is to say, of cases where the predicted future is modified as a result of some action prompted by the prediction: as when, for example, some-

---

[1] Cicero, *de div.* I. 125 f.; I. 82.   [2] Above, p. 159.
[3] Cicero, *de div.* I. 126–8.   [4] *Def. orac.* 24, 423 c.
[5] Cf. Louisa E. Rhine, 'Precognition and Intervention', *Journal of Parapsychology* 19 (1955), 1–34; Ian Stevenson, 'Precognition of Disaster', *Journ. Amer. S.P.R.* 64 (1970), 187–210.

Supernormal Phenomena in Classical Antiquity 183

one dreams of being shipwrecked and in consequence cancels his passage on a ship; in the event the ship is wrecked but the dreamer is not involved. That no one can escape his destiny is an assumption illustrated in the folklore of many peoples, including the Greeks (Oedipus is the stock example). But actual behaviour in Antiquity did not reflect this assumption. In Classical Athens it was customary to 'avert' (*aphosiousthai*) the consequences of an unfavourable dream by prayer or sacrifice, or by the simpler magic of 'washing off' the dream or 'telling it to the sun'.[1] Even the Stoics admitted that it was possible to evade the predicted future by such means (if no intervention were possible, what providential purpose could precognition serve?). This did not, according to them, violate determinism, for the 'precognitive' experience and the resulting intervention were in their view equally determined.[2] To which an Epicurean critic replied that if so, the warning had no value: 'for we shall intervene if fated to do so, and fail to intervene if fated not to, however many prophets have warned us'.[3] The critic seems to have the better of the argument.

To judge by surviving specimens, the empirical evidence on which the Stoics relied was by modern standards of the poorest quality. As Cicero pointed out, much of it consisted of anecdotes attached to famous names—Simonides, Alexander the Great, Hannibal, and the like—which were culled from the pages of historians and biographers. '*Quis auctor istorum?*' he asks: 'On what authority do such anecdotes rest?'[4] We shall never know. First-hand ancient reports of precognitive experiences are almost unknown; we seldom have any assurance that the experience was reported before its fulfilment;[5] and the interval between the two

---

[1] Prayer and sacrifice, e.g. Aesch. *Pers.* 201 ff.; *Cho.* 31–46; Theophr. *Char.* 16 (28 Jebb), every time he has a dream the Superstitious Man runs to the *oneirocrits* to ask what god he should sacrifice to. Washing off the dream, Aristoph. *Ran.* 1338 ff. Telling it to the sun, Soph. *El.* 424 and schol. ad loc.; Eur. *I.T.* 42. Similar protective rituals are prescribed in the Egyptian and Assyrian dreambooks (cf. Oppenheim, op. cit. 239). Psychologically they are easy to understand, as providing a discharge for anxiety, but logically they seem to imply either that the dream has causative force—as in modern theories of type (*c*)—or that it expresses a divine intention (which can be reversed); if it were a mere sign of a fixed future there would be no point in annulling it.
[2] Seneca, *Nat. Q.* 2. 37–8 (probably following Chrysippus).
[3] Diogenianus *apud* Euseb. *Praep. Evang.* 4. 3.   [4] *De div.* 2. 135–6; cf. 2. 27.
[5] An exception is the prediction of the Persian defeat at Plataea (Hdt. 9. 16 where the last words of the chapter show that Herodotus realized the importance of this requirement).

events is rarely stated. The only instance known to me which satisfies the first two of these elementary conditions (though not the third) is the dream experienced by Cicero during his exile, in which the ghost of Marius (who had himself suffered exile) led him to Marius' temple of Virtus and promised that he should find safety there; it was in this temple that the decree for his recall was later passed. This dream struck the impressionable Quintus as remarkable, but not his harder-headed brother, who sees in it only daytime residues (he had been thinking much about the example set by Marius) plus a chance coincidence of location. But such as it was, it was his sole experience of a 'precognitive' dream.[1] Rather more striking, and doubtless equally genuine, is Quintus Cicero's dream that his brother Marcus was almost drowned when crossing some wide river on horseback—which duly came to pass (how soon, we are not told). This conforms to a standard modern type of 'crisis-dream'. But it too failed to impress the sceptical Marcus, who refuses to see in it more than a natural expression of brotherly anxiety (Freud would have said, of repressed jealousy directed against his more famous and successful brother); coincidence would in his view sufficiently explain the rest.[2]

Little would be gained by enumerating other, less well attested, examples. But it may be of interest to list, for what they are worth, some general points of agreement between ancient and modern testimony.

In the first place, the content of precognitive dreams is in neither case randomly determined: some selective principle is at work. Aristotle remarks that such dreams mostly concern our personal friends, the reason being that we recognize and attend to stimuli (*kinēseis*) which originate with them; and modern inquiries confirm his remark if not his reason.[3] Moreover, a disproportionate number of ancient 'precognitions' seem to concern deaths or (like Quintus Cicero's dream) violent accidents, and the same is true today. (Modern writers conclude 'that an emotional shock is a factor tending to generate precognitive experiences'—or is it merely that shocking dreams are more often remembered?)[4]

[1] *De div.* 1. 59; 2. 140–1.   [2] Ibid., 1. 58; 2. 140.
[3] Aristotle, *de div. per somn.* 464^{a}27; cf. Stevenson, op. cit. 200.
[4] 'The themes of precognitive experiences (as of most other spontaneous ESP experiences) are mostly serious and shocking events such as deaths and accidents' (Stevenson, 200). Out of 349 cases examined by Saltmarsh (*Proc. S.P.R.* 42 (1934),

Secondly, some 'precognitive' dreams have distinctive marks by which it is thought they can be recognized. One such mark is recurrence, where the same dream is dreamt more than once by the same person or (less often) by different persons.[1] Another is often called *enargeia*, the absence of the usual dream symbolism: this was thought to be characteristic of the 'god-sent' dream, which normally gave its message *en clair*, and the same is generally true of modern 'precognitive' dreams.[2]

What is perhaps more significant is that in Antiquity as today intuitive 'precognition' emerged in states of what we should call 'mental dissociation' and only in these: in dreams (much the commonest channel then as now);[3] in waking states ranging from slight distraction[4] to the hallucinations of the dying or the mentally disturbed; and in 'mediumistic' states voluntarily induced. About the last class something has been said in connection with oracles; but since it was often exploited independently of the official oracles and for purposes other than precognition it will be convenient to give it separate treatment.

III. 'MEDIUMISTIC' AND ALLIED STATES

From the belief that certain mental states are favourable to the emergence of supernormal phenomena it is logically a short step

49 ff.) 99 were concerned with deaths (p. 56). Shock as a factor: Stevenson, 201. In Antiquity, from Homer onwards, diviners were commonly taxed with being 'prophets of evil' (*Iliad* 1. 106 ff.).

[1] For dreams recurring to the same dreamer see Artemidorus 4. 27; Aesch. *P.V.* 655; Herodotus 7. 14; Cicero, *de div* 1. 54, 55, 57, etc.; to a different dreamer Herodotus 7. 15–18 and p. 169 above. For discussion of modern instances, Saltmarsh 57.

[2] For this sense of *enargeia* cf. Aesch. *P.V.* 663, Hdt. 8. 77. All save one of the dreams in Homer are *en clair*, as are most of those described by Cicero. Such dreams are called 'theorematic' by Artemidorus (1. 2, p. 4. 22), 'visions' by Macrobius (*in Somn. Scip.* 1. 3. 9), and sharply distinguished from ordinary symbolic dreams. Modern precognitive dreams are nearly always *en clair*: Saltmarsh (58) found symbolism in only 5 per cent to 6 per cent, Stevenson (199) in $12\frac{1}{2}$ per cent. On the reason for this see my remarks in *Journ. S.P.R.* 28 (1934), 206.

[3] 'The precognitive dream is by far the commonest reported psychic incident at the present time' (D. J. West, *Proc. S.P.R.* 48 (1948), 265); the same was true in Antiquity.

[4] We owe to Aristotle the significant observation that precognition occurs when 'the mind is not occupied with thoughts but as it were deserted and completely empty, so that it responds to an (external) stimulus; similarly some "ecstatics" precognize because their internal stimuli are completely suppressed' (*de div. per somn.* $464^a 22$ ff.). He also recognized that dreams and the hallucinations of the sick have a common cause (*de insomniis* $458^b 25$ ff.).

to the deliberate induction of these states. Of the various devices which have been employed to that end in different societies one of the simplest and most widely used is the practice of prolonged staring at a translucent or shining object which enables a minority of persons[1] to see a series of hallucinatory moving pictures 'within' the object; it seems to be in effect a method of dreaming without going to sleep or, as Myers put it, 'a random glimpse into inner vision'. In modern Europe it is best known under the name of 'crystal-gazing', but the crystal, though an impressive stage property, is inessential; I know in fact no certain instance of its use before Byzantine times.[2] I shall adopt the old English term 'scrying', which is neutral as to the nature of the translucent object or 'speculum'.

The ancients were acquainted with at least two methods of scrying, which (as Delatte[3] showed) were distinct in origin, although the same sensory automatism underlies both. In one method, for which the term 'catoptromancy' has been coined, the speculum is a mirror. It appears that it was sufficiently familiar in fifth-century Athens to furnish Aristophanes with the material for a joke: in the *Acharnians* Lamachus uses his shield as a mirror after it has been burnished with oil and pretends to see in it the future condemnation of Dicaeopolis for cowardice. The Alexandrian scholars understood this as an allusion to scrying, and I have little doubt that they were right—no other explanation really fits.[4] Later references to catoptromancy are sparse, other methods

---

[1] Myers estimated that perhaps one man or woman in twenty can procure hallucinations by scrying, and that of these successful scryers again perhaps one in twenty obtains in this way 'information not attainable by ordinary means' (*Human Personality*, I. 237). The ancient and medieval use of young boys for the purpose may have somewhat increased the proportion of successes; see below, p. 190. William of Auvergne judged from personal experience that among boy and girl scryers possibly one in seven or one in ten might succeed (Delatte, *Catoptromancie*, 30).

[2] 'Cristallomancy' appears for the first time under that name in Byzantine books of magic (Delatte, 174 ff.). It seems that certain gems, credited with magical properties, were used in connection with 'hydromantic' scrying as early as Pliny's time (*N.H.* 37. 73. 3), but whether as the actual speculum is not clear. In the sixth century, however, Damascius saw a holy stone, 'round and whitish', which was certainly used for scrying: see below, p. 191.

[3] Delatte, *Catoptromancie*, a work of wide learning to which I am heavily indebted.

[4] *Ach.* 1128 ff. and scholia ad loc.; cf. Delatte, 133 ff. For the shield used as a mirror cf. Pherecrates, frag. 145. 11 f. Kock. The *Acharnians* passage seems to be the only solid piece of evidence for scrying in Greek lands before the first

having come into fashion; but it was known to Iamblichus as an alternative to hydromancy,[1] and it was allegedly used in A.D. 193 by the Emperor Didius Julianus to ascertain his future, employing a mirror 'in which boys with their eyes blindfolded and their heads enchanted are reported to see things'.[2] We also hear of scrying in a mirror suspended over a holy well or spring (thus combining the virtues of mirror-magic with those of water-magic) : this was done in Pausanias' day at a spring beside the precinct of Demeter at Patras with the object of foreseeing the course of a patient's malady;[3] it was still practised fairly recently on the island of Andros, for the more cheerful purpose of enabling a young girl to see the image of her future husband.[4]

The alternative and in later times more frequently mentioned method, which ancient authors call indifferently lecanomancy ('divination by bowls') or hydromancy ('divination by water'), used as speculum a simple vessel of water (as some modern scryers have done),[5] with or without the addition of a film of oil. This

century B.C. The well-known red-figure vase in Berlin (Beazley, *A.R.V.* 739. 5) which shows Aegeus consulting the legendary Delphic prophetess Themis has sometimes been interpreted as a scene of hydromancy (A. B. Cook, *Zeus*, ii. 206, etc.) or of catoptromancy (Delatte, 186) ; but in the absence of any evidence for scrying as a Delphic method I hesitate to give the guess much weight. Cf. P. Amandry, *La Mantique apollinienne à Delphes* (1950), 66 ff. and T. J. Dunbabin, *B.S.A.* 46 (1951), 65 f.

[1] *De myst.* 2. 10 (p. 94. 3 Parthey). Iamblichus thinks both these techniques inferior to his own 'theurgic' methods.

[2] *Historia Augusta, Didius Julianus* 7. The blindfolding (*praeligatis oculis*) has naturally puzzled interpreters: cf. Myers, *Classical Essays* (1883), 65 ; Ganszyniec in Pauly–Wissowa xi. 28, s.v. κατοπτρομαντεία; Delatte, 140 f. One or two modern scryers have claimed to be able to see visions in total darkness without a speculum ; Delatte suggests that this may be the case here, the mirror being a mere symbolic appurtenance. But it seems more likely that the late and careless compiler has misunderstood or misrepresented the source which he is abbreviating: the scryer may well have been blindfolded during the preliminary incantation (to keep him from gazing prematurely), just as his eyes are to be kept closed or covered for a time in the hydromantic rituals prescribed in the Griffith–Thompson demotic papyrus, col. iii. 14 f., xiv. 24, etc. (cf. A. Abt, *Die Apologie des Apuleius von Madaura und die antike Zauberei* (1908), 248 f.).

[3] Paus. 7. 21. 12. The speculum was the mirror, which was not submerged but suspended at water level; but the prophetic virtue was thought to reside in the *pneuma* coming up from the 'truthful' water. The spring in question is still credited with healing powers (Herbillon, *Les Cultes de Patras* (1929), 24, 28). Such rituals are parodied by Lucian, *Vera Historia* 1. 26. Cf. Halliday, *Greek Divination* (1913), 151 ff.; Delatte, 135 ff.

[4] Sir Rennell Rodd, *Customs and Lore of Modern Greece* (1892), 185.

[5] e.g. Mrs. Verrall found a glass of water as effective as a crystal (*Proc. S.P.R.* 8 (1892), 473).

technique was borrowed, as the ancient writers acknowledge,[1] from the Middle East where it had a long history. It seems to have originated in Babylonia as a purely ominal mode of divination, from the shapes which oil assumes when poured on to the surface of water (like our Hallowe'en divination from melted lead or white of egg poured into water).[2] But concentration on observing the omens will have induced hallucinatory visions in a certain number of subjects, and in course of time more significance was attached to the vision than to the omen. The oil could then be dispensed with, though it was often retained out of respect for tradition or to give increased luminosity. By the time it reached the Greco-Roman world—in the first century B.C. or earlier, probably via Egypt—the transformation of the rite seems to have been complete. This is obviously the case where water alone is used, and we can probably assume it wherever a detailed vision is described. An excellent though late instance is the 'holy woman' known to the philosopher Isidore, who 'would pour clean water into a glass goblet and used to see down in the water inside the goblet phantasms of coming events; and the predictions she made from her vision regularly came to pass.'[3]

The purpose of the rite was most often precognition, either by direct vision as in the case of the holy woman or by inducing a god or daemon to appear in the speculum and answer questions.[4] Spells for evoking a god in this way are given in the magical papyri; and this is perhaps the explanation of Varro's curiously worded story about the boy who foresaw (and described in a poem of 160 verses!) the future course of the Mithridatic war by watching an image or phantasm (*simulacrum*) of the god Mercury in water.[5] Varro locates the story at Tralles in Caria. Is it pure

[1] Varro *apud* Aug. *Civ. Dei* 7. 35; Strabo 16. 2. 39; Pliny, *N.H.* 37. 192.
[2] H. Hunger, *Becherwahrsagung bei den Babyloniern* (diss. Leipzig, 1903).
[3] Damascius, *vita Isidori, apud* Photius, *Bibl.* cod. 242. 191 (p. 268 Zintzen).
[4] According to Varro (*apud* Aug. *Civ. Dei* 7. 35) the original purpose of hydromancy was 'to see in water the images of gods', and this is the usual aim of the hydromantic spells in the papyri, e.g. *P.G.M.* iv. 161 ff.
[5] Varro *apud* Apuleius, *Apol.* 42. *Simulacrum* is ambiguous: it could refer to an effigy of Mercury engraved on the inside of the bowl or to a hallucinatory image seen in the water by the boy. The former view gets some support from a spell in the Griffith-Thompson demotic papyrus where a figure of Anubis is to be engraved within the bowl (col. xiv, p. 101)—though the surfacing of oil would there make the figure invisible to the scryer. But the second view, which is Abt's, fits Varro's opinion better (see preceding note). The boy's report of what he saw was presumably amplified and versified later by the magician or priest, as was

coincidence that a century later the same little town produced the medical charlatan Thessalus, who has left us a highly coloured account of his search for magical knowledge? The quest brings him to Egyptian Thebes, where he meets a priest 'who could procure personal[1] visions by means of a bowl of water'; after ritual fasting the priest obtains for him a vision of Asclepius, who appears seated on his throne (in the bowl of water?) and answers his questions on astrological botany.[2]

Scrying was practised under the aegis of religion. We possess the epitaph from the year A.D. 129 of a priest of Dionysus at Salonica who was also an official 'hydroscopist' or scryer.[3] The magician in Thessalus' story is likewise a priest; the 'vision' is preceded by ritual fasting and incantations and is described with all the solemn trappings of a theophany. But similar methods could also be employed for less exalted purposes. Varro's contemporary Nigidius Figulus, a Neopythagorean much addicted to magical practices, used incantations to enable certain boys to discover, probably by scrying, the whereabouts of a missing sum of money.[4] So too a Christian dignitary, Sophronius, Bishop of

the custom at Delphi and other oracles. (But the whole story may of course be, like so many political oracles, a *vaticinatio post eventum*.)

[1] αὐτοπτικήν: i.e. without using proxy scryers.
[2] Text, ed. H.-V. Friedrich, *Beiträge z. Klass. Philol.*, Heft 28 (1968). Translated and discussed by Festugière, *Revue Biblique*, 48 (1939), 45 ff. (cf. also *Rév. d'Hermès* i. 56 ff.). That the author can be identified as Thessalus of Tralles was convincingly argued by Cumont, *Rev. de Phil.* 42 (1918), 85 ff. Much has been made of his 'vision'. Festugière, who takes it as an honest description of a personal experience, thinks it can be explained only by 'hypnotism' or by fraud on the part of the priest; he excludes scrying on the ground that the god is seen seated on an actual material throne. But why is the priest's skill in lecanomancy mentioned if it leads up to nothing in the event? I think we are probably meant to suppose that Thessalus, who is seated opposite the throne, sees it reflected in a bowl of water and then sees a phantasmal Asclepius occupy the phantasmal throne: the scryer employed by Bishop Sophronius (see below, p. 190 n. 1) has a closely similar vision of 'a man seated on a golden throne'. However, this is perhaps (with all respect to Festugière's great authority) a pseudo-problem. The purpose of Thessalus' 'vision' is after all to lend supernatural confirmation to a collection of astrobotanical lore—a type of pious fiction of which later Antiquity offers numerous examples. In some MSS., for greater authority, the part of Thessalus is played by Asclepius himself and that of Asclepius by Hermes Trismegistus.
[3] Quoted by Nilsson, *Geschichte der griech. Religion*, ii. 509, from Heuzey et Daumet, *Mission arch. de Macédonie* (1876), 280.
[4] Varro *apud* Apul. *Apol.* 42. The method employed is not stated, but the context and the use of 'boys' in the plural make scrying the most probable; Abt's argument to the contrary (p. 251) seems very weak.

Tella, was accused in the year 449 of scrying to discover the identity of a thief.[1] And we even hear of a Christian charioteer who consulted the monk Hilarion as to the reason for his ill success in the games; the monk caused him to scry in a cup of water, where he perceived that his chariots were 'bound' (*dedemenoi*) by a spell which his opponents had cast.[2] In this sphere as in others the advent of Christianity failed to abolish pagan practices, as is clear from the later history of scrying, both at Byzantium and in the medieval West.[3]

Some features of the ancient usage are deserving of notice. In the first place, where the scrying is done by proxy, the proxy, both in Antiquity and in the Middle Ages, is almost invariably a boy or a team of boys below the age of puberty. The primary reason for this choice is no doubt a ritual one: sexual purity is a common ritual requirement in magical operations. But Apuleius[4] was probably correct in remarking that an *animus puerilis et simplex* is especially suited to this purpose. Piaget has shown that the sharp distinction between fancy and objective vision is slow to develop in children—they see faces in the fire or landscapes in the clouds more readily than adults.

Secondly, the source of the vision is assumed to be external to the scryer, and its content is largely determined by the contemporary culture-pattern. Most often a single figure is seen, as in the 'god-sent' oracular dream, and this figure is taken to be, in Varro's words, 'the image of a god' (or, less frequently, the image of a dead man).[5] The images of contemporary events which have

---

[1] See E. Peterson, 'Die Zauber-praktiken eines syrischen Bischofs', *Miscellanea Pio Paschini* (1948), 1. 95 ff., reprinted with additions in his *Frühkirche, Judentum und Gnosis* (1959), 333 ff. The detection of thieves was a frequent motive for scrying in the Middle Ages (cf. Delatte, 16, 25, 29, etc.), as also among modern primitives (Andrew Lang, *The Making of Religion* (1898), 90 ff.).

[2] Quoted by Casaubon on *Historia Augusta, Didius Julianus* 7. But in Jerome's Latin version of the story, *vita Hilarionis* 20, the scrying is omitted: Jerome may not have wished to attribute a pagan practice to his hero.

[3] On scrying in medieval and later times see Delatte, 13–132 and 154–84; also T. Besterman, *Crystal-gazing* (1924).

[4] Apuleius, *Apol.* 43. Cf. T. Hopfner, 'Die Kinder-Medien in den griechisch-ägyptischen Zauberpapyri', *Recueil Kondakov* (1926), 65 ff.; A.-J. Festugière, *Révélation d'Hermès* i. 348–50; and below, p. 201. Keith Thomas cites the view of a seventeenth-century magician: 'When a spirit is raised none hath power to see it but children of eleven & twelve years of age, or such as are true maids' (*Religion and the Decline of Magic* (1971), 268).

[5] Varro, *apud* Aug. *Civ. Dei* 7. 35. But Thessalus is offered a choice between a vision of a god or one of a ghost, and a similar option is implied at *P.G.M.* iv.

chiefly interested modern students of the subject are relatively seldom reported in Antiquity: the clearest case is that of the boy employed by Sophronius, who is said to have had on one occasion a veridical vision of the bishop's son riding out of Constantinople on a black female mule in the company of two other men.[1] A curious feature is that auditory as well as visual hallucinations are sometimes apparently involved. The papyri promise that a god will appear in the vessel and *answer the inquirer's questions*, as Asclepius does in the narrative of Thessalus. The scrying-stone which Damascius saw uttered 'a sound like a thin whistling', which a priest proceeded to interpret; with this we may compare Psellus' complaint that the spirits which enter the water speak indistinctly on purpose, wishing to leave themselves a loophole in case their predictions prove false.[2] In modern times auditory automatism has occasionally been procured by applying a shell to the ear, but it is very rarely reported as an accompaniment of scrying: I have seen accounts of only two such cases.[3] Here also we should probably make large allowance for the influence of the culture-pattern: the ancient scryer, accustomed to the spoken oracle delivered in the first person and to the oracular 'message-dream', may have expected (and *been* expected) to hear as well as see, and his expectation may on occasion have been rewarded.[4] (It is perhaps worth adding that Hippolytus includes in his

227 and 250. Necromantic scrying is also referred to by Pliny (*N.H.* 37. 73. 192) and in the *Cyranides* (p. 30. 24 Ruelle).

[1] See Peterson, 100. It seems that this vision was the outcome of a special ritual: the boy scried first in a pit filled with water and oil, then in white of egg, and the same picture appeared in both media.

[2] *P.G.M.* iv. 227 ff.; Griffith–Thompson pap., col. xiv. 27; Damascius *apud* Photius, *vita Isidori* 203 (p. 276. 22 Zintzen); Psellus, *quaenam sunt Graecorum opiniones de daemonibus* (Migne, *Patr. Gr.* 122, 881B: from Proclus?). It is tempting to include here (with Delatte, 104 n. 4) the famous anecdote in Petronius about the sibyl 'suspended in a bottle' who was questioned by certain boys, 'What is it you want?' and answered 'I want to die' (*Sat.* 48). But Ampelius (8. 16) knows of the bottled sibyl as a temple exhibit, which seems to tell against Delatte's suggestion.

[3] In one of these, the Salis experiment reported by Mrs. Henry Sidgwick, *Proc. S.P.R.* 33 (1923), 41 ff., the auditory automatism was provoked by post-hypnotic suggestion. The other is a case published by H. Silberer, *Zentralblatt f. Psychoanalyse* 2 (1911), 383 f., and quoted by Hopfner, 'Kindermedien', 73. On 'shell-hearing' see Myers in *Proc. S.P.R.* 8 (1892), 492–5; and on the problem generally, Delatte, 177 f.

[4] Cf. Keith Thomas, *Religion and the Decline of Magic*, 89: 'In hallucination, no less than in ordinary vision, human perception is governed by stereotypes inherited from the particular society in which men live.'

collection of conjuring tricks a device which could be used to fake both visual and auditory automatism: a cauldron of water with a glass bottom is placed over a small skylight, and the scryer, gazing into the cauldron, sees (and perhaps hears?) in its depths certain demons, who are really the magician's accomplices seated in the room below.)[1]

Spontaneous auditory automatism appears to have been less frequent in the Greco-Roman world than it was among the Jews. But there is one celebrated exception—the 'daemonic sign' of Socrates. From childhood onwards (as Plato tells us) he was accustomed to hear an admonitory voice which dissuaded him from some intended course of action—often a seemingly trivial action—but never offered positive counsel.[2] The experience, he thought, was all but unparalleled,[3] and he took it seriously, believing the voice to come from a source outside himself which he called 'daemonic' but did not attempt to specify more closely. Whether the voice was fully externalized as an auditory hallucination or reached his consciousness only as an inward monition we are hardly in a position to decide.[4] Later antiquity assumed it to be the voice of an indwelling personal daemon, a sort of guardian angel or spirit guide,[5] but it does not appear that Socrates or his immediate disciples made any such claim (though his accusers may well have understood it so). Nor does it seem from the examples—whether actual or merely typical—which are quoted by Plato and Xenophon that its warnings were based on anything that we should call supernormal precognition; it is only in later works, such as the spurious dialogue *Theages*, that

---

[1] Hippolytus, *Ref. omn. haer.* (ed. Wendland, *G.C.S.* vol. xxvi), 4. 35. Cf. Ganschinietz, 'Hippolyts Capitel über die Magier', *Texte und Untersuchungen*, 39 (1913). Modern use of a similar device is reported by F. Podmore, *Modern Spiritualism* (1902), 11. 249 f. But conscious fraud seldom plays a part in modern cases.

[2] Plato, *Apol.* 31 d, 40 a.   [3] Plato, *Rep.* 496 c.

[4] In one place Socrates is made to say 'I seemed to hear a voice' (*Phaedrus* 242 b), but this is hardly decisive, and the frequent description of the experience as a 'sign' or 'signal' (*sēmeion*) perhaps points rather (as Myers thought) to an inward sense of inhibition.

[5] See the lengthy discussions in Plutarch, *gen. Socr.* 20; Apuleius, *de deo Socratis* 17 ff.; Maximus of Tyre, *orat.* 8–9; Proclus, *in Alc. i*, pp. 78–83 Creuzer; Olympiodorus, *in Alc. i*, pp. 21–3 Creuzer: Hermeias, *in Phaedrum*, pp. 65–9 Couvreur. Olympiodorus actually equates the 'daemon' with the Christian 'guardian angel'. But Hermeias comes nearer to the modern view when he speaks of the daemon as the supra-rational personality which controls the *whole* of our life, including involuntary functions like dreaming and digestion.

Socrates is represented as making oracular predictions about public events.¹

Auditory and visual automatism have their counterpart in motor automatism, the unconscious muscular action which accounts for the phenomena of automatic writing and drawing, table-tilting and the so-called 'ouija-board'. We do not hear of graphic automatism or jumping tables in Antiquity, but we possess a detailed account of a magical operation performed in the year A.D. 371 whose principle was that of the ouija-board.² It is for once well attested, being based on the confession of one of the participants, who were subsequently brought to trial for treason. Their instrument, produced in court at the trial, was a tripod of olive wood which supported a circular metal dish on whose rim were engraved the 24 letters of the Greek alphabet. Above the dish the operator held a ring suspended on a very light linen thread. After prolonged incantations, addressed to 'the deity of precognition' (unnamed), 'at last', says the confession, 'we got the thing to work'.³ The ring began to swing from letter to letter, picking out words, and eventually spelt out 'hexameter verses appropriate to the questions addressed to it'.⁴ Then someone

---

¹ [Plato], *Theages* 128 d ff. The examples given in this dialogue are very different from anything we hear of in the genuine works of Plato; Socrates appears as a sort of 'Wundermann' after the style of Pythagoras. With A. E. Taylor (*Plato, the Man and his Work*³, (1929), 532 ff.) I should incline to attribute the *Theages* to the miracle-mongering circle of men like Xenocrates and Heraclides Ponticus. Further apocryphal tales of Socrates' prophetic powers were collected by Antipater; Cicero offers specimens (*de div.* 1. 123).

² The fullest and most trustworthy account is that given by Ammianus, 29. 1. 25–32. Other sources include Sozomen 6. 35; Zosimus 4. 13 f.; and Socrates 4. 19.

³ *movimus tandem*: not, as Andrew Lang understood it, 'we got the tripod to move'—for that would have been irrelevant to the purpose intended—but simply 'we got things going, obtained a result'. The unnamed deity (*numen*) is presumably Apollo, since the *mensula* was constructed 'after the fashion of the Delphic tripod'. The church historian Socrates speaks of necromancy, but by his day the word had lost its specific meaning and become a general term of abuse like the Latin *nigromantia*. The Byzantine writers Zonaras and Cedrenus assume that the letters were picked out by a live cock (electryomancy, a form of ominal divination); their opinion cannot, however, weigh against the contemporary authority of Ammianus.

⁴ For responses in verse cf. *P.G.M.* iv. 161 ff. and my *Greeks and the Irrational* 92 f. Ammianus quotes some tolerable Greek hexameters which appear to have been spelt out by the ring. They predict the death of Valens 'when battle rages on the plains of Mimas', and Ammianus later (31. 14. 8 f.) reports a claim that the prediction was in the event obliquely confirmed; but this may be merely the gossip of pious pagans, anxious to defend Apollo's veracity.

asked the question they had come to ask: 'What man shall be Emperor after Valens?' Slowly the ring started to spell: *theta*, then *epsilon*, then *omikron*. 'Ah,' they said, 'Theodorus!' and went home.[1] But they were mistaken, as the event proved. One of them happened to mention the little experiment to a friend—or what he thought was a friend. Soon after, all of them were arrested, tried, and executed; and to be on the safe side, though he denied all knowledge of the affair, Theodorus was executed also. Nevertheless it was the ring that had the last laugh. Seven years later Valens was killed. The name of his successor was Theodosius.

Modern experience suggests that the operator at that fatal séance was probably as innocent of conscious fraud as his too inquisitive employers. To the best of my knowledge it is the only certain example of the use by ancient diviners of a ouija-like technique.[2] But the same principle of unconscious muscular pressure may account for the curious belief that certain very holy statues when carried on the shoulders of priests or other ritually pure persons guided their involuntary movements and thus gave oracular responses by signs in place of speech. This was from an early date the practice at the Egyptian oracle of Zeus Ammon, where a corps of eighty priests carried in procession an ancient wooden statue, 'moving involuntarily (αὐτομάτως) wherever the god's will directs their course'. Diodorus says this was a unique oracular method, but Macrobius records a similar procedure at Baalbek (Heliopolis) with a statue of Egyptian provenance: there the bearers 'are moved by the divine spirit, not of their own volition, but carry the statue wherever the god propels it'. Macrobius further cites as a parallel 'the oracular moving statues

---

[1] Some translators, taking *cum adiectione litterae posterae* with what precedes, make the ring spell out THEOD- (as it certainly would have done in a fictitious narrative). But the words make better sense if construed with what follows: the meaning then is that when the ring in its slow progress had got as far as THEO- an impatient sitter supplied the next letter.

[2] Marinus' statement that Proclus 'tested the divinatory power of the tripod' (*vit. Procli* 28) does not necessarily refer to an experiment of this kind: the magical papyri prescribe the use of tripods for a wide variety of operations. Richard Wünsch compared the table of divination found at Pergamon (*Antikes Zaubergerät aus Pergamon*, 1905). But if Wünsch's explanation of the use of the Pergamene table is correct, the superficial similarities conceal what is, from the modern standpoint, a basic difference: the Pergamene device worked on the principle of a roulette table, not on the principle of a ouija-board; the outcome was determined not by human action, conscious or unconscious, but purely by chance.

of the Fortunes which we see at Antium'. But the technique no doubt had its origin in Egypt.[1] One other form of automatism remains to be discussed— automatic speech. This involves a much more profound degree of dissociation than the types so far considered, and has correspondingly made a much deeper impression on the popular imagination at all periods. It is often accompanied by bizarre and startling manifestations. A female automatist will suddenly begin to speak in a deep male voice; her bearing, her gestures, her facial expression are abruptly transformed; she speaks of matters quite outside her normal range of interests, and sometimes in a strange language or in a manner quite foreign to her normal character; and when her normal speech is restored she frequently has no memory of what she said.[2] Everything happens, in fact, as if an alien personality had taken a temporary lease of her body and used her vocal organs as its instrument, speaking of itself in the first person and of the automatist in the third. It was inevitable that such phenomena should be taken nearly everywhere at their face value—as they still are by many persons in our own society—and interpreted as cases of possession by an external spirit. And when once possession was accepted as a *vera causa* it was almost equally inevitable that the notion should be extended to cover a wide range of unexplained pathological conditions. In Antiquity not only were cases of epilepsy and delusional insanity put down to the intervention of hostile demons, but even such things as sleepwalking and the delirium of high fever were popularly ascribed to the same cause.[3] My concern here, however, is

[1] Zeus Ammon: Diodorus 17. 50. 6; Curtius Rufus 4. 7. 23. Baalbek: Macrobius, *Sat.* 1. 23. 13; cf. also Lucian (?), *de dea Syria* 36 f., who describes with miraculous embellishments a like practice at Hierapolis. For the Egyptian origin see Parke, *The Oracles of Zeus*, 200; for the explanation, R. Vallois, *Rev. des études grecques*, 44 (1931), 121–52. A similar belief is held today concerning a statue of the Virgin at Salamis. I cannot deal here with the wider topic of animated statues in general, most recently discussed by P. Boyancé in *Rev. Hist. Rel.* (= *Annales du Musée Guimet*), 147 (1955), 189–209.

[2] A wide range of examples, historical and contemporary, will be found in T. K. Oesterreich's still indispensable book, *Possession, Demoniacal and Other* (1921; Eng. trans. 1930, repr. 1966). J. Beattie and J. Middleton (eds.), *Spirit Mediumship and Society in Africa* (1969), also offer rich comparative material.

[3] See *The Greeks and the Irrational*, 65–8, 83–5; and for a fuller treatment the excellent little book of G. Lanata, *Medicina magica e religione popolare in Grecia* (1967). It has recently been argued (W. D. Smith, 'So-called possession in preChristian Greece', *T.A.P.A.* 96 (1965), 403–26) that there is no real evidence for a belief in possession in the classical period of Greek literature. And it is

only with those cases of true automatism which are of potential interest to the psychical researcher.

States of 'possession' are everywhere viewed with a mixture of fear, curiosity, repulsion, and religious veneration, compounded in proportions which vary with the nature of the symptoms displayed and also with the belief-pattern current in each society. Where the condition is persistent and accompanied by grossly pathological behaviour, the possessing agent is assumed to be an evil spirit and ritual techniques of exorcism are developed—often with the effect of inducing by suggestion the symptoms they are designed to cure. In Antiquity exorcism was practised by Jews, Egyptians, and Greeks before it was taken over and institutionalized by the Christians.[1] But where the symptoms are benign, as they normally are in true automatism, the 'possessed' are highly valued as channels of communication with the supernatural world; 'mediumship' is deliberately sought, is ritually controlled and canalized, and in many societies acquires high religious and social importance. The most influential of all Greek religious institutions, the oracle of Delphi, owed that influence entirely to the powers attributed to an entranced woman, the Pythia. The belief almost universally held by pagans and Christians alike, over a period of more than a millennium, that through the lips of the Pythia an alien voice spoke in the first person, cannot be dismissed as a simple product of conscious fraud or even as a *fable convenue*. Nor is the old Stoic explanation by mephitic vapours

certainly true that not every reference to demoniacal 'attacks' (*ephodoi, epibolai*) need be taken as implying such a belief. But as regards 'divine' possession the words *entheos* ('having a god inside one') and *enthousiān*, which were in common use from the fifth century B.C. onwards, and *katechesthai* ('to be occupied by god', Plato), testify directly to the belief. And the 'god's use of the first person in Delphic responses would be hard to explain otherwise, even if we had not Plato's explicit statement (whether seriously meant or not) about 'oracle-givers and inspired prophets' that 'it is not they who speak, since their intelligence is not present, but the god himself who speaks to us through them' (*Ion* 534 d).

[1] For detailed descriptions of Jewish and pagan exorcism see Josephus, *Ant. Jud.* 8. 2. 5, and Philostratus, *vit. Apoll.* 3. 38 and 4. 20; for an Egyptian exorcist formula employing Jewish and Christian *nomina sacra*, *P.G.M.* iv. 1227 ff. Further passages are collected in J. Tambornino's useful book, *De antiquorum daemonismo* (R.G.V.V. vii. 3, 1909), 75 ff. All these texts are relatively late; and it seems likely that the practice of formal exorcism, as distinct from simple rites of purification, only developed *pari passu* with the growing fear of demons which characterized the Roman Imperial Age (cf. W. D. Smith, op. cit. 409). On the growth of Christian exorcism see Harnack, *Mission and Expansion of Christianity* (Eng. trans. 1908), 1. 125–46, and K. Thraede in *R.A.C.* vii, s.v. 'Exorzismus'.

Supernormal Phenomena in Classical Antiquity 197

any longer tenable: there are no vapours at Delphi, and the geologists assure us that there can never have been any.[1] It remains to accept the view to which all analogy points, that the entranced woman was a vocal automatist, what we now call by the question-begging term 'medium'.

Our information about the psychology of the Pythia is regrettably scanty, but what we have is consistent with this view.[2] The onset of trance was induced by such ritual acts as sitting on the god's holy seat, touching his sacred laurel and drinking from a holy spring—all of them actions charged with auto-suggestive power. The trance could of course be simulated. But Plutarch tells us of a recent Pythia who on one occasion began to speak in a hoarse voice and throw herself about as if possessed by an evil spirit, then rushed screaming from the sanctuary, and actually died within a few days. He seems to have had this story from one of those present, and if so it is good evidence that as late as the first century after Christ the trance was at least sometimes genuine.[3]

Again, all our sources testify to the singularity and obscurity of the Pythia's utterances. In her normal personality she was a perfectly ordinary woman who had no special gifts or special knowledge.[4] When she became possessed (*entheos*) she did not 'rave' or foam at the mouth—it was Roman poets like Lucan who first popularized that notion—but she spoke in riddling symbols. Heraclitus[5] remarked that 'the god of Delphi neither declares the truth nor conceals it, but points to it': the Pythia supplied *pointers* which the priests had to interpret and amplify. The same thing could be said of many modern 'trance-mediums'. They

[1] See A. P. Oppé's now classic paper, 'The Chasm at Delphi', *J.H.S.* 24 (1904), 214 ff.; and P. Amandry's careful discussion, *La Mantique apollonienne à Delphes* (1950), chap. xix.

[2] I have discussed the function of the Pythia more fully in *The Greeks and the Irrational*, 70–5 and 87–93.

[3] Plutarch, *def. orac.* 51. There is no reason to doubt the correctness of his report. I have myself seen a medium break down during trance in a somewhat similar way, though without the same fatal results. Changes of voice are characteristic of mediumistic possession, both savage and civilized; and cases of 'demoniac' possession ending in death are reported by Oesterreich, 117 ff., 222 ff.

[4] Plato, *Phaedrus* 244 a–b; Aelius Aristides, *orat.* 45. 11 Dind. Plutarch describes the Pythia of his own day, whom he knew personally, as a woman of honest upbringing and respectable life, but with little education or experience of the world (*Pyth. orac.* 22). The same is true of some famous modern mediums like Mrs. Piper and Mrs. Leonard.

[5] Heraclitus, frag. 93 Diels-Kranz. Cf. Aesch. *Ag.* 1255; Soph. frag. 771 Pearson; etc.

speak as a rule quite calmly, but their answers to questions are commonly indirect and frequently cryptic; their communications tend to take the form of a chain of symbolic images, linked by association rather than logic. And behind the stylized diction of extant Delphic responses we can still at times detect traces of their possible origin in just such a mode of speech. Between the Pythia's words and the published response we must indeed allow for an extensive process of interpretation and reshaping, a process which must often have been governed by rational considerations of policy. Nevertheless the famous ambiguity of the responses need not always have been due to the calculating caution of a hard-headed priesthood; it may very well have originated in many cases with the entranced woman on the tripod.

The Pythia was unique in the lofty status accorded to her throughout the Greek world and beyond it, but she was not unique in kind. Plato couples with her 'the priestesses at Dodona' as examples of persons who possess the divine gift of prophecy but can exercise it only in the state of trance (*maneisai*), and adds that there are other instances too familiar to need mention.[1] And if we can trust Aelius Aristides there were still trance mediums at Dodona in the second century A.D.; he supplies the interesting information that on awaking 'they know nothing of what they have said', which indicates a relatively deep degree of dissociation.[2] It also appears, from such evidence as we have, that trance mediumship was practised in the Roman Imperial Age, if not earlier, at the two great Apolline oracles of Asiatic Greece, Didyma (sometimes called Branchidae) and Claros. According to Iamblichus the priestess at Didyma after contact with a sacred spring was possessed by the god and predicted the future.[3] For Claros we have in addition the more reliable evidence of Tacitus and Pliny: there the functions of the Pythia were discharged by a priest who after drinking from a sacred spring uttered prophecies in verse, though he was generally (like the Pythia) an unlettered

---

[1] *Phaedrus* 244 a–b. I cannot agree with Professor Parke (op. cit. 83) in rejecting this explicit testimony: see *Hermathena* 1968, 88 f. If Plato's statement needs support it can be found in Sophocles, frag. 456 Pearson, where the Dodonaean priestesses are described as θεσπιῳδοί, a word which surely implies at least some form of inspired utterance.

[2] Aristides, *orat.* 45. 11. He speaks as if this were still true in his own day; and with his lifelong interest in oracles he is unlikely to have relied on pure hearsay.

[3] *De myst.* 3. 11, pp. 123. 12 ff., 127. 3 ff. Parthey.

person; his predictions (like those of the Pythia) were, we are told, enigmatic 'as is the way of oracles'.[1]

Apart from the official oracles classical Greece also knew of private persons who possessed or claimed to possess the gift of automatic speech. They were known as 'belly-talkers' (*engastrimuthoi*),[2] since they were believed to have a daemon in their bellies which spoke through their lips and predicted the future. It seems that like modern mediums they spoke in a state of trance, for an old Hippocratic casebook compares the stertorous breathing of a heart patient to that of 'the women called belly-talkers'.[3] The name of one of them, a certain Eurycles, has come down to us, but it does not appear that he was regarded with much reverence: Plato calls him 'that queer fellow (*atopos*)', and Aristophanes uses him as material for a joke.[4] Later ages took such persons more seriously. They went by the more respectful name of 'pythons', and a speaker in Plutarch draws the crucial (and psychologically inescapable) comparison between these private mediums and the Delphic Pythia, though only to reject it.[5]

The 'possession' of both Pythia and pythons was, so far as we know, auto-suggestively induced.[6] But in the Egyptian papyri, both Greek and demotic, we find spells by which a magician may induce it. To quote a single Greek example, the great Paris papyrus gives an elaborate recipe for summoning a 'god' to enter into a child or adult and speak through him.[7] The ceremonial culminates in a sevenfold repetition of a magic formula in the medium's ear, after which we are told that the medium will fall

[1] Tacitus, *Annals* 2. 54; Pliny, *N.H.* 2. 106; Iamb. *de myst.* 3. 11, p. 124. 9 ff. Parthey. It is noteworthy that sacred springs play a part at all three of the major Apolline oracles (the one at Didyma is now inscriptionally attested, Wiegand, *Abh. Berl. Akad.* 1924, Heft 1, p. 22). Was their sacredness the starting-point which determined the location of the oracles? Pliny asserts that drinking the spring at Claros shortened the drinker's life, but its waters, which are still available to the curious, appear to be perfectly wholesome.

[2] Mistranslated 'ventriloquists' in many of the older books and in L.S.J.; rightly corrected to 'mediums' in L.S.J. Suppl.

[3] Hipp. *Epid.* 5. 63 (= 7. 28). For the stertorous breathing of entranced mediums cf. Amy Tanner, *Studies in Spiritism* (1910), 14.

[4] Plato, *Soph.* 252 c; Aristoph. *Wasps* 1019.

[5] Plutarch, *def. orac.* 9. Clement of Alexandria says they were still esteemed by the masses in his day (*Protrept.* 2).

[6] 'It is sometimes asked, how much control has the subject... over the onset of his trance? The answer is, about the same control as ordinary people have over falling asleep' (Beattie and Middleton, *Spirit Mediumship and Society in Africa* (1969), 4).   [7] *P.G.M.* iv. 850–929.

down and remain motionless; to awake him, the magician must recite another formula and then make a noise like a dog. What are we to make of this prescription in the light of modern experience? The 'falling down' of the medium has been compared to the falling down of a boy in the house of Apuleius the novelist, which was attributed by Apuleius himself to epilepsy, but by his accusers to magic.[1] The monotonous formulas with their long lists of *nomina sacra* etc. might serve the same purpose of inducing a suitable mood as does the hymn-singing or soft music customary at the beginning of a spiritualist seance; and the sevenfold whispered repetition might have a hypnotic effect (though I can find no clear evidence that 'hypnotic' as distinct from 'mediumistic' states were known in Antiquity).[2] It is perhaps more relevant to recall that Mrs. Piper, the most celebrated of modern voice-mediums, would at the onset of her trance fall into a state of total unconsciousness in which her body slumped forward and had to be supported.[3]

But the fullest and most interesting descriptions of mediumistic trance which have come down to us are due to members of the late pagan religious sect who called themselves 'theurgists'—men who not only talked about the gods as theologians did but *acted* upon them. Theurgy,[4] like spiritualism, may be described as

[1] Apuleius, *Apol.* 42. Cf. Abt, op. cit. (p. 187 n. 2 above), 232 ff., and Hopfner, 'Kinder-Medien' (p. 192 n. 4 above).

[2] Hopfner thought the procedure in the Egyptian spells 'obviously' hypnotic. He compared the experiment described by Aristotle's pupil Clearchus in which a magician with a $\psi υχουλκὸς$ $\dot{ρ}άβδος$ ('magnetic wand'?) 'drew out' the soul of a sleeping boy, leaving his body inert and insensitive to pain (Proclus, *in Remp.* ii. 122. 22 ff. Kroll = Clearchus frag. 7 Wehrli). We are not, however, told that the boy was in anything other than a natural sleep, and it is in any case very doubtful if the alleged experiment ever took place—it comes from a work of fiction, Clearchus' dialogue *On Sleep*. More suggestive of hypnosis is Apuleius' description (*Apol.* 43) of boys 'lulled to sleep either by the influence of spells or by soothing odours', who lose contact with their surroundings and predict the future 'as though in a kind of stupor' (*velut quodam stupore*).

[3] R. Hodgson, *Proc. S.P.R.* 13 (1898), 397 f. At an earlier stage in her career Mrs. Piper showed epileptoid symptoms—convulsive movements and grinding of the teeth—at the beginning of her trance (Mrs. Sidgwick, *Proc. S.P.R.* 28 (1915), 206 f.), a fact which may help to explain the frequent confusion in antiquity and the Middle Ages between epilepsy and 'possession'. Psellus similarly speaks of mediums ($κάτοχοι$) who bite their lips and mutter between their teeth (*C.M.A.G.* vi. 164. 18).

[4] I deal here only with those theurgic operations which involve mediumship, and with them only summarily. For a more general account of theurgy and a fuller statement of the ancient evidence I must refer the reader to my paper in *J.R.S.* 37 (1947), reprinted as an appendix to my *Greeks and the Irrational*. On

magic applied to a religious purpose and resting on supposed revelations of a religious character. Its practitioners were not motivated by scientific curiosity: by using certain magical techniques to establish communication with the Unseen they hoped to secure the salvation of their souls as well as the more immediate benefits resulting from foreknowledge of the future. But as witnesses they have the advantage over the authors of the magical papyri of being educated and thoughtful men who appear to speak, in some cases at least, from personal experience. Their sacred book, the *Chaldaean Oracles*,[1] is unfortunately lost, but numerous fragments of it and descriptions of the rituals based on it are preserved by the later Neoplatonists—Porphyry, Iamblichus, Proclus, and others—and by the Byzantine occultist Michael Psellus (b. 1018), who had access to material that has now perished.

It is clear that the theurgists used mediums and that they had a technique for throwing them into trance, probably by such ritual acts as the putting on of a special dress, which would operate autosuggestively. The medium is called *docheus*, 'the recipient', or by the older term *katochos*, 'the one who is held down'; the word *meson*, the literal Greek equivalent of the English 'medium', is actually suggested in one place by Iamblichus, but rejected as too presumptuous.[2] Not everybody, says Iamblichus, is a potential medium; the best, he thinks (in agreement with Apuleius), are 'young and rather simple persons'.[3] A distinction is drawn between trance automatism, in which the medium's personality is completely in abeyance, so that a normal person must be present to look after him, and automatism without trance, which the medium can both induce and terminate at will (both types are familiar today).[4] The symptoms of trance are said to vary widely with different communicating 'gods' and on different occasions:

its religious purpose see now A.-J. Festugière, 'Contemplation philosophique et art théurgique chez Proclus', in *Studi di storia religiosa della tarda antichità* (1968).

[1] Most of the fragments are collected in W. Kroll's Latin work, *De oraculis chaldaicis* (1894). See also H. Lewy, *Chaldaean Oracles and Theurgy* (1956), and my review, *Harv. Theol. Rev.* 54 (1961), 263–73.   [2] Iamblichus, *de myst.* 3. 19.

[3] Ibid. 3. 24, p. 157. 14 Parthey. Cf. above, p. 190. So too Olympiodorus thought 'young boys and country folk' most apt for mediumship (*in Alc.* 8. 12).

[4] Cf. ibid. 3. 4, p. 109. 9, and the clearer statement of Psellus, *Scripta Minora* i. 248. 13–30, based on Proclus. Two grades of demoniacal possession are similarly distinguished by Origen, *de princip.* 3. 3. 4. The first type is exemplified in the automatism of Mrs. Piper, the second in that of Mrs. Coombe-Tennant ('Mrs. Willett').

there may be anaesthesia, including insensibility to fire; there may be bodily movement or complete immobility; there may be changes in the quality of the voice.[1] Porphyry tells us that the 'gods' come at first reluctantly, but more easily when they have formed a habit[2]—that is, no doubt, when a trance personality has been built up. He adds a warning about the dangers of mediumship, which is elaborated by Psellus: the medium may be obsessed by 'material spirits', whose intrusion and violent movements the weaker mediums cannot endure.[3] Most of these observations can be paralleled from the classic study of Mrs. Piper's trance phenomena by Mrs. Henry Sidgwick;[4] the resemblances are too close to be dismissed as accidental.

Of actual mediumistic utterances delivered at private seances, or what purport to be such, a number of specimens have survived. Most of them come, via the church historian Eusebius, from the great collection of so-called 'oracles' made by Porphyry.[5] Some of them afford clear evidence that the state of possession was deliberately induced: for example, one begins: 'Serapis, being summoned and housed in a human body, replied as follows.'[6] Often they speak of the medium in the third person, just as modern 'controls' do, and give directions for his comfort or for terminating the trance. 'Close the sitting,' says one of them, 'I am going to speak falsehoods.'[7] In exactly the same way a modern medium exclaims 'I must stop now or I shall say something silly.'

The supernormal phenomena most often associated in Antiquity with possession, whether spontaneous or induced, are precognition, clairvoyance, and 'speaking with tongues' (the last especially but not exclusively among Christians).[8] Psellus expresses the general view in his statement that possession may be recognized

[1] Iamblichus, *de myst.* 3. 4 f.   [2] Porphyry *apud* Euseb. *Praep. Evang.* 5. 8.
[3] Porphyry, loc. cit.; Psellus, *Scripta Minora* i. 249. 5. Cf. above, p. 197, and below, p. 209.   [4] *Proc. S.P.R.* 28 (1915); see especially chap. vi.
[5] *Porphyrii de philosophia ex oraculis haurienda reliquiae*, ed. G. Wolff (1856, repr. 1962). Cf. Myers, 'Greek Oracles', in Abbott's *Hellenica*, 478 ff.
[6] Porphyry *apud* Firmicus Maternus, *de err. prof. rel.* 13.
[7] Porphyry *apud* Euseb. *Praep. Evang.* 6. 5; cf. *Proc. S.P.R.* 38 (1928), 76.
[8] See E. Lombard, *De la glossolalie chez les premiers chrétiens* (1910). The Delian priestesses who 'could imitate the speech of all men' (Homeric *Hymn to Apollo* 162 ff.) and the inspired priest at the Ptoan oracle in Boeotia who answered a Carian inquirer in his own language (Herodotus 8. 135) seem to be early pagan examples: both are described in the same terms as 'a great marvel'. Similar marvels have been ascribed to possessed persons among African primitives (Beattie and Middleton, op. cit. 6, 29, 132, etc.) and to certain modern 'mediums'.

Supernormal Phenomena in Classical Antiquity 203

'when the subject is deprived of all activity . . . but is moved and guided by another spirit, which utters things outside the subject's knowledge and sometimes predicts future events'.[1] How strong this tradition was is shown by the acceptance of it in an official Catholic document, the *Rituale Romanum*, which to this day cites among the criteria of possession 'the ability to speak or understand an unknown language, and to reveal things distant or hidden'. Some of Porphyry's 'gods' venture upon explicit answers to such questions as 'Will it be a boy or a girl?'[2] This, it may be thought, was risky. But false answers were accounted for by 'bad conditions',[3] or by the disturbed state of the medium's mind or the inopportune intervention of his normal self;[4] or again by the intrusion of a lying spirit who 'jumps in and usurps the place prepared for a higher being'.[5] All these excuses recur in the literature of spiritualism. The last especially must have come readily to hand, since it does not appear that the theurgic communicators ever furnished proofs of their identity (nor is it easy to see how a non-human spirit could provide such proofs).

In addition to revealing past and future through the medium's lips the gods also vouchsafed to the theurgists visible signs of their presence. Sometimes these could be observed only by the operating priest (*klētōr*), but on other occasions they could be seen by all who attended the sitting.[6] To these physical phenomena the best-known witness is Iamblichus. He does not give his evidence as lucidly as we could wish, and some writers have built too much on certain of his rather vague phrases. But he appears to allege that there may be dilatation or levitation of the medium's person; that lights may be seen, sometimes by all present, at the moment when the medium is falling into or emerging from trance; and that the operator may see spirit forms entering the medium's body (this last he calls 'the most important sign').[7] These are the

---

[1] *De operatione daemonum* 14 (Migne, *Patr. Gr.* 122, p. 852).
[2] *Apud* Euseb. *Praep. Evang.* 6. 1. The prediction, though attributed to 'Apollo', was apparently based on astrology.
[3] Porphyry *apud* Euseb. *Praep. Evang.* 6. 5; Proclus, *in Remp.* I. 40. 18 ff.
[4] Iamblichus, *de myst.* 3. 7, p. 115. 10 Parthey.
[5] Synesius, *de insomn.* 142 A (*Patr. Gr.* 66, p. 1300); cf. Iamb. *de myst.* 3. 31, p. 177. 12 ff.
[6] Cf. Proclus, *in Remp.* ii. 167. 15 ff. on visions and voices perceptible only to those qualified by 'hieratic power' or natural aptitude; Psellus, *Expos. Or. Chald.* 1136 D Migne; Bidez in *Mélanges Cumont*, 95 ff.
[7] Iamblichus, *de myst.* 3. 5, p. 112. 2; 3. 6, p. 112. 10.

most clearly attested phenomena.[1] To the psychical researcher it is a familiar-sounding list. The apparition of lights, which seems to have been the most frequent phenomenon, is frequent also in the modern seance-room. Levitation and dilatation have been ascribed to the modern mediums Home and Peters. And the 'spirit forms'—which may appear either as shapeless masses or in recognizable shapes[2]—are suggestive, as Hopfner and others have noticed, of the so-called 'ectoplasm' which modern observers claim to have seen emerge from, and return to, the bodies of certain mediums.

The similarities between ancient theurgy and modern spiritualism appear too numerous to be dismissed as pure coincidence. How then should we account for them? Not, I think, by literary tradition or any diffusionist theory. In the middle of the nineteenth century, when spiritualism first arose, little was known about theurgy even by professional scholars, and anyhow the first spiritualists were not learned people—their main or only source-book was the Bible. We seem driven to recognize a case of like causes independently producing like effects. This does not imply that either the causes or the effects were necessarily supernormal. Dissociation is a psychological condition which occurs with varying degrees of intensity in all cultures, from New Guinea to Haiti and from third-century Rome to twentieth-century London. Its causes are not understood, and in the absence of understanding its more extreme symptoms are inevitably taken at their face value and interpreted as signs of possession. The 'possessed' in turn are seen as spokesmen for the supernatural: their utterances acquire religious authority, and for the true believers that authority is confirmed by the experience of symbolic physical phenomena. Lights are of course the most natural of all

[1] We also hear of 'autophonic' oracles, i.e. what spiritualists call 'the direct voice' (one which dispenses with the use of the medium's vocal organs). Proclus offers a theoretical explanation of such voices, *in Crat.* 77, p. 36. 20 Pasquali. This type of miracle had long been familiar in Jewish religious tradition (cf. Philo, *de decal.* 9). According to Lucian, Alexander of Abonuteichos occasionally reproduced it with the help of a speaking-tube (*Alex.* 26; cf. Hippolytus, *ref. omn. haer.* 4. 28). For a possible but not entirely clear allusion to so-called 'apports' and other physical feats see Iamb. *de myst.* 3. 27, p. 166. 15, and my note, *The Greeks and the Irrational*, 311.

[2] Proclus, *in Remp.* i. 110. 28; Psellus, *Expos. Or. Chald.* 1136 c. Modern 'ectoplasm' is said to behave in a similar manner. But whereas the spiritualist values above all the anthropomorphic materialization, the theurgist prefers the unshaped, since gods have no material form.

symbols for that inward illumination which the believer desires and expects.[1] And levitation too has an obvious symbolic value: since heaven is in the sky or beyond the sky, it is natural that the soul should strain in that direction and natural that it should be thought on occasion to carry the body a little way with it. Hence levitation is everywhere the mark of a very holy man: it has been attributed to Indian fakirs, Jewish rabbis, Christian saints, and Moslem mystics.[2] And the believer also longs to see and touch the divine substance. That substance, or a half-material emanation from it,[3] is for the time being housed in the possessed organism, but he can hope to catch a glimpse of it, at least with the spiritual eye, as it enters or leaves the medium's body. We shall understand neither theurgy nor spiritualism if we see them only as superstitious pseudo-sciences and ignore the element of religious experience. Both of them use magical techniques, but both use them in the service of religion.

Close as the parallelism of the two cults is in many ways, it is not exact. For one thing, the feats of 'psychokinesis' (movement

[1] Cf. W. Beierwaltes, *Lux Intelligibilis* (diss. Munich, 1957). Several of the spells in the magical papyri also promise lights or luminous apparitions (iv. 692, 1106, etc.), as do the *Chaldaean Oracles* (*apud* Proclus, *in Remp.* i. 111). It should be added that for the lights to be effective the sittings must have taken place in the dark or in near-darkness, and that in these conditions the phenomenon is easy to simulate: Hippolytus proposes a simple if rather hazardous way of doing it (*ref. omn. haer.* 4. 36).

[2] A useful collection of evidence will be found in O. Leroy's book, *La Lévitation* (1928), though probably few readers will accept his conclusion that *real* levitation is a privilege confined to good Christians. In Antiquity levitation was ascribed to Indian sages (Philostratus, *vit. Apoll.* 3. 15); to Iamblichus himself (Eunapius, *vit. soph.* 458. 31 Boissonade); to the theurgist Chrysanthius (ibid. 504. 22); and to Jesus (*Acta Johannis* 93). But the practice had its dangers: the Montanist Theodotus, attempting it on an unsound theological basis, fell to the ground and was killed (Eusebius, *Hist. Eccl.* 5. 16. 14); Simon Magus in a like situation broke his leg (*Acts of Peter* 32). For the subjective *feeling* of being levitated cf. *P.G.M.* iv. 537 ff.; for the appearance of bodily dilatation in trance, Virg. *Aen.* 6. 49, Ovid, *Fasti* 6. 540.

[3] To the Neoplatonist, as to the spiritualist, the 'materialization' of immaterial beings presented a difficult problem. Porphyry seems to have suggested that the spirit forms were somehow built up by the psychic power of the medium or generated out of matter 'taken from (existing) organisms' (the medium's body, as in spiritualism? or the bodies of sacrificial animals?). Iamblichus rejects this on the ground that the lower cannot generate the higher, *de myst.* 3. 22. Proclus attempts a compromise: what is seen is not the god in person but an emanation from him which is partly divine, partly mortal in character; and even this is seen only with the eyes of the spiritual or astral body in whose existence the Neoplatonists (like some spiritualists) firmly believed (*in Remp.* i. 39. 1 ff.).

of physical objects without contact) which have been attributed to several modern mediums are missing, so far as I know, from the repertoire of the theurgists, unless we so interpret a passing reference to 'tying and untying sacred bonds and opening things locked' (*de myst.* 3. 27, p. 166. 17). Their absence is the more striking since the possibility of such happenings was entertained by other ancient occultists and was linked by them with the state of possession, though not in the spiritualist manner. Thus we are told that the Jewish exorcist Eleazar, when he gave public demonstrations (as he once did for the Emperor Vespasian), would place close by a cup of water or a footbath and would require the exorcized demon to overturn it in order to prove to the observers that he had really left his victim.[1] A very similar tale is told of Apollonius of Tyana. There the demon, being required to furnish proof of his withdrawal, volunteered to overturn a neighbouring statue and proceeded to do so, whereupon the possessed youth 'awoke as if from sleep, rubbed his eyes', and resumed his true personality.[2] These questionable anecdotes represent Antiquity's nearest approach to experimental psychokinesis. Presumably the theurgists considered such trivial antics beneath the dignity of their gods—who in any case were accustomed to give, not take, orders.

This brings us face to face with the basic difference between theurgy and spiritualism. With all their similarities there is associated one fundamental contrast: what the spiritualists ascribe to the activity of a discarnate human mind the theurgists normally attribute to gods or non-human daemons. In this they agree with the preponderant weight of ancient opinion. The *possibility* of communication with the dead was seldom denied save by Epicureans and sceptics, but the prevalent pattern of belief did not encourage it. On the orthodox pagan view only the unquiet dead—those who had died untimely or by violence, or had failed of due burial—were earthbound and available. And since these were thought to be angry and dangerous spirits, their company was not as a rule desired; those who sought it were suspect

---

[1] Josephus, *Ant. Jud.* 8. 2. 5.
[2] Philostratus, *vit. Apoll.* 4. 20. A Christian version of the same story turns up in *Acts of Peter and Simon* 11; cf. also Marcus Diaconus, *vita sancti Porphyrii* 61, and *Vitae Patrum*, Migne, *Patr. Lat.* 72. 760. A partial modern parallel may be seen in a case reported by Richet where a 'poltergeist' on two occasions overturns a chair *at the request of the investigator* (A. R. G. Owen, *Can We Explain the Poltergeist?* (1965), 331 f.).

Supernormal Phenomena in Classical Antiquity 207

of exploiting it for the unholy purpose of magical aggression. Necromancy did exist, not only as a romantic theme in the imagination of poets from the *Odyssey* onwards but also as an occasional practice in real life.[1] But it existed under a cloud, in the face of strong public disapproval and (at least in Roman times) of severe legal penalties.[2] It had no place in religious life[3] and was commonly thought of as a foreign importation.[4] In Cicero's days it seems to have enjoyed a certain vogue in decadent Neopythagorean circles; he mentions two such amateurs.[5] Later we meet it as a charge brought by suspicious emperors against dangerous aristocrats and by hostile historians against wicked emperors,[6] while at the other end of the social scale we hear of charlatans who for a few pence offered to 'raise the ghosts of heroes', i.e. of the dead.[7] The practice was associated, in the popular mind at least, with the digging up of recently buried corpses to obtain power over them, and even with ritual infanticide for a like purpose.[8] It is not surprising that the word

[1] For a short account of ancient necromancy see Cumont, *Lux Perpetua* (1949), 97-108.
[2] For Roman legislation against necromancy see Mommsen, *Strafrecht* (1883), 642 n. 2, and A. A. Barb in *The Conflict between Paganism and Christianity* (ed. Momigliano, 1963) 102-11. Plato had already proposed solitary confinement for life as a suitable penalty for those who 'fool many of the living by pretending to raise the dead' (*Laws* 909 b).
[3] The 'oracles of the dead', like the one at which Periander consulted his dead wife Melissa (Hdt. 5. 92), hardly constitute an exception, since they were not necromantic in the ordinary sense. They seem to have been mostly incubation-oracles at which the inquirer hoped to see the dead in a dream. See *The Greeks and the Irrational*, 111, and S. I. Dakaris, *Archaeology*, 15 (1962), 85-93.
[4] Necromancy was considered especially as a Persian practice (Pliny, *N.H.* 30. 14; Strabo 16. 2. 39; etc.). It was in fact, as Cumont says, endemic throughout the semitic East (*Lux Perpetua*, 99). But 'psychagogues' were already known though not much esteemed in fifth-century Greece (Eur. *Alc.* 1128 and schol.; Aristoph. *Birds* 1555).
[5] Appius Claudius Pulcher, *de div.* 1. 132, *Tusc.* 1. 37; Vatinius, *in Vat.* 14. Cf. the magical experiments of Nigidius, above, p. 189.
[6] Tiberius: Tacitus, *Ann.* 2. 28. Nero: Pliny, *N.H.* 30. 1. 6; Suetonius, *Nero* 34. 4. Caracalla: Dio Cassius 77.
[7] Celsus *apud* Origen, *c. Celsum* 1. 68. Cf. also Lactantius, *Div. Inst.* 7. 13. 7.
[8] Cf. Cicero, *in Vat.* 14; Lucan 6. 533 ff.; Servius on *Aeneid* 6. 107; Libanius, *Orat.* 1. 98, *Decl.* 41. 7; Chrysostom, *Hom. in Matth.* 28, p. 336 B-D Montfaucon. In the great purge of A.D. 359 even visiting a graveyard in the evening was enough to incur a charge of necromancy (Ammianus 19. 12. 14). On the social reasons for the fear of necromancy, and of sorcery in general, in late Antiquity see now Peter Brown, 'Sorcery, Demons, and the Rise of Christianity', in *Witchcraft Confessions and Accusations* (ed. Mary Douglas, 1970), a brilliant essay which appeared too late for me to make full use of it.

'necromancy' was corrupted in the Middle Ages into 'nigromancy', the Black Art, and became a general term for sorcery: it was already a black art in Imperial Rome. This picture has little in common with the mild activities of modern spiritualists. Both the motives of the client and the methods of the necromancer are as a rule very different. The most frequent motive seems to have been a desire for power over others or a desire to know the future; a wish to meet 'the loved ones' or a 'scientific' curiosity about the condition of the dead is rarely mentioned.[1] And the techniques of the necromancer, so far as they are known to us,[2] appear to have been purely magical and compulsive: the dead come unwillingly, because they have to; there is no indication that mediums were employed. The possibility of occasional *spontaneous* possession by the dead was admitted by the theurgists (see below); but outside theurgy our only witnesses to this possibility, so far as I know, are Jewish and Christian writers. Josephus and Justin[3] maintain that in cases of possession the so-called daemonic agents are really the spirits of the wicked dead, but Justin admits that this is not the general assumption; everybody, he says, calls the possessed 'demoniacs' (*daimonioleptoi*). Tatian and Tertullian,[4] like most of the later Fathers, are of the opposite opinion: so-called spirits of the dead are really demons. Under exorcism, says Tertullian, they sometimes give themselves out to be relatives of the possessed, sometimes to be gladiators or beastfighters (persons who have met a violent end), but are later forced to confess their true nature. And he offers the theory that in such cases the agent is that particular 'personal' demon or familiar spirit who haunted the man in question during his lifetime and drove him to his evil end. It is

[1] Nero's abortive effort to appease the ghost of his murdered mother (p. 207 n. 6 above) hardly qualifies for the former category. The hero of the pseudo-Clementine *Recognitions* proposes to consult a necromant 'as if I wanted to inquire into some piece of business, but actually in order to find out whether the soul is immortal' (1. 5). This, however, is pious Christian romance, not real life. Philostratus makes the ghost of Apollonius warn people against such impertinent curiosity (*vit. Apoll.* 8. 31).

[2] About necromantic methods serious writers give us little information; probably they had little to give. We are dependent on a few magical recipes in the papyri and on the sensational but untrustworthy descriptions offered by poets and novelists (Lucan 6. 420–761; Statius, *Theb.* 4. 406 ff.; Apuleius, *Met.* 2. 28–30; Heliodorus 6. 14 ff.).

[3] Josephus, *Bell. Jud.* 7. 6. 3; Justin, *Apol.* 1. 18.

[4] Tatian, *adv. Graecos* 16; Tertullian, *de anima* 57.

hard to see why this bizarre speculation was introduced if not because the trance intelligence appeared to show supernormal knowledge of events in the life of the person it claimed to be, or at any rate identified itself in some way as being in fact that person. This seems to be as near as we get in antiquity to 'evidence of survival' in the sense familiar to students of Mrs. Piper and Mrs. Leonard.

Cases of disputed identity—ghost or non-human spirit—were also known to the theurgists.[1] Porphyry in a cautious mood had asked how he was to distinguish the higher ranks of being— gods, archangels, angels,[2] daemons, planetary rulers—from mere 'souls'. To which Iamblichus replies that each class of being has its characteristic appearance, attributes, and modes of behaviour, and proceeds to give a lengthy but not very informative list of these distinctive features.[3] He admits, however, that the lower orders of spirits do on occasion simulate the higher. This happens when the operators are ignorant or impure; such operators may even attract to the seance the evil spirits called *antitheoi*.[4] Iamblichus himself is credited with having unmasked a *soi-disant* Apollo, evoked by an Egyptian magician, who was in reality only the ghost of a gladiator.[5] But such cases are exceptional. The theurgist was not interested in demonstrating survival, which he took for granted; his object was to achieve communication with divine beings and by their aid to transcend earthly experience and 'ascend to the intellectual fire'.[6]

In any social group which assigns religious value to 'mediumship' its apparent function is to alleviate the characteristic

[1] Confusion on this subject was made easier by the popular belief that privileged human souls might be promoted after death to the status of 'daemon'. The notion is as old as Euripides (*Alc.* 1003); it was widespread in Roman times (Max. Tyr. 9. 6; Apul. *de deo Socratis* 14. 3; etc.) but the theurgists reject it, just as they reject any blurring of the line which separates 'daemons' from 'gods' (Proclus, *in Alc. i*, p. 70 Creuzer).

[2] On pagan (originally Persian) angels and archangels see Cumont, *Rev. Hist. Rel.* 72 (1915), 159–82.

[3] Porphyry's question is quoted by Iamblichus, *de myst.* 2. 3, p. 70. 8. Iamblichus' reply occupies the rest of Book 2. Cf. also Aeneas of Gaza, *Theophrastus*, p. 61 Boissonade.

[4] *De myst.* 2. 10, p. 91. 7 ff.; 3. 31, p. 177. 7 ff. The danger of intrusion by these *antitheoi* was known to the Egyptian magicians (*P.G.M.* vii. 634) and also to Heliodorus (4. 7. 13). They seem to correspond to the *devas* who serve Ahriman, the Persian Satan. Cf. W. Bousset in *Arch. f. Rel.* 18 (1915), 135 ff.

[5] Eunapius, *vit. soph.*, p. 473 Boissonade.

[6] Iamblichus, *de myst.* 3. 31, p. 179. 8.

anxieties of the group in question by neutralizing or 'disproving' any force which threatens it. For the nineteenth-century spiritualists the threat came from the progress of science, which was gradually undermining the authority of the Bible.[1] For the theurgists of the third and fourth centuries it came in part from the progress of Christianity, which was undermining belief in the old gods, in part from the insecurity of a visibly decaying culture, which inspired in pagan and Christian alike an overwhelming need to escape from earthly conditions.[2]

The survey of ostensibly supernormal phenomena in the ancient world which is here offered makes no pretence of completeness; it covers only selected areas of ancient belief and practice. But it has, I hope, served to illustrate both the differences between the ancient and the modern evidence on these matters—differences largely conditioned by the dissimilarity of the cultural background—and also the indications of a possible underlying identity of experience in certain of the happenings described. For the rest, I can still only echo as I did in 1936 the words of Augustine: 'If anyone can trace the causes and modes of operation of these visions and divinations and really understand them, I had rather hear his views than be expected to discuss the subject myself.'[3]

[1] Cf. A. Gauld, *The Founders of Psychical Research* (1968), chaps. i–iii.
[2] Cf. my *Pagan and Christian in an Age of Anxiety* (1965).
[3] *De Genesi ad litteram* 12. 18.

INDEX OF PASSAGES DISCUSSED

AESCHYLUS
   Ag. 206–23: 57; 883: 46
   Cho. 910: 60 n. 2
   Eum. 690–5: 48 f.; 704–6: 49 f.; 858–66: 51 f.; 996–1002: 52 f.
   P.V. 190–2: 40 f.; 425–30: 38; 442–506: 5 f.; 981: 41
   frag. 282 Lloyd-Jones: 43 n. 1
   schol. *P.V.* 94: 39 n. 2
AMMIANUS MARCELLINUS
   29. 1. 29: 193 n. 3
   29. 1. 32: 194 n. 1
ANDOCIDES
   1. 130: 158 n. 1
APULEIUS
   Apol. 42: 188 n. 5; 189 n. 4
ARISTOPHANES
   Ach. 1128–31: 186
ARISTOTLE
   de div. per somn. 464^{a}1: 163 n. 4
AUGUSTINE
   contra Academicos 1. 6 f.: 175 f.
   de cura pro mortuis 12 (15): 174 n. 2
CHRYSIPPUS
   frag. 1205 Arnim: 172 f.
CICERO
   de div. 1. 57: 172 f.; 1. 58 f., 2. 140 f.: 184
CLEARCHUS
   frag. 7 Wehrli: 200 n. 2
DIODORUS
   1. 6. 3–1. 8. 9: 9–11
EURIPIDES
   Ba. 115: 88 n. 3; 1264–84: 83 n. 2
   Hec. 799–801: 85 n. 5
   Hipp. 189–97: 86 f.
   Supp. 195–218: 7
   Tro. 885 f.: 85 n. 5
GORGIAS
   frag. 3 Diels–Kranz: 95
HERODOTUS
   1. 47: 166
HESIOD
   Works and Days 106–201: 3 f.

Historia Augusta
   Didius Julianus 7: 187 n. 2
Inscriptions
   S.I.G. 1157: 167 n. 5
   I.G. iv². 1. 121–2 (= Edelstein, *Asclepius* i. 221 ff.): 168–71
MARINUS
   vit. Procli 28: 194 n. 2
MOSCHION
   frag. 6 Nauck: 43
Papyri
   P. Oxy. 1381: 170; *P. Oxy.* 2256 frag. 9a: 43 n. 1
   P.G.M. iv. 850–929: 199 f.
PAUSANIAS
   7. 21. 12: 187
PETRONIUS
   Sat. 48: 191 n. 2
PLATO
   Epist. vii, 335 a: 122
   Laws 896 e: 116
   Tim. 37 c: 120 n. 3
PLOTINUS
   Enn. 4. 9. 3: 165 n. 8
   Enn. 5. 1. 8. 10: 126 f.
PLUTARCH
   def. orac. 51: 197
   gen. Socr. 20, 589 b: 164
   Q. conv. 8. 10. 2, 734 f: 161 f.
   Theseus 22: 148
PORPHYRY
   vit. Plot. 14: 129
PROTAGORAS
   frag. 4 Diels–Kranz: 96 f.
SENECA
   N.Q. 3. 27–30: 21
SOPHOCLES
   Ant. 332–75: 8
   O.R. 895: 75
TERTULLIAN
   de anima 57: 208 f.
THESSALUS
   1. 11–24 Friedrich: 189 n. 2
XENOPHANES
   frag. 18 Diels–Kranz: 4

GENERAL INDEX

Names of authors, ancient or modern, are in general indexed only where their views are discussed or quoted; bare references are not as a rule included. All Greek words are transliterated in this index.

Abt, A. 188 n. 5, 189 n. 4
Adkins, A. W. H. vi, 56
Adrastus 72
Aegeus vase 186 n. 4
Aeschylus, and Athenian politics 45–53; freedom and necessity in 57–9; *pathei mathos* in 59–62; presuppositions of 55–7; on progress 5–7; *see also* Zeus
 Eumenides 6, 43, 155
 Oedipodeia 69
 Oresteia 45–63
 Prometheus Lyomenos 35, 38–41; *Pyrphoros* 38 f.; *Vinctus* 5–7, 29–44
alastōr 55–7, 60, 81
Albicerius 175 f.
Alcidamas 101
Alcmaeon of Croton 124
Alexander of Abonuteichos 167, 204 n. 1
Alexander of Aphrodisias 136
allegory in Greek tragedy 44 n. 1, 52, 75
amnesia after trance 195, 198
Amphiaraos, oracle of 166
Anacharsis, Letters of 21
Anaxagoras 9–11
Andocides 158 n. 1
Andrews, K. 147
angels, pagan 209
Anonymus Iamblichi 99 f.
Anthesteria 147
Antiochus of Askalon 127
Antiphon (the *oneirocrit*) 178; distinct from the sophist 178 n. 7
Antiphon (the sophist) 94; distinct from the politician 101
Antisthenes 162
antitheoi 209
Antium, moving statues at 194 f.
Apollo 50, 161; *see also* Delphi
Apollonius of Tyana 171 f., 206, 208 n. 1
'apports' 204 n. 1

approach, monitions of 174
Apuleius 190, 200
Archelaus (the philosopher) 9, 11, 20 n. 1, 94, 100
Archer-Hind, R. D. 115
Archimedes 18
Areopagus 47–50, 62
Aristides, Aelius 198
Aristippus 13 n. 2
Aristophanes 74, 98, 152, 186, 199
Aristotle, on divination 163; on *hamartia* 64–8; on moral failure 82; on active Nous 136 f.; on recurrent catastrophes 14; on precognition 176, 180–2, 184, 185 n. 4; on progress 15 f.
Armstrong, A. H. 138
Arnott, P. 37 n. 3
Artemidorus 169 n. 2, 172 n. 1, 178 n. 1, 179
Artemis 87, 151
Asclepius 74, 161, 169
askēsis 82
astral body 205 n. 3
astral theology 124 f.
Athena 46 f., 62, 154 f.
Augustine 170 f., 173–6, 210
automatism, auditory 191–3; motor 193–5; visual, *see* scrying; vocal, *see* 'mediumship'

Baalbek, oracle of 167, 194
Badham, C. 38
Bagehot, Walter 1
battles, supernormal knowledge of 163 n. 4, 173
Beattie, J. 199 n. 6
Benedict, St. 171
Bevan, Edwyn 161
Bidez, J. 122
Blass, F. 48, 53
Bowra, Sir Maurice 71
Bradley, F. H. 133, 137

General Index

Branchidae, oracle of 198
Bréhier, E. 133
Brimo 149
Brimos 149
Britomart 151
Brown, Peter 207 n. 8
Burnet, J. 94, 96
Bywater, Ingram 67

Callicles 104 f.
Campbell, Lewis 42
Cary, Joyce 138
catastrophes, recurrent 14, 18
catoptromancy 186 f.
caves, sacred 144 f., 151
Chaeremon 8
Chaffin Will case 171
Chaldaean Oracles 201
chance 13, 16, 112, 115
Choerilus 11
Christian assumptions, misleading 71, 76, 140 f.
Chrysippus 159, 172 f.
Cicero, Marcus, on divination 164, 172 f., 182; on precognition 176 f., 183 f.
Cicero, Quintus, dream of 184
clairvoyance 118, 159-76, 202 f.; medical 169, 180
Claros, oracle of 168, 198 f.
Clean Monday 147
Clearchus 200 n. 2
Clement of Alexandria 116
Cole, T. 11, 18 n. 5
conflict, psychological 111 f.
contemplative life 85, 134
Corfidius 170 f.
Cornelius, Gaius 173
Cornford, F. M. 115, 120 n. 3
corpses, chained or mutilated 152; discovery of missing 170
Corybantes 161
Critias 8, 97
Croesus 166
Crossman, Richard 102
crystal-gazing 186; *see also* scrying
Ctesias 13
Cumont, F. 122
curse, inherited 69, 80, 82
cyclic view of history 3 f., 12, 18; *see also* Great Year
Cylon 50 f.
Cynics 13, 17

daemonion: see Socrates
daemons, the dead as 209 n. 1; evil 55 f., 195, 206, 208 f.; of the individual 208
Damascius 191
Daube, B. 45 n. 6
dead, the, become daemons 209 n. 1; earthbound, fear of 152, 157 n. 2, 206; possession by 208 f.; ritual salvation of 149; tendance of 147, 151 f.; *see also* necromancy
Delatte, A. 157 n. 1, 186, 187 n. 2, 191 n. 2
Delphi, oracle of 75, 80, 119, 166, 177, 186 n. 4, 195 n. 3, 196-8; Earth oracle at 160 n. 2
Democritus, anthropology of 9-11; on divination 161-3, 181 f.; on origin of religion 19; on research 12; on social questions 94
dēmos, in Aeschylus 46
Denniston, J. D. 36
design, argument from 7 f.
determinism 18, 64, 69-71; *see also* free will
Dicaearchus 16 f.
Didius Julianus 187
Didyma, oracle of 198
Diels, H. 9 n. 4
Dill, Sir Samuel 26
Dio Chrysostom 21
Diodorus 9-11, 20 n. 1
Diogenes of Apollonia 89
Dionysus 88 f.
Dissen, L. 42
dissociation, mental 185, 204
divination, by the dying 180 n. 5; ominal and intuitive 160, 182, 188; Pergamene table of 194 n. 2; and religion 160 f.; *see also* clairvoyance, 'mediumship', precognition, telepathy
Dodona, oracle of 168, 177 n. 3, 198
Dörrie, H. 54 n. 1
Dover, K. J. 45, 47 n. 1, 48, 50, 52
dreambooks 178 f.
dreams, 'aversion' of 183; clairvoyant 168-71; coinciding with crisis 172 f.; medical 180 f.; oracular 177 f.; precognitive 184 f.; reciprocal 175; recurrent 185 n. 1; simultaneous 169 f.; symbolism in 179; theories of 161-4, 179-82
dualism, Platonic and Zoroastrian 123

'ectoplasm' 204
Edelstein, Ludwig 1, 13 f., 15, 19
education 103
ego, the, in Plotinus 135–7
Ehrenberg, V. 75
Eiresione 147 f.
Eleazar 206
Eleusinian Mysteries 145, 148 f.
Eliot, T. S. 113
enargeia 185
engastrimuthoi 199
Engels, F. 15
entheos 195 n. 3
Ephorus 13
Epicureans 183
Epicurus 17, 161
Epidaurian temple record 168–71
epidosis 1
epōidai 111 n. 1
Er 123
Erchia, calendar of 153 n. 1
Erinyes 51 f., 55 f., 59
errant cause 115 f.
Eudoxus 123–5
Euphorion 38
Euripides 7, 100 f.; irrationalism of 78–91; studies neurosis and insanity 83; and philosophy 79–81, 89 f.; and Plato 83–5; and Shaw 80, 88; and Socrates 79, 82, 84, 89 f.
  Bacchae 30, 87–9
  Hippolytus 81 f., 86 f.
Eurycles 199
'evil eye' 162, 165
exorcism 196, 206, 208
extrasensory perception: *see* clairvoyance, precognition, telepathy

farmer's year 145 f.
festivals 146–9
Festugière, A.-J. 108 n. 1, 189 n. 2
Field, G. C. 117
Finley, J. H. 12
firstfruits, dedication of 147 f.
Forms, Platonic 14 f., 120, 130, 137
Forrest, W. G. 166 n. 2
Fraenkel, E. 21, 58, 60 n. 1
free will 57–9, 131 f.; *see also* determinism
Freud, Sigmund 70, 77, 135, 136 n. 1, 179, 181 n. 3, 184
Friedländer, P. 139 n. 1

Galen 112 n. 1
Gandillac, M. de 132
Gatz, B. 1 n. 2
Gercke, A. 34
glossolalia 202 f.
God, love of 140; *see also* Zeus
gods, mythological, Euripides' view of 85–9; Homeric view of 143; Plato's view of 118 f.; Protagoras' view of 96 f.; Sophocles' view of 74–6; not timeless 42 f.; as trance personalities 201–3, 206, 209; visions of 169 f., 188–90; *see also* religion
Golden Age 3, 17, 19, 21; *see also* primitivism
Golden, L. 42 n. 2
Goldschmidt, V. 3
Gomme, A. W. 70
Gorgias 83, 100 f., 104; not a 'philosophical nihilist' 94 f.
grace, divine 132, 138
Great Year, 3 f., 14, 21
Groeneboom, P. 47, 53
Groningen, B. A. van 2
Grossmann, G. 41 n. 3
Grote, G. 92
Grube, G. M. A. 116, 121 n. 1
guilt 55 f.
Guthrie, W. K. C. 1 n. 2, 22, 92 n. 1

Hackforth, R. 109 n. 1, 110 n. 6
Halliday, W. R. 160
hamartia 64–8
Harrison, E. 36
Harrison, Jane 148 n. 1
haunted houses 157 n. 2
Havelock, E. A. 1 n. 2, 9 n. 5
Headlam, W. 59 n. 3
Hecate 161
Heliopolis: *see* Baalbek
Heracles 154
Heraclitus 98, 164; on Delphi 197; on divine justice 76; on Great Year 14 n. 2
Herington, C. J. 37 nn. 1–3
Hermann, G. 31, 39
Hermes 151
Hermotimus 171
Herodotus, on *nomos* 98; on progress 12
'Heroes' 74, 152 f.
Herzog, R. 169 f.
Hesiod 3 f., 150
Hey, O. 67 n. 1

General Index

Hilarion 190
Hipparchus 18
Hippias (the sophist) 11, 94, 98, 100, 105
Hippocratica 147, 199; on dreams 179 f.; on progress 11 f.
Hippodamus 12
Hippolytus (Christian Father) 149, 167, 191 f., 205 n. 1
holy ground, continuity of 144 f.
Homer, religion in 143 f.; not a Sacred Book 142
Hopfner, T. 200 n. 2, 204
Horace 21
human condition, the, Euripides on 84 f.; Plato on 109–14; Sophocles on 77
Huxley, Aldous 138
hydromancy: *see* lecanomancy, scrying
hypnosis 200
Hyrcanus, John 173

Iamblichus 201–3, 205 n. 3, 209
immoralism 102–5
incest 100
incubation 168
individualism 101, 103 f.
inspiration 117 f.
intellectualism 108 f., 111 n. 3
internationalism 100 f.
Io 34
irrationalism, of Euripides 78–91; growth of 90; Plato and 106–25; as Zeitgeist 106 n. 2
Isidore, the philosopher 188
Isocrates 13, 142

Jacoby, F. 49 n. 1, 62
Jaeger, W. 122
James, William 96
Jerome, St. 190 n. 2
Johnson, Samuel 74
Josephus 208
justice, divine 54–7, 76, 89, 97
Justin Martyr 208
Juvenal 21

Kalchas 160 f.
katechesthai 195 n. 3
kernos 144
Kirkwood, G. M. 73
Kitto, H. D. F. 30, 57 n. 3
Klees, H. 166 n. 2

Knox, B. M. W. 70 f., 75
Koestler, A. 114
Kore, *anodos* of 148
Korope, oracle of 167
Kranz, W. 30, 37
Kronos, life under: *see* Golden Age
Kypris 87

Lambert, G. W. 165 n. 8
Lang, Andrew 156
law: *see nomos*
Lawson, J. C. 152
lecanomancy 187 f., 189 n. 2
Leibniz 135
Leonard, Mrs. Gladys Osborne 197 n. 4
Leroy, O. 205 n. 2
Lesky, A. 56 n. 5, 58
levitation 203–5
Lewis, David 156 n. 1
liberalism, reasons for failure of 102–5
Libya 47
lights, supernormal 203
Livingstone, Sir Richard 45, 52
Lloyd-Jones, H. 59
Longinus 129
Lucian 21, 49, 158 n. 1, 167
Lucretius, on progress 20

Macrobius 167
magic, agricultural 146–9; use of boys in 190, 201; Plato on 117; and religion 148, 201, 205
magnet 165
Maine, Sir Henry 1
Manilius 22 f.
manteis 117
mantikē: *see* divination
Marcus Aurelius 24, 103, 113
'materialization' 205 n. 3
'mediumship' 195–206
Megara, two travellers at 172 f.
'melancholics' 163 n. 3, 181
Melian dialogue 104
Menander 153
Menon 104
Mercury 188
Middleton, J. 199 n. 6
Mopsus, oracle of 167 f.
Moschion 8, 43
Müller, K. O. 48
Murray, Gilbert 87, 90, 156
muscular pressure, unconscious 194
Mycale, rumour at 173

Myers, F. W. H. 156, 159 f., 176, 186
mysticism, Platonic 118; Plotinian 137–9
myths, anti-progressive 3; of Plato 9, 120–2

Nature 115 f., 134; *see also phusis*
Necessity 115 f.; *see also* determinism
necromancy 117, 190 n. 5, 207 f.; and spiritualism 208 f.
Nietzsche, F. ('Nitch') 104 f.
Nigidius Figulus 175, 189
Nilsson, M. P. 124 n. 8, 157 n. 1
nomos 94, 124 n. 8, 157 n. 1
Nous, in Plotinus 135–7
Numenius 127 f.
nymphs 151

One, the Plotinian 137
oneirocrits 178 f.
Oppenheim, A. L. 178
oracles 69, 72, 119, 166–8, 196–9; 'autophonic' 204 n. 1; Chaldaean 201; of the dead 207 n. 3; *see also* Delphi, Dodona, etc.
Orphic poems 142
'Orphic–Pythagorean' doctrines in Plato 122
over-determination 56
Ovid 37

Page, Sir Denys 57, 59
Paley, F. A. 30
Pan 151
panspermia 147
Parke, H. W. 167 n. 5, 193 n. 1
peithō 56, 83, 95
Periander 170
Petronius 191 n. 2
Phaleas 103
Pherecrates 10 n. 1
philotheos 140
phusis 81 f., 94, 97–9, 104 f.; *see also* Nature
Piaget, J. 190
Pindar 137
Piper, Mrs. L. E. 197 n. 4, 200, 201 n. 4, 202
Plato 102 f., 128 f., 142 n. 2, 155; and the irrational 106–25; on education 103; and Euripides 83–5; on evil 111 f., 115 f.; on foreign travel 98; on magic 117; myths of 9, 120–2; on necromancy 207 n. 2; on parricide 72; on partial catastrophes 14; on possession 195 n. 3, 198; on progress 14–16; on Protagoras 9, 95 f.; on Sophists 92 f.; *see also* Forms, Zoroastrianism
[Plato], *Epinomis* 112, 124 f.; *Second Letter* 119, 128; *Theages* 193 n. 1
Plato, the comic dramatist, 6 f., 31
Pliny the Elder 23
Plotinus 24, 90, 126–39; relationship to Plato 127–9; on the intelligible world 132–4; on mystical union 137–9; on Outgoing and Return 129–32; psychological discoveries of 135–7; on the sensible world 134; on 'sympathy' 165
Plutarch 148, 161 f., 164, 168, 182, 197, 199
Pohlenz, M. 30
politics, Athenian, Aeschylus on 45–53, 62
pollution 72
poltergeists 158
Polybius, on progress 18, 21
Pompeius Trogus 21
Pomponius 175
Porphyry 129, 137, 202 f., 205 n. 3, 209
Posidonius 111 n. 3, 159; anthropology of 18 f., 21; on divination 163 f.
'possession', spontaneous 195 f., 208; induced, *see* 'mediumship'
Potidaea 47 n. 2
precognition 162, 176–85, 188, 193 f., 202 f.
priests 142; as magicians 189
primitivism 2, 13 f., 15, 17; *see also* Golden Age
Proclus 194 n. 2, 205 n. 3
Prodicus 7, 81, 94
progress, ancient opinions on 1–25, 109; in Heaven 41–4; of scholarship 26–31
prokopē 1
Prometheus 5–7, 31–43
Propertius 37
prophecy: *see* precognition
Protagoras 7, 79, 83, 89 f., 94, 103; on gods 96 f.; on *nomos* 99; on progress 9 f.; not a subjective idealist 95 f.
Psellus 191, 201–3
Psyche, the, in Plotinus 135–7
'psychokinesis' 158 n. 1, 205 f.
purification of Orestes 50 f.

General Index

Pythagoras 171
Pythagoreans 14, 111, 119, 122 f., 163 n. 5
Pythia 196–8; *see also* Delphi, oracle of
pythons 199

rationalism 78 f., 107 f.; decline of 90 f.; of Plotinus 127
rebirth in animal form 113 f.
recurrence, eternal 3 f., 14
Reinhardt, K. 5, 10, 42 n. 2, 58, 164
Reitzenstein, R. 122, 174 n. 2
religion, of Euripides 86–90; Minoan and Mycenaean 144 f.; of the ordinary man 140–55; of Plato 119–25; modern survivals of ancient 144 f., 147, 151 f., 154, 187, 195 n. 1; *see also* Athena, gods, magic, Zeus
Renan, E. 124 n. 7
retrocognition 160 n. 3
Richardson, N. 156 n. 1
ritual 141; fixity of 144–5
rivers, crossing 150
Robertson, D. S. 37–9
Robin, L. 20 n. 2
Rome, eternity of 22
Romilly, Mme de 1 n. 2, 14 n. 1
Rose, H. J. 174 n. 2
Russell, D. A. vi
Rutilius Namatianus 22

Sacred Books 142
sacred places: *see* holy ground
sacrifice 150, 153 n. 1
Ste Croix, G. de 1 n. 2
Saturnia regna: *see* Golden Age
Say, Thomas 171
Schadewaldt, W. 58
Schmid, Wilhelm 34–7
Schoemann, G. F. 31 f.
scrying 186–92
sealed letters, reading of 167
self: *see* ego
self-consciousness 136
self-sufficiency 13, 105
Seneca, 19, 131; on progress 23; on world destruction 21 f.
Serapis 202
Sextus Empiricus 95 f.
Shaw, G. B. 80, 88
Sibyl, bottled 191 n. 2
Sigeum 47 n. 2
Sikes, E. E. 32
Simonides 2

sin 140
sixth sense 162
Skira 146
slavery 101
Smertenko, Clara M. 50 f.
Smith, W. D. 195 n. 5, 196 n. 1
Snell, B. 57
Socrates 7, 109, 110 n. 6, 124; *daemonion* of 108 n. 1, 164, 192 f.; *see also* Euripides
Solmsen, F. 53, 62 n. 2
Solon 154 f.
sophistēs 35 n. 1
Sophistic Movement 92–105: *see also under names of individual sophists*
Sophocles 79, 98, 124, 198 n. 1; influence on Aeschylus 37; dream of 168 n. 7; on progress 8, 12
   Oedipus Rex, free will in 57 n. 2, 69–73; *hamartia* in 65–9; religion in 73–7
Sophronius 189–91
Sosipatra 172 f.
Spoerri, W. 1 n. 2, 10 n. 5
'spirit forms' 203–5
spirits, intrusive 202 f., 209
spiritualism and theurgy 204–10
springs, holy 145, 199 n. 1
Spyridon 170
stars, divinity of 124
statues, moving 194 f.
Stenzel, J. 135
Stoics 17 f., 105, 131; on divination 159, 161; Plotinus' relation to 129, 133; on precognition 182 f.; on vapours at Delphi 196 f.
Strabo 21
subconsciousness 135
sun, divinity of 124
Swinburne, A. C. 91
'sympathy', occult 165
Synesius 179 n. 2

Tatian 208
Taylor, A. E. 115, 120, 193 n. 1
technē 11, 108
teleology 115
telepathy 159–76
Tertullian 208 f.
Theiler, W. 132
Theocritus 17
Theodorus 194
Theodosius I, Emperor 194

Theognis 140 n. 2
theophilēs 140 n. 3
Theophrastus 16 f.
Theseus 7
Thesmophoria 146
Thessalus of Tralles 189, 191
theurgy 200–4; and spiritualism 204–10
thieves, detected by scrying 189 f.
Thomas, K. 190 n. 4, 191 n. 4
Thomson, G. 30, 32 n. 1, 37
Thomson, J. A. K. 32
Thucydides, on progress 11–13
thumos 81
Thyestes 67
Tillich, P. 56 n. 4
'tongues, speaking with' 202 f.
Toomer, G. J. 158 n. 1
trance, mediumistic 197, 199–202
transmigration: *see* rebirth
Treitschke, H. von ('Tritch') 104 f.
Trouillard, J. 132
tychē: *see* chance

Unconscious, the 135–7
Utopias 13, 15, 17

Valens 194
Valerius Maximus 172 f.
Vandvik, E. 33 f.
Varro 170 f., 175, 188, 190
Vellacott, P. H. 68 n. 1
Vernant, J. P. 3 n. 3
Verrall, A. W. 48, 78, 85
Verrall, Mrs. A. W. 156
Vian, F. 44 n. 1
Virgil, on Golden Age 4, 21

'virtue', can it be taught? 81–3, 109
Vitruvius 22 f.
voice, change of in trance 195, 197, 202; 'direct' 204 n. 1

Wackernagel, J. 36
Walbank, F. W. 119 n. 7
Waldock, A. J. A. 68, 73
Walton, F. T. 171 n. 1
Walzer, R. 106 n. 1
Weil, H. 42, 53
Wellmann, M. 167
West, D. J. 185 n. 3
Westphal, R. 36, 39
Whitman, C. H. 75
Wilamowitz, U. von 29, 41, 49, 59, 65, 118, 122
'Willett', Mrs. 201 n. 4
William of Auvergne 186 n. 1
Willson, St. J. B. W. 32
Wolf, F. A. 28
Wünsch, R. 194 n. 2

Xenophanes 4 f., 6
Xenophon 7, 13, 166

Yeats, W. B. 3, 37
Yorke, E. C. 36

Zeno of Citium 17
Zeus 140, 145, 155; in Aeschylus 31–4, 40–4, 54, 56 f.; Ammon 194; in Euripides 85; Ktesios 150; of underworld 150; *see also* Dodona
Zoroastrianism, and Plato 117, 122–5
Zuntz, G. 52